MYTHS OF
MASCULINITY

▰▰▰▰▰▰▰▰▰▰▰▰▰▰▰▰▰▰▰

MYTHS OF MASCULINITY

WILLIAM G. DOTY

CROSSROAD • NEW YORK

1993

The Crossroad Publishing Company
370 Lexington Avenue, New York, NY 10017

Copyright © 1993 by William G. Doty

Printed in the United States of America

Library of Congress Cataloging-in-Publication Data

Doty, William G., 1939–
    Myths of masculinity / William G. Doty.
        p. cm.
    Includes bibliographical references and indexes.
    ISBN 0-8245-1233-2
    I. Title.
    BF692.5.D67   1993
    155.3'32—dc20   93-25481
                                                          CIP

Contents

v

Preface

Had James Hillman's term "revisioning" not been overworked, I would have led it into my title, since it has been important to me for a long time as a way to name the revisionary, even revolutionary endeavor I support enthusiastically. But part of the title or not, the enterprise is there, and I reflect upon what I am doing in light of Adrienne Rich's use of the concept as well:

> Re-vision — the act of looking back, of seeing with fresh eyes, of entering an old text from a new critical direction — is for us more than a chapter in cultural history: it is an act of survival. Until we can understand the assumptions in which we are drenched we cannot know ourselves. . . . We need to know the writing of the past, and know it differently than we have ever known it; not to pass on a tradition but to break its hold over us.[1]

My work looks back at myths of the past, but it also looks sideways at the stereotypes of our own day, and toward the future shapings of human gendering. I engage theory as well as narratives, images as well as ethics, and, as part of the drenching in knowledge of ourselves, at popular as well as scholarly materials. Revisioning in the senses of re-seeing and re-vising the traditional, of re-exploring and re-appropriating rich mythical narratives and figures that are still useful in the present, and re-valuing as we heed the desperate imperative to reshape a culture that seems to be sprawling out of bounds and destroying more than it is saving: yes, this "is an act of survival" that we dare no longer leave to someone else in another generation.

■ ■ ■

That this book appears as what Christine Downing names in her Acknowledgments as a "twin" to her *Gods in Our Midst* (1993) delights me considerably. For nearly thirty years we have explored the goddesses and gods in tandem, almost always reading each other's work and responding critically. Sometimes we have discovered ourselves telling as

vii

our own story something that originated with the other, but always the myths and images have mattered to us deeply, and we have sought to share our concern and our dedication to the nobility of the instructive stories, while remaining cautious before the cheap and tawdry.

Sometimes *Myths of Masculinity* reflects directly my own personal experience and sometimes it reflects the experiences of others, shared throughout the very large range of published materials on men's issues. Making one's way through that literature can be almost overwhelming — my annotated working bibliography now runs to over a hundred pages — but there are a number of key works, and I have tried here to refer to many of them (a companion reader on men's issues will be available soon). The book will be useful in courses and discussion groups as portions of the men's movements develop out of the beginning stages and begin to delve more deeply and reflectively into the many concerns that have become evident in gender studies contexts. At the end of the last chapter I give a brief list of important beginning readings, and the cumulative References to this volume will provide the necessary bibliographic information. Bibliographic citations in the text refer to that reference section (by author, date, and page(s); when there are multiple authors, I have cited only the first).

■ ■ ■

One of my own preferences — that Greek names ought to be transliterated, rather than replaced by later Anglicized-Latin equivalents — is only partly satisfied here, because it seemed too awkward to some advance readers to follow my constant giving of both names (Narkissos/Narcissus). I've compromised by using the Greek names where the material I look at is primarily Greek (hence Hermes and Herakles and not Mercury and Hercules), but the Latinate forms where even strict classicists give in to English usage (hence Narcissus and not Narkissos, Oedipus rather than Oidipous). I use the Greek transliteration *phallos* to indicate the symbolic signifier, not the physical penis (phallus).

■ ■ ■

The work represented here reaches back to the early 1970s in several studies of the many-figured Hermes, and to involvement with feminist critical theory even before that. I have been aided by extraordinary audiences at slide-lectures on Hermes, and later on Revising Our Myths of Masculinity (especially at St. John's, Hobart and William Smith, Syracuse, and Alabama): their lively responses told me years ago that a men's new-consciousness was aborning, as repeatedly witnessed in the men's movements of the 1990s. Two chapters were originally presentations at meetings of the Society for Values in Higher Education, and some of the theoretical emphasis first surfaced in Doty (1987).

I am grateful to Gregory Vogt for sharing his own books (1991; Vogt and Sirridge 1991) and his works and ideas in process, his enthusiasm, and his fishing stories; and to both Greg and Hank Lazer for critical readings, at about half-way. Since September 1986, the Hairy-Chested Men's Group of Tuscaloosa has sought to keep each other honest to ourselves and to each other. We've now been through birth, death, marriage, legal process, divorce, book publications, promotions, fathering, and mentoring. Never quite focal to the group's sessions, these materials nonetheless were influenced by these brothers. And thanks to others along the way: Julio, Clay, Joan, Georgette, Ute, Mathew, and the magical hexagonal cabin on Chunk's Brook in Vermont, where the mythical figures were dreamed and most of the first draft was written. I appreciate the cooperation of Galeria Durban/Cesar Segnini in Caracas in providing a photograph of Agustín Cárdenas's sculpture, "Narcissus," reproduced in Chapter 4.

Part One

MYTHIC AND HEROIC MODELS FROM ANTIQUITY TO OUR OWN DAY

Chapter 1

Introducing Heroic Masculinity in Myths and Contemporary Culture

*Mythical figures or events are those imbued with an aura of
specialness: they are privileged, exemplary, larger-than-life phenomena which distill in peculiarly pure form some collective
meaning or fantasy. We can thus speak of "the myth of Jimi Hen-
drix," as we would not speak of the myth of Jimmy Carter.*
                                                (Eagleton 1991:189)

*These are perilous times to be a man in America. There are
forces afoot that have changed men's sense of themselves, blur-
ring what once seemed clear-cut modes and models of manhood.
John Wayne is dead, and we have not yet picked his stand-in.*
                            (Daniel Goleman, foreword to Garfinkel 1985)

Sidetracked somewhere today between the irrational Rambo-style killer
and the ineffective wimp, traditional models of heroic masculinity increasingly seem merely mystifying and misleading. But they may be
explored usefully still, in terms of underlying mythical models, as possible re-imaginings of the nature of masculinity. We ignore the familiar
models at our peril if we laugh them away along with the childhood
fairy tales, because re-examined carefully they can illustrate an important range of experiences of being male that otherwise get shouted down
by the cheap-shot advertisers on the children's television programs and
in the beer, cigarette, or deodorant ads for adults.

  We can learn to recognize the contemporaneity and complexity of
many of the mythical models of masculinity: Hermes is not just a Hellenic deity, but a psychological component of who I am today as I make
my troubled way through the twentieth-century questioning of the nature of patriarchal values conveyed by dominant images of masculinity.
Herakles is not just a figure of musclebound, yes-man barbarism, but
a figure who like Hermes has feminine aspects, if we review the entire
range of stories about him. <u>In this book these and other figures from</u>

3

the past whose contemporary relevance remains quite powerful will be explored alongside today's unique issues of masculinity.

Often persons who have been introduced to these sorts of materials remark that they suddenly see Hermes or Dionysos or some other figure becoming evident in their own lives. They recognize in themselves herculean overreaching, narcissistic absorptions in their cars or muscles, friendships dominated by one-sided warlike (Ares-like) competition, and, occasionally, the gift of relationship that echoes the love between Enkidu and Gilgamesh. The "gods" are still "alive," still providing ways to learn to recognize aspects of our societies and parts of ourselves. Even a very secularized society has privileged models, or quasi-divine figures, and it provides systems of interpretation that accord more or less viability to now this, now that model, although our depth finding self-consciousness about such interpretive and evaluative systems may be undervalued and underdeveloped.

Sigmund Freud, so proud of identifying the role of religion as a crutch for the immature neurotic, worshiped *unser Gott Logos* (our god, logos), that is, rationalistic scientific analysis. More recently we have realized how logos-rationality can easily be misworshiped, at the price of losing Eros, the divine figure who models moral and emotional *connections,* in opposition to the *isolation* and *separation* of scientific analysis. Furthermore religious and political values underlie decisions about who does which research or which portions of the population merit which expenditures (for instance, research on AIDS affecting women and children has been funded much more extensively than that affecting males), and how a nation can be mobilized to defend its "natural right" to have access to the earth's petroleum resources — certainly the ultimate background to the recent Persian Gulf invasions from both sides.

Any national group can consider itself divinely supported because of the belief that the deities simply must be on its own side, and what's more, today we seem to become godlike creatures as we manipulate genetic patterns and create new forms of life. But as Ginette Paris notes, the classical position was not so much to *imitate* the gods and goddesses — in that direction lies the Greek concept of hybris, or the modern psychological taint of "inflation" — as to *learn* from them and their errors and overreaching (1986:171). Hence as we learn to resymbolize and reinterpret the mythical figures for our own times and contexts, we must remain alert to the negative, shadowy, excessive side of mythical or legendary figures, and not just revel in their sunlit glories. Such careful analysis will question just how the mythical figures manage to bridge cultural oppositions and deal with the strong dualities that are often reinforced by creation myths and hero legends. Examining relationships among siblings in myths, for example, discloses ways the personality traits carried by the deities were thought to interact, both in harmony and in discord — we'll examine those doubling dynamics in two chapters on mythical brothers. Following criticism of the typical scientistic splitting of logos and eros, Chapter 10 attends to the ways Apollonian logical rationality gets contrasted with the erotics of his brother Dionysos.

Revoicing Masculinity More Deeply

The project here is intended as a contribution to the assembling of the male person, an endeavor faced inescapably when the contemporary self seems only painfully stitched together, if not indeed, as many women claim today, abusive and tyrannical. Recently many men also have claimed to have been abused and tyrannized, and have flocked to involvement in "the men's movement," ignoring for the moment how loosely that movement has to be defined to include all its aspects (for a moderate statement of the oppression and woundedness of contemporary males, see Kipnis 1990). Speakers such as poet and translator Robert Bly command tens of thousands of dollars in lecture fees; groups of chanting, drumming men around campfires seek to get in touch with "the wildman within," enchanting mass media reporters as well as some of the men themselves; and small men's groups comparable to the consciousness-raising groups that heralded the feminist revolution have appeared across the continent.

Such groups and their national umbrella organizations span a spectrum from pro-gay activist to anti-liberal "save the family" positions, so just recognizing that a group exists does not mean that one approves or disapproves. The initial intention here is to indicate and explore the contemporary interest in "masculinity," however defined, but increasingly treated in terms of various appropriate "masculini*ties*," rather than a single normative "masculinity." The range of options within the men's movements and the theoretical and political issues behind the calls for change are charted in Chapter 3. Partly this book grew out of dissatisfaction with the superficiality of the literature on cultural materials available in much of the men's movement, a number of representatives of which pride themselves on avoiding analysis and intellectual reflection. I understand the way academic discussions and intellectualizing can keep anyone from facing crucial personal issues, and if I've been successful, I've avoided that trap. But I think the obverse can also be a trap: the necessary work of getting men in touch with feelings and expressivity is not all the men's movements ought to be about; it is not just the highly emotional work of weekend conferences and therapy groups. It is also the assignment of wordsmiths, mythographers, and iconographers who plumb long-term cultural models — and this book takes that assignment very seriously.

I cite and quote a lot in this book because it is not just my book; it represents a series of depth trenches into the literature of the men's movements; not my own brilliance, but ours, that's what I've sought to represent. We, not just I, are clarifying and disciplining the approaches that future gender awareness will follow as it alters what has become merely customary in our own day. The recommended bibliography in Chapter 12 provides some samples of the wide range of published materials; it is selected from several hundred recent works on masculinity annotated in my own electronic bibliographic system. Increasingly bookstores have added Men's Studies sections where the reader can find many of these works, and mail order shops will provide lists and ship copies.[1]

Reaching sideways to build upon analyses of contemporary cultural images and issues, the book also plunges into the mythical depths beyond merely contemporary agendas. While many rich models of masculinity available in mythological materials are being ignored, this book reclaims some of them for our own day. It begins to revoice some of the masculine figures the way a number of women have revoiced feminine figures (examples: Downing 1981, Walker 1983, Bolen 1984, and Paris 1986). When a British socialist-feminist, Lynne Segal, states that "it is women who have taken the initiative in beginning to explore what men want, in explaining the ways of men," she graphs correctly the time lag in which male authors came onto the scene rather tardily (1990:60). Also in the more explicit feminist and gender-analysis scholarship, women have had the leading roles.

My own involvement with the feminist rethinking of our cultural history began in the late 1960s, and this book taps that resource freely, but it does not so much address the problematic expressions of masculinity today seen from feminist perspectives, as the possible corrective resources for the problematic that I read out of several traditions of myths about men — "myths" in the false sense of negative stereotypes, but also "myths" in terms of the cultural storehouses of wisdom and information that our vast number of mythologies provide as ever available resources for change and growth. *Myths of Masculinity,* then, in both senses: correcting unhealthy stereotypes of gender dominance (myths as negative/abusive stereotypes), and regarding myths more appropriately as narratives and themes from our cultural storehouses of knowledge that remain essential and relevant today. Of course personal feelings and emotional expression are important, but myths supplement those modes of knowing and living, adding an important long-term dimension.

We can voice masculinity more richly and broadly by including a larger range of experiential knowledge, passed along through myths, than we are accustomed to recounting in a society that seems to have lost its ability to remember even the most recent historical developments. For example, it was astonishing to see the widespread acceptance of camouflage clothing outfits in the late 1980s: something inconceivable immediately after our humiliating inability "to win" in Vietnam. Likewise, at first it was inconceivable that Congress did not resist the warmongering of President Bush in the Persian Gulf; it was as if Vietnam had never happened. No wonder that within a decade of the Vietnam war students could not identify which side the United States had supported.

Ours is a society seemingly obsessed with the latest and best, or at least the most recent. Freud might focus upon the Oedipus and Jocasta myths, and Carl Jung upon archetypes and medieval alchemy, but contemporary academic psychology seldom engages mythological figures, in seeming contrast to the widespread popular recognition of their influence in literature and the arts (one example: the admitted influence of Joseph Campbell's study of the hero-monomyth upon George Lucas's *Star Wars* film trilogy). Instead of needing even more studies citing meaningless statistics that pile up in undigested heaps, understanding the function of stereotypes and false projections about other people needs to be complemented by understanding fundamental cultural elements, repeated situations, and archetypal scenarios.

Asking questions in greater depth than customary, we can look beneath the contemporary manifestations at some of the ways mythical figures and images continue to be extremely influential even in a time when we can no longer remember just which god or goddess goes with just which animal or pictorial image. My project is less a debunking program than a retrieval of aspects of masculine traditions that got lost when people suggested that some "natural" way of "being male" had been the norm always, and in the process dissolved the specific socio-historical contexts that produced particular ethnic perspectives. It is easy to believe that "essential masculinity" is identical with what one's own culture admires only so long as one remains ignorant of the great range of types of masculinity in other cultures. Revisioning explorations have the benefit of questioning the socio-historical construction of masculinities, asking about the validity of the models we explore and the prospects for growth through liberations yet to come. Cultures are always re-imagining, re-interpreting; they do not simply locate objective patterns to be replicated, divine models that determine ever after who gets to be called "male" and who "female." And we are already well along on the path of reconsidering the qualities that characterize each gender, as well as how they will relate to one another in the twenty-first century, so we need to look repeatedly at the rich store of information and theory that has been developed from a number of directions in psychology, sociology, political theory, and gender studies.

Recovery from Patriarchy

So this book is not so much an exposé as a cautious work of resistance to many of the modern institutionalized heterosexualisms in which patriarchy, misogyny, gay-bashing, rape, repressive and arbitrary authoritarian treatment of women, and abuse of children and other males flourish. Others have written *against* many of the prevailing models; here the emphasis is upon recovering positive mythic models that have been set aside by the simplifying reductionism of our public discourse, by our impatience with complexity or extensive detail or subtlety.

Again and again I find myself working against established *ideologies*, against the framing stories that have become normative versions of what it means to be a male. These normative versions more often than not turn out to be *stereotypes*, common negative and demeaning assumptions that are often oversimplified and simplistic, tired and worn-out ways of responding to situations that no longer confront us.[2] Over against such essentialist models I prefer more archetypal models, meaning no particular slant toward Jungian psychotherapy or Northrop Frye's charting of the four archetypes of the seasons that he thought underlay all of the world's literature, but rather "generative models," "ideal forms," that bring a number of similar materials into a household. The archetype is the generic, the general — not necessarily the most appropriate, but repeated often enough that we can learn from it to recognize *typical* ways in which we are culturally predisposed to evaluate this or that heroic figure, to accept or reject this or that mythic narrative as essential to our well-being as a society.

Mythological stories and figures have much to teach about refurbishing the notion of the masculine self. Myths provide *projective psyche models* for contemporary life even when they are materials no longer immediately familiar. The child's use of heroines or heroes models how one might develop by identifying imaginatively with a range of mythic figures. Of course one can also get absorbed in the figure and never outgrow an adolescent identification with the macho king of the hill! But other models do not stress conquering and ruling-over, and this book includes some of those models as resources for our lives. The significance of a culture is revealed in its rituals and myths, and I suspect that the most significant cultures in the long run are those that allow for the greatest number of stories.

Contemporary masculinity may be imaged more adequately from mythic stories, although the mythic shapes are not always positive — I have a lot of trouble with Ares, for instance, and malfunctional aspects of Narcissus are obvious in the cases of narcissistic individuals who never relate to others satisfactorily. The externally directed energies of Dionysian extroverts may lead them to an endless series of momentary encounters rather than anything lastingly satisfying. Some of the masculine myths and hero legends here are not immediately familiar to everyone, although several are part of our long-term heritage from Greece (Narcissus, Ares, Hermes). They reach across the millennia, in some cases (Gilgamesh), or outside the usual focus of Western attention (the Navajo hero twins). Hence the mythical stories in Chapters 4–10 are summarized and the history of their transmission to us recapitulated before each discussion. Additional background information, relevant textual sources, and bibliography are suggested at the end of each of those chapters.

The focus is upon honing our questions and seeking new insights, rather than upon establishing definitive interpretations. After two context-setting chapters elaborate the contextual issues by which masculinity is questioned and subsequently revisioned today, seven chapters alternate between the mythico-heroic accounts and contemporary significances. Chapter 11 provides revisionings of the classical model of the hero. What is often identified as "the postmodern" situation comes out there especially — it is a perspective that refuses to stipulate any one normative gender pattern or conservatively to advocate return to any singular canonical set of hero models. Such advocacy would in fact do violence to the original panoplies of ways in which legends and myths are passed along in specific family and social contexts, and it would put me in the awkward position of the old "patriarchy," controlling access to tools as a form of exerting authority over the canon.

That phrase "the patriarchy" is used here loosely, as it is often used in feminist literature, to refer to the non-reflective domination of societies

by males, based on unself-conscious assumptions about male superiority and a millennia-long suppression of difference.[3] To posit and worship
an original male-female difference, as most of the West does in reiterat-
ing the biblical creation narratives, is already to claim a "natural" basis
for what is in effect a political hierarchy with women consistently the
inferior members. The situation now seems patently stupid, yet ever
more energy is exerted to maintain the sort of power relations by which
women are trivialized and considered inferior. Perhaps it is especially
within capitalism that we are so oblivious to the ways specific forms of
power relations are coded as "natural," so that "the personal is the political," the slogan of the feminist movement, comes as a great shock as well
as a liberating insight into the *institutional* forms of gender oppression
that transcend any liberal male's desire not to be sexist.

But being sexist can mean remaining blind to the socio-political
problematics now facing masculinity itself. Perhaps there are other ways
of being male than those that have become customary, other significant ways of naming what is most wondrous about human beings than
merely pointing to sexual differentiation. Perhaps there are new lessons
to learn from materials previously overlooked and to unlearn from what
has been tyrannical there. Emmanuel Reynaud's powerful *Holy Virility:
The Social Construction of Masculinity* (1983) is a good place to begin to
re-examine the basic Judaeo-Christian gendering myths, biased as they
are by an ideologically implicit separation between male and female.
Gregory Vogt's *Return to Father: Archetypal Dimensions of the Patriarch* contrasts a negative "dualistic" patriarchy with the "homologous
patriarchy" that he thinks can replace it usefully. The former, practiced
by men or women, represents "an attitude and an attempt to create an
all-encompassing (economic, political, sexual, spiritual) system which
aspires to domination by conscious control of all people, places, and
things both organic and inorganic. [It is] a pattern of prowess, competition, and strength exercised for the exclusion of others for political,
social, and economic control" (1991:6, 9). On the other hand, what Vogt
calls "homologous patriarchy" would treasure collective values and be
conservationist in outlook, celebrating the continuity of being that is
evident across the entire universe.

Patriarchy is about control or mastery, and John Brenkman (1976)
does a superlative deconstruction or anti-patriarchal analysis of the
Echo and Narcissus section of Ovid's *Metamorphoses*, emphasizing
how achieving "mastery" of a text, which can then be said to have
one meaning, is defeated already by Ovid's writing, in which he sets
in motion oppositional voices that intensify rather than resolve power-

ful conflicts of the mythical narratives themselves. When I move into mythological narratives and themes, I now keep in mind deconstructionist questions: What in this text goes against what it *appears* to be saying? What elements of the story provide elements of its *undoing* in contrast to its establishment as a norm? In what ways are we caught up into the story so that we lose sight of the fact that unconsciously we have become an actor within it, assuming that its features are "natural" or divinely given? At which points does a particular narrative free us from the claims it apparently makes upon us?

Jeffrey Weeks reminds us that the important social factor of gender construction is not just the repression of one unified position, such as might be represented by patriarchy or capitalism in isolation, insofar as "power does not operate through single mechanisms of control. It operates through complex and overlapping — and often contradictory — mechanisms which produce domination *and* opposition, subordination *and* resistances" (1986:37). Criticism of the masculine image of the Marlboro cowboy would have to deal with the positive quality of frontier adaptability as well as the negative individualism of the non-social horse rider impressing a false order upon the natural environment. Our hopes of finding a single problem "to fix" are shattered upon the realities of social constructions that have both long histories of how they came into being and wide-ranging forms in which their influences are expressed across many different elements of the cultures in which we are reared.[4] In spite of the American penchant for assigning simple and single causation to complex issues, it *is* possible to avoid the Band-Aid approach that sells well in the mass media because it is so reductionist and trivializing, in order to bring serious attention to the importance of ongoing political planning and social action. Band-Aids are fine for first aid, but useless for repair of cultural dysfunctions that have complex, historically generated origins.

Asking Important Questions, Feminism, and Gender

In reflecting upon mythic and heroic models, a more nuanced type of cultural reflection is involved — the mythic-heroic dimensions are not comparable to short-term first aid but to involvement in long-term cultural therapy. Myth is never simplistic or temporary; it does not lie around waiting to be slapped onto a particular trouble spot, but it initiates constant reflection and reconsideration, asking what aspect of masculinity might be most appropriate in each given situation, how the traditional heroic might need to be revised to provide adequate long-range solutions. Myth is above all polyvalent rather than singular; it is complex and overlapping rather than simple and linear. Hence it is a category fruitful for the necessarily complex rethinking of masculinity in our postmodernist complexity. My approach is neither strongly reverential toward myths as such, nor do I argue that the heroic figures were always ideal models of healthy masculine identity. Instead I see the heroic figures and mythical stories as modeling *possible* enactments of selfhood, possible ways masculinity in particular might be shaped positively *or negatively,* but I do not assume that traditional heroes and myths are automatically appropriate for all situations. Being oriented to mythic figures does not require living in a fully mythic universe, or becoming uncritical; such mythic figures will be resources for analyzing and exploring modes and phases of masculinity if they are not treated as timeless answers that must be engraved in stone or simplistic correlations such as one finds in pop psychology or astrology columns. What I can promise is that the mythical models will provide more options to the usual gender modelings, additional ways of insighting masculinities from the vantage points of a rich panoply of cultural values lost to the casual view of those who only heed the most popularly represented hero images of a society.

A *men's* movement corresponding to the history of the *women's* movement will most likely have to undergo many years of arguing and debating before it identifies the most important issues and models, answers the most important questions, or develops the most useful analytics. The historical reviews of the initial manifestations of the men's movements by Kenneth Clatterbaugh (1989 and 1990) already provide part of the necessary tool kit to map the field as men seek to escape some of the gender traps into which the society, even academic scholarship, is often betrayed. Perhaps The Men can learn from The Women to value plurality and minority positions, since a bland vanilla milkshake platform is no longer effective in American politics over the long run, even if it still appeals temporarily to many voters. Such a platform ought not to be expected to work in terms of men's issues, either — there is too much at stake. If we are not recognizing and listening to the several elements of our society now being repressed and devalued, American democracy is not fully underway yet, an insight recognized by the organizers of the annual conferences of the National Organization of Men Against Sexism (NOMAS, until 1990 the National Organization for Changing Men), in featuring program units on gay bashing, child abuse, violence against spouses, and African-American male survival. Where else in contemporary political discourse does one hear such issues being addressed consistently and repeatedly?

Individual change is still crucial, essential; but structural political change remains even more important, both in the feminist sense that "the personal is the political," and insofar as gender issues trail long historical streamers that affect thousands of human beings over a long period of time. Perspectives that only repeat a masculine essentialism lacking any connection with the social, historical, and economic factors that produce it fail to raise the questions necessary for honest social responsibility and cultural growth.[5] Susanne Langer suggests that the most important thing about a culture is not how it resolved problems, but how it managed *to ask important questions,* and her suggestion affects the questions raised by the mythical stories and figures: Where have we come from? Where are we headed? Ought we to be imagining ourselves differently? Whose imaginings are most provocative in thinking through gender issues today? Where are the points in the culture where the mythic models get translated into everyday life and imagery?

It will be obvious that some of Langer's "important questions" surface in the revisioning and rethinking of some of the traditional gender models that will be discussed in Chapters 2, 3, and 11, and as different conceptions and experiences of masculinity enrich our contemporary gendering. For me these important questions are often derived from feminist discourse, since I regard twentieth-century feminist scholarship as one of the major intellectual advances of our time, and it is difficult to imagine writing in a pre-feminist mode ever again. Likewise we learn a great deal from feminist politics, even if we must now take into consideration the anti-feminist backlash originating from males who consider that their own personal rights have been compromised repeatedly by "strident" feminists (see the accounts of the backlash phenomenon in Faludi 1991 and Astrachan 1986). We may have to endure a period of prolonged confusion as anti-feminist, pro-masculinist voices are heard and the men's/fathers' rights advocates have their own day in court.

In some cases feminist insights are insights attained from other modes of social analysis and politics as well, but I find it easy to articulate portions of what I incorporate in my work as a result of influences stemming from feminist ways of thinking and operating:

- Developing self-consciousness of presumptive gender dominance: taking Man as the generic for Human, or presuming to speak for another group of which one is not a member ("what women really want is . . . ").

- Honing one's ability to empathize with an utterance or text in ways that go beyond mere abstraction, "rational" analysis of it — hearing the submerged voices, the countertrends suppressed as being "unnatural."

- Attending to the socio-historical sites of the image or text — how it was produced and how it was inserted into the cultural economies, including communications media.

- Investigating the micro- and macro-interactions of family and individual and society from the stance of "the personal is the political," so that one comprehends defensively the implicit and unself-conscious power of social institutions, which always claim to operate "for your own good."

- Recognizing that masculine (if not indeed patriarchal) perspectives have controlled language in terms of who has been allowed to write or be published as well as what could be expressed in language; the male has usually been understood as the universal, the female as the particular — and hence inferior — and a great mass of writing by women was never allowed into print. Issues of freedom of expression for all voices within masculinities can hardly avoid ties to movements for free speech and access to media led by women and ethnic-racial-sexual minorities.

- Learning that the competitive, hierarchical organizational model that dominates our society — a chairperson with assistants of increasingly reduced rank — is not necessarily more productive of true knowledge than informal collaborative methods.

- Questioning the liberal ideal of equality as an issue of one's attitude or willpower, seeing instead the need to change society by means of gaining control over the various forms of power exerted throughout the legal system, seldom impartially with respect to gender or race or economic class.

- Noting how personal and shared experience can be as valuable as abstract ideas, how males also can learn to discipline their emotions and not be so fearful of them, how males can come to appreciate the feeling and affective bases of action on the part of other males, and how they too can learn to operate not just competitively, but out of concern and love for others of both genders.

- Experiencing just how limiting it is to follow the bourgeois emphasis upon individualism — coming to see how much of our experience is shared, how it is shaped especially by our common language, literature, arts, media, and economic system. Again the *common* experiences, the disciplines of the *polis* or city-state, politics: it should be evident that much of the excitement of contemporary gender studies derives from a sense of recovering positive *communal and political* values in the face of the capitalistic fragmentation and commercial competition that have nearly undone the American experiment and made politics a bad word.

These remarks have not been attached to particular positions within the recent "second" or "third wave feminist" movements — the time of grand harmonious colloquy was very brief indeed, and as in any other personal and intellectual movement, very strong disagreements soon appeared among branches of feminists. But "feminist" can still be used in a general manner that appreciates its contributions without buying into any particular system or school of thought. Nor does this book feature a particular site within Women's or Men's Studies, as they have multiplied across the academic scene — nor within Gender Studies, although gender-related issues are seen now increasingly as deserving long-term reflection (the first substantial study of academic Men's Studies: Brod 1987; the *Journal of Men's Studies* began publication in the summer of 1992).

Elizabeth Minnich's comments about gender are typical of the feminist critique that many men find painful and would like to forget, but her remarks convey economically some of the raw edges of the "problem of masculinity" that will be engaged throughout this book:

> Gender, in its broadest sense, is the term feminists use to evoke the conceptual and experiential, individual and systemic, historical and contemporary, cross-cultural and culture-specific, physical and spiritual and political construction of what it means to live in a world that has created them not human, but always woman or man (a division that is not a dualism but a hierarchical monism). Humans are, then, either men or the lesser beings created for them (by Nature? by God? by History? — various languages are used) called "women." For those of us who live enmeshed in that system which is, of course, shaped by the root problem and its related conceptual errors, to be human, sexed, and uniquely individual at once is virtually impossible. Both the generic and the particular are formed/informed/deformed by the hierarchy that made some males into Man and the rest of us into failed men, deviants, primitives, saints, or whores. (1990:136–37)

The last sentences of Minnich's remarks demonstrate that "gender" can no longer remain an apparently simple social science term that merely reflects the passing impact of culture upon one's biological constitution. *Gender is not something neutral, but has been experienced as a complex aspect of a historical economic system of masculine repression of women.* Hence Gender Studies now names much more than cool social-psych studies or sociological data analysis. It becomes a matter of the moral rights of "The Other," however comprehended, or of, as Gayatri Spivak argues (1989), a matter of "cultural politics." Not just description but proscription; not just observational analysis but demands for moral behavioral changes — the old models of disinterested sciences accumulating non-materialistic/transcendent knowledge are little respected today, as opposed to the recognition that even the most abstract scientific methodologies are sited firmly within politically determined frameworks of specific institutions funded by specific companies or their subterfuge funding agencies, or of governmental policies.

Sexualities and Masculinities

This book seeks models alternative to those that have led to our current state of affairs. It does so by probing models that are no longer always recognized as twentieth-century icons, but that nonetheless are rooted firmly within our Western heritage. The scope here is limited to the West, although Westerners have only begun to appreciate fully the cultural achievements of the East. When the two are brought into comparative interaction, mutually beneficial results often occur. See for instance the volume that resulted when a Western art professional looked at traditional Japanese woodblock prints from a men's movement perspective, Roger Keyes's *The Male Journey in Japanese Prints* (1989). Although one might suppose traditional art history would be little affected by gendering issues, Keyes learned to recognize elements of the woodblocks that both reflect Japanese gender models and raise insightful questions about American models. Other examples would include the recent translation into English of *The Great Mirror of Male Love,* seventeenth-century stories of Japanese homosexual love (Saikaku 1990), or David Gilmore's comparative summary (1990) of masculinity as experienced in China, Greece, North America, Japan, India, East Africa, and elsewhere.

Attending to cross-cultural representations of gender display and understanding of gender relations from different cultural heritages help us to understand just how artificially the categories "essential" or "natural" are constructed. <u>Too frequently what are taken to be biological</u> <u>givens are charted, overlayered with recent social values, and the end</u> <u>product is then treated as having been "natural" or "god-given" from</u> <u>the start.</u> The issue is more complicated when we recognize that we have no access to pure "nature," that any "natural" behavior has been inescapably shaped by human culture. Often to speak of "nature" has meant indulging in what historian John Winkler refers to as "andro-centric protocols," namely, in reports on how women behave or ought to behave that have little relationship to the actual ways in which they do behave or have behaved, but instead represent male ideals with respect to the other gender (Winkler 1990:8). Modern researchers of the role of women in antiquity, for example, have had to learn to understand many of the descriptions of how women acted not as reflexive descriptions but as idealizing projections of the ways many men *wanted* women to behave. <u>"Natural" sexuality usually turns out to be nothing</u> <u>more than the particular morally determined range of expression con-</u> <u>sidered appropriate ("natural") by a particular set of ethical teachings</u> (*moral* derives from *mos*, custom, not from some eternally valid set of culturally transcendent guidelines).

Jeffrey Weeks's *Sexuality* can be cited again as representing the now common anti-essentialist position that argues against the claim that the primary gender determinations are either physiological or biological or cultural: "I am suggesting that what we define as 'sexuality' is *an histori-cal construction*, which brings together a host of different biological and mental possibilities — gender identity, bodily differences, reproductive capacities, needs, desires, and fantasies — which need not be linked together, and in other cultures have not been" (1986:15, my emphasis). Sexuality, Weeks observes, "is something which society produces in complex ways. . . . Sexuality is not given, it is a product of negotiation, struggle, and human agency" (25).

Just as Weeks would argue that there is no singular *sexuality* but "various forms of sexuality: there are in fact many sexualities," so I and many others argue that there is no single *masculinity* but various forms of masculinity, *many masculinities*. An article by a gay apologist, Stephen Donaldson, proclaims that there is no single way of being gay: "I don't believe in a single homosexuality, but in many homosexualities, and I most emphatically don't believe in 'the homosexual' " (*RFD* no. 67, Fall 1991:14). At the other extreme we can refer to the single slickly produced issue of *Men's Life* that was published in 1990, wherein any questioning about the nature of the masculinity represented by upper-class dominant white men was hooted down in the article that claimed to make "lunch meat of the so-called sensitive 'New Man.' " During the writing of this book I was astonished to see the conservative reaction to the men's movements in special sections or issues of popular magazines such as *Esquire, Newsweek, Men's Journal,* and *Gentlemen's Quarterly.* The very thought of questioning the established versions of macho masculinity evidently threatens the writers charged with representing the clientele/purchasers of these magazines. It would be hard to find a clearer instance of the importance of long-term analyses of masculinity within historical periods and specific ethno-social situations and a focus upon some of the mythic contexts that shape our imaging of masculinities. Such contexts are *not* uniformly homophobic, anti-progressive, reactionary, defensive, the way these articles have been.[6]

But I state "some of the mythic contexts," because only a very small selection of them has recently had much influence. Aaron Kipnis notes that:

> over the last few millennia only a few mythological images have served as our cultural foundations for masculinity: the youthful, invincible hero, like Hercules; the war-making gods like Ares; or the dominant elder male like Moses who rules in the name of an all-powerful, god-in-the-sky. This wrathful Solar/Sky God is known as Apollo, Zeus, Jove, Indra, Jehovah [i.e., Yahweh or the Lord — WGD], Allah and by many other names. The so-called patriarchy evolved from these images. (1991:1)

While Kipnis is correct in asserting that a very small range of patriarchal figures has been dominant, it ought to be clear by now that I hope to redirect attention to other neglected figures from whose stories we have much to learn, figures whose "spiritual" significance I readily admit, but not in the usual pious overtones. The contours of male spirituality will engage us explicitly rather seldom in this volume, although my profession is that of academic Religious Studies, and I teach a course in Men and Spirituality.

Curiously enough, although like Kipnis we turn instinctively to a short list of masculine heroes and mythic figures when we start to reflect on mythology or heroes, that short list itself has become a selective canon that has screened out a richly contoured assembly of other figures — figures who function to carry forward "important questions" about our social order and our ideals of individual success. Recovering some of the depth insights of the cultures producing those myths and heroic figures will engage us for a long time to come, even when we begin with experiences close to hand. Hence in concluding an essay on myths of and about friendship, for instance, I suggested that the "recovery" has to begin by studying approaches to mythic materials as such, before we delve more deeply into individual figures (Doty 1992).

Overview

Chapters 2 and 3 explore aspects of "the problem of masculinity" and how mythic materials permeate societies even when they are not explicitly recognized; there I review the context of the present-day men's movement and its many different aspects. Readers will find these the most historically and theoretically oriented chapters; they differ in style and tone from the rest of the book, and there as in this chapter and Chapter 11, I have used subtitles to clarify the sequence of the several topics treated.

In Chapter 4, the scope reaches back behind the Greek myths to Mesopotamia, indeed to what is most likely the first Western myth (although our texts of it are relatively late). The love of Gilgamesh, the ruler of the city Uruk (contemporary Warka, Iraq), for the famous wildman of the countryside, Enkidu, and their subsequent assault on the divine order, bears re-examination not only because of the richness of its modeling of male-male companionship, but because of the role of the prototypical femme fatale, Ishtar, who is the city's agent in bringing Enkidu "down" from nature to culture. We will puzzle through why our culture has so little advice to give on the nature of friendship between two members of the same gender.

In Chapter 5, attention is directed to that most apparently masculine of all heroic prototypes, Herakles (the Roman Hercules). Apparently non-masculine qualities in Herakles will be indicated as well as reflections upon the appropriateness of the Roman treatment of the macho jock or pimp Hercules as a figure of derision. Chapter 6 engages the figure of Narcissus, a figure entirely familiar from the yards of muscled skin exposed in the latest fashions and music business — Peter Watrous (1991) has reported on the increasing nudity of male singers on the American stage and in musical videotapes, and any supermarket magazine rack will have at least five or six magazines devoted to the new muscular physique. In this chapter I argue both that we do not do well as a culture in learning how to love our own beauty appropriately, and that there is in general a narcissistic problematic with reference to masculinity.

In Chapters 7–9, we look at additional Greek figures, namely, Hermes (the Roman Mercury), Ares, and then the pair Apollo and Dionysos.

Stories about these figures will provide us insights into forms of masculinity that are not simplex but complex. They represent ways of modeling multiplicity and fluidity that make some of our contemporary ego-psychology paradigms seem ridiculously rigid and elementary. In Hermes, Apollon, and Dionysos, the feminine element is *not* something to be rigidly excluded; indeed, as we shall see, it is precisely the arbitrary cultural bifurcation of masculine and feminine, rationality and emotionality, that has determined (and warped) Western models of masculinity. For instance, in the figure "insatiate of war," as the Greeks called him, Ares (assimilated to the Roman Mars), the figure most like the public male ideal of the post–World War II period, so painfully pilloried in Jason Miller's play *That Championship Season* (1972). Why the John Rambo movies provide for many people a respite from the dishonor of our defeat in Vietnam is perhaps not such a mystery if an Ares prototype remains at work in our culture.

In Chapters 9–11, several myths and images take us toward further balancing of supposedly "masculine" and "feminine" qualities. The Navajo twin-hero myth in Chapter 9 is an example of the American cross-continental theme of the two brothers (or a brother and a sister pair) who are important in the mythical primal times; repeatedly we find that the extroverted, aggressive brother is only able to clean up the primal landscape, killing off the evil creatures who threaten all life, because his introverted, passive brother has been guarding and nurturing the *souls* of both. Chapter 11 reviews the classical male hero pattern (the "monomyth") before looking at the recent development of heroine-models and lunar-heroes that complement traditional masculine solar-hero models such as the warrior, the conqueror, or avenger. The strong link between myths and hero/ine models necessitates looking at recent heroic images as well as those of mythic antiquity, and this chapter sketches some of the ways in which we may evaluate both contemporary and future hero/ines. The concluding Chapter 12 names themes that readers are invited to help develop, and annotates twenty or so publications on masculinity currently available.[7]

Part Two

MASCULINITIES AND MYTH TODAY

Chapter 2

The Myth... and the Myths... of Masculinities

We do not ask whether Dürer or Degas represents the human nude more correctly. Instead we see them — along with the science of anatomy — as different systems of notation.... Should not the same be true of different modes of historical figuration?

(Brown 1989:114)

The boys gave him a fishy look when he drove back up the road toward the camp, as if they had finally recognized who he was out of the haze of their past, and weren't amused to see him still around. (Ford 1976:195)

Meanings of "Myth"

The term "myth" is used here in specific ways: first with reference to the secondary sense of "falsehood" or "stereotype," as when someone debunks a perspective felt to be partial or incorrect. In that case "the myth of masculinity" might well be a put-down rather than the object of serious study. And second to recall the sense in which myth represents the underlying belief-system of a culture, its primary networks of meaning and significance. In that case "the myth of masculinity" might refer to the values assigned in our gender systems, as made evident in ideologies and social hierarchies, in the amount paid one or the other gender (women still earn sixty cents for every dollar earned by males), and so forth. And of course myth also refers to story or narrative, to specific emplotments of meaning by which a culture herds its shared significances into the corral of social amiability.

The various meanings do not create problems as they overlap, once it is clear that this book is not merely a debunking. In fact it is only realistic to recognize that the various meanings shade in and out all the time. The specific context should make clear which sense I have in mind in each instance in this book. And the various contexts should make clear that I do not believe in any overarching "myth of masculinity": I think there are many myths of masculinity, both in the sense of many stories by which masculinity comes to be configured and emulated and in the sense of underlying patterns by which teachers and parents force roles upon children according to whether they are biological males or females.

A survey of a number of myths of masculinity would demonstrate that ours is a culture with many such myths — like genes, some are predominant and others recessive, some helpful and others harmful, dysfunctional. There are a number of masculinities at work within our society, various versions that are determined by an individual's ethnic background, socio-economic class, and employment. Gaining awareness of as many of the myths of masculinities as possible, one gains a resource useful in getting out of the current crisis of dysfunctional masculinity by finding resources other than those of the dominant tough-guy macho avenger who gives golf-cart interviews that barely suppress his disdain for those who haven't landed near the top of the dominant socio-economic hierarchy.

While medical evidence has demonstrated repeatedly how significantly worse off males are than women in our society, change in lifestyle is still left to the cardiac recovery specialist, rather than systematic alteration of the causes of stress in the male gender role. Our culture ought to be more farsighted, looking at the ultimate mythical scenarios that have been dominant, scenarios that have undergirded a dualistic gender splitting and the package of male stress syndrome we expect allopathic medicine to treat at a time when it is usually too late.

To say that one "ought to" consider different myths concerning gender than those that shape one's own immediate culture introduces an admonitory, moral aspect that I sometimes feel unsure about. Yet I have no trouble telling students in an Introduction to Religious Studies or Humanities class that they "ought" to take seriously Taoist or Buddhist teachings as I try to convince them of the importance of "the other" or "difference" in construction of a meaningful self. Indeed, other societies conceive the self differently, and that conceiving is linked to various conceptions of deities or other supernatural or transcendent forces, the purposes of life, and guidelines for ethical behavior that often contrast sharply with the common Judaeo-Christian and Euro-American consensus. This book challenges that consensus with respect to the ways we imagine masculinity and with respect to the calm, cool, scientific voice with which authors hide their own involvement. It conveys personal judgments of writings and aspects of the men's movements, and tracks issues that are central to attempts to revision masculinity today. These issues form the contexts in which specific myths and heroes are heeded, and most of this chapter is devoted to clarifying the social and historical factors that regulate what gets heeded or considered too far out.

The "Difference" of Contemporary Masculinities

In short, this book studies *difference* with respect to masculinity. Some of its materials are unfamiliar to many Americans, and furthermore these materials often challenge the pervasive view that there is an essentialized, unequivocal "masculinity," opposed to which one images only the deviance or inversion or lack of successful socialization that sex-role sociology and psychology have presumed (see the critique by Carrigan 1987:165). The cultures engaged include several that may be unfamiliar even to many educated persons. And the types of masculinity modeled here are often explicit contrasts to the prototypical male-hero models of the movies or the newsstand. I believe "masculinity" need not be uniformed or essentialized; I'd even suggest that it hurts all of us to assume that there is one standard way of being "male" or "female," any single normative type of gender discourse or modeling imposed upon the young. Asserting that there is only gender specificity and singularity goes against the bodily awareness and knowledge that each of us experiences personally as the opposite pole from the social values of the statistical majority. Dream transformations remind us constantly that we are simultaneously both male and female at some elemental, primal level, for all the day-to-day imbalances and cruelties of our jobs and responsibilities that depend upon simple role definitions and gender assignments.

We need not delve deeply into dreams or the language of the soul or psyche, i.e., *psychology*, to recognize that soul (Greek *psychē*, Latin *anima*) is never just individual; it is always shaped and expressed historico-culturally and physiologically and environmentally. "My experiences" are "mine" in that I am situated here as a result of a very long historico-cultural development. My experiences are part of a very complex network of historical and economic and political factors conveyed by all the communications media, ranging from grandfathers' stories to the latest music video or the fascinating hypertexts made possible by recent advances in computer engineering. Hence in this book I seek to complexify, not to simplify as I push for recognition of the extended period of our cultural development in which important perspectives often have been forgotten or suppressed. I add examples beyond those strictly necessary, and I promote the value of a richly contoured perspective that may have to be reviewed many times before it becomes personally rewarding. We have to confront ideas and values, complex types of narratives and reflective metanarratives, as well as the overlayered iconographies and symbolics by which gendering is conveyed — the explicit as well as the implicit instruction that seeks always to influence us to fulfill gender roles one way or another.

Meanings that are important enough to structure our ethical behaviors are never simple sets of do's and don't's, and any list of moral standards needs a good scrubbing now and then as our society changes and we relate to different contexts, act in different and often more complexly structured relationships. My arguments for complex and multiple images of selfhood, for repeated forays into our own histories and into the rich storehouses of traditions from other cultures, recognize that the contemporary world has infinite arrays of possible choices and that a retreat into the simple fundamentalist dichotomy between absolute good and absolute evil represents a prescription for schizophrenia. There are valuable models worth emulating, ways of being male and female not encompassed by the repetitive evening television news or entertainment programs, and we ignore them at the cost of becoming mindless tools of an oppressive system in which one or another commercial group determines the small range of behaviors appropriate to "an American male," at the cost of losing the sense of multiplicity and excitement that might well be the hallmark of our era. I like Lynn Segal's summary statement in this respect:

> Male sexuality is most certainly not any single shared experience for men. It is not any single or simple thing at all — but the site of any number of emotions of weakness and strength, pleasure and pain, anxiety, conflict, tension and struggle, none of them mapped out in such a way as to make the obliteration of the agency of women in heterosexual engagements inevitable. Male sexuality cannot be reduced to the most popular meanings of sex acts, let alone to sex acts themselves. It becomes intelligible only if placed within actual histories of men's intimate relationships with others — or the lack of them. (1990:215)

The same author suggests that *"a diversity of 'masculinities' jostle to present themselves as the acceptable face of the new male order"* (293; similar opinions are expressed in Seidler 1989 and Brittan 1989).

Expanding Our Logic

It is crucial today to distrust simplistic teachings and to complexify our manner of thinking. We get trapped too easily in the simplicities of the *Playboy* or *Reader's Digest* mentality and can count and imagine only in that awful binary way: 0:1; yes:no; male:female. For one example among many, Elizabeth Minnich in *Transforming Knowledge* (1990) refers to a very different way of thinking found in India, the Jaina system, a seven-pointed logic, rather than the two-point oppositional "is:isn't" logic that Westerners assume to be the way humans think. In the Jaina system the excluded middle is not only raised up, but honored in all its proliferations, so that its followers are able to encompass a rich texture of ways of being right. The excluded middle includes the sort of positional perspectives we are beginning to find necessary if we are to move through contemporary cultural multiversity with any equanimity and poise at all. Minnich gives as an example the work of Gandhi, who was reared in Gunjarat, the area of India where Jaina teachings were most influential.

Minnich points out that in a multiple-optioned logical system the options are not merely "something is" versus "something is not," but between the extremes lies "a third possibility: that in one aspect something is, but in another it is not. That possibility recognizes different elements of existence as relative rather than absolute, i.e., another possibility to our exclusionist logic is that something exists, 'but its nature is otherwise indescribable'" (Minnich 1990:114; she quotes A. L. Basham). Minnich is concerned to re-examine the notion of knowing, and she applies the multi-optioned logic template to the familiar parable of the several blind persons who come across an elephant, the person who encounters the tail asserting that the elephant is like an enormous snake, the one who encounters a leg that the animal is like a huge tree, and so forth. Her point is that we usually laugh at the parable, finding its "truth" to be that only an impartial sighted onlooker will tumble to the true nature of the beast, yet the parable actually makes the point that it is only the holistic knowing of each, the combined knowing of separate parts, that satisfactorily represents the full Gestalt of "the elephant": "The point is . . . that knowledge requires many of us, and that even apparently incompatible models or metaphors can provide part of the picture — if we can give up the notion that there is one right way of knowing it, that only one paradigm can or must rule" (Minnich 1990:114).

Minnich's discussion of Jain logic and the elephant parable provides an occasion to look at gender "differences" in a richer, more rewarding manner than those customary in our social sciences today. Simple reference to the sort of hippie androgyny that was promoted in the 1970s is not sufficient: gender confusion is painful for all concerned, and extremely few of us seem genetically or socially programmed to be ambisexual throughout our lifespans. Freud's claim that every infant is bisexual — his term was "polymorphously perverse" — was tempered by his observation that at any given time the individual acts from the perspective of a single gender alone.

But recent ethnographic accounts have given the lie to the usual "as the child is reared, so is the adult" precepts familiar in the West. Gilbert Herdt has authored or edited a number of publications (1981, 1982) about several Melanesian societies in which males are both homosocialized and homosexualized during their initiatory years. According to the underlying cultural beliefs, if boys do not receive semen orally from older men, they will not become males. But having done so, at maturity they marry and continue both homo- and heterosocial life, although their primary sexual activity will be heterosexual except when initiating a new batch of young men. Doubtless such a society would not have originated the terms "homosexual" and "heterosexual," which became common in Western discourse only in the early part of this century.

Reflecting upon Melanesian concepts of gender from the perspective of feminist anthropology, Marilyn Strathern (1988) reflects at length upon gendering as part of the social construction of reality. To make her points, she has to utilize an entirely different basic metaphor than that of market production and consumption upon which our own social relations are structured, and the discussion gets very technical, but she demonstrates how gendering is a *processual* activity, not a physiological matter of genitals and hormones. Following the Melanesian examples, we might get beyond the domination of gender study by issues such as the sexing of men and women, the individual's self-concept of sexual identity, and how to reprogram gender stability, to the ways in which the process of gendering actually structures various relational networks.

To be sure, initially we have to stretch significantly the boundaries of our customary socialization when Western concepts of single and unitary masculine identity leave us baffled by Melanesian males who flaunt their maleness by revealing that they contain within themselves *not only* maleness, but in addition that which in their culture is considered to be essentially female. Westerners expect maleness to represent "ultra-highest-degree" male qualities defined primarily by binary and exclusive opposition to female traits, but in the Melanesian societies Strathern treats, the *inclusion* of the opposite is valued highly (1988:122–23).

Hence what it means to be "male" or "female" in some Melanesian societies depends upon where and how one is related to another person: one may well be *positionally* a "female" to a male initiator, later a "male" to a male initiate, and a "male" to a female. Yet that third stage of gender would include a strong "female" component as the man has incorporated femaleness as part of his "maleness," and in this model, become *much more* "male" as a result.

Closer to home, American novelist Ursula Le Guin's *The Left Hand of Darkness* (1969) is set on a faraway planet locked in the midst of an ice age of universal proportions. A brilliant sustained experiment in gender modeling, the novel portrays a situation in which physiological sex is fully hermaphroditic — *positionally* hermaphroditic, since at the periodic times of sexual arousal, each of two persons in a pair-bond chooses whether to be male or female for the period of estrus. What might have been a very difficult scenario to imagine is sensitively modeled by Le Guin, as she highlights the confusion of off-planet visitors from places like Earth, who are nonplused in meeting a hirsute male who refers to the child he has borne during a period when "he" was a female.

Beyond the subtle exploration of the ways gender identities determine much of daily human contact and the romantic escape-motif in which the off-worlder is saved by the figure who seems initially to be his betrayer, Le Guin also makes sure that we get her points about (1) how superficial gender distinctions can be, and (2) what the successive genderings on the ice-clad planet make possible: It is a world without war (since there's no need for nasty displays of masculinist virility, although there is some pretty dreadful competitiveness nevertheless), without sexual hang-ups (no Oedipal-Jocastic patterns, since children see parents variously as male and as female), and without gender-specific employments (since it is not just females who have the child-rearing roles and anyone can follow the heart's desires).

Reimagining Binary Opposition

Discussing a novel primarily regarded as being within the literary genre of speculative or science fiction helps illustrate that *gendering is an imaginative construction.* I do not mean that it is made up at the beginning of each millennium, and various gender models then pass a board of judges, but I have in mind Tom Moore's rather striking reminder that "gender is one of the grand *metaphors* for the human condition" (1990:125) — not biologically innate so much as channeled according to the social and mental models portrayed in myths and hero ideals; not "something in the blood" but socially determined by the imaginations of our literature, our arts, and our religious moralisms.

Richard Dellamora (1990) explores how writers in the Victorian period such as Melville, Wilde, Whitman, and Swinburne gave birth to the rhetorics in which later generations would be able to talk about their masculinity; and historians have demonstrated how various images of masculinity have imagined and articulated specific historical settings.[1] What might seem a transcendent, ahistorical masculine ideal, such as men's physical strength, turns out to be quite recent, established only a few decades ago, and indeed it replaced the earlier predominant ideal of the sensitive, caring male whose primary role was to serve and improve the divinely ordained social order.

Changes in the American family structure led to the Victorian sentimentalizing of women, and the development of separate gender realms divided male and female sociality just as the Industrial Revolution scattered the family members across specialized job sites. Subsequently women became the primary, if not sole, parents responsible for the home and childrearing. More recently, after the beginnings of *gay* liberation (the famous Stonewall Inn bar incident, 27 June 1969), *male* liberation took on different contours than it had earlier in the 1950s and early 1960s when it was primarily an adjunct to the women's liberation movement. The subsequent emphasis upon the feeling, supportive male sponsored by pop psychology in the 1960s and 1970s was driven underground in tandem with the resurgence of the frontier-looking Republican administration, beginning with Ronald Reagan's imperial but know-nothing presidency.

These instances illustrate just a few of the ways in which historical periods and socio-political contexts determine ways masculinities will be shaped, but most frequently gender is construed abstractly today, as if it had always and everywhere meant one gender versus another, as if masculinity ought to be defined as the exact opposite of femininity, rather than as (perhaps) one point on a continuum or spectrum of personality. Serious dangers derive from operating as if the binary opposition came down from the heavens on a golden platter, and later I will call into question some of the ways we use binarism to exacerbate a clash between male-ness and female-ness, or between the Apollonian and the Dionysian, the macho and the wimp, and so forth. Eve Kosofsky Sedgwick (1990) notes how the binary contrast between one thing and another was a particular development of the Modernist period in our thinking, just as she notes how the development of the concept of homosexuality toward the end of the last century left many homosexual persons feeling that they were neither female nor male, but stranded in a non-gendered never-never land. The same absolutist binarism contributed to the standard psychiatric treatment of homosexuality as an *inversion* of "normally gendered" sexuality.[2]

Binarism has left such a trail of oppositional imagining and speaking that today straight-identified heterosexual men have almost no vocabulary with which to discuss bodily or emotional contact with other males that doesn't feel "homosexual" to them, and hence threatening (Dellamora 1990:5). Likewise males fear any even faintly sexual contact with other men because that would either "make them queer" or disclose that they had been latent homosexuals all along (the so-called homosexual panic). Anything that attracts men to other men must, by such simplistic logic, be *sexual,* the only one of the languages of relationship in which we develop sophistication beyond a junior-high-school level (hence I argue for an athletics or aesthetics of friendship, Doty 1992). Accordingly the normative "masculine" often means that one is sexually repressed, as well as "rational," interpreted as being cold and scientific, non-attached, impartial — all those ways of detaching oneself from feeling relatedness.

Lewis Hyde refers to *eros* as "the principle of attraction, union, involvement which binds together" as opposed to *logos,* "reason and logic in general, the principle of differentiation in particular" (1983:xiv). Hyde makes eros carry rather a different load here than it would have in classical culture (Halperin 1990 consistently parallels it with "sexual passion"), but his distinction between differentiation and separation (scission, science) on the part of logos and synthesis and relationship on the part of eros is useful. The second half of our century has witnessed several attempts to rejoin logos and eros, but the binary way of opposing them as "natural" opposites like oil and water returns repeatedly, in everyday diction as well as in scholarly analysis.

On another pairing, that between masculinity and rationality, Victor Seidler's *Rediscovering Masculinity: Reason, Language, and Sexuality* is especially useful. Seidler's book investigates the Kantian ethical tradition concerning the will, a tradition in which feelings and emotions must come from someplace outside the male, defined as *the rational* animal to whom feelings and emotions would be foreign (1989:24). Such a view negates the historical construction of our reality when it denies that the emotions are shaped in any way other than by the (feminine) *materiality* (*mater* = feminine, fleshly, maternal) that a real ("rational") man will learn to subdue. Supposedly rational men do not *have* needs, they *master* them, and since we cannot admit that we have needs, we become rather unskilled at giving to others in ways that will satisfy their needs. The model likewise understands "falling in love" only negatively as something that happens to us, just what the Greeks expressed in the metaphor of the irresistible arrows of the god Eros.

And this dominant Greco-Roman and Jewish-Christian perspective understands human nature as essentially untrustworthy: "We cannot trust it, nor can we expect good to come from it. We have to look beyond ourselves and our human nature for our notions of justice and morality," and certainly we will not look to *women*, who as representatives of *materiality* as contrasted to (masculine) spirituality are suspect from the outset. Likewise they are involved in the messy particularity of life as actually lived out, in history and family rather than in transcendent ideas; "what women have to say is branded with the status of the particular, whilst men offer what they see as an encompassing and objectively-grounded account" (Seidler 1990:38, 123). In another essay, Seidler discusses the connection between emotionality and *madness*, which is what males have been taught to fear when they experience sexual impulses — which therefore must represent non-rationality and hence animality, nature as opposed to civilization (1987:87).

In a related critique, Arthur Brittan notes the common male assumption that reason is "genderless, not contaminated by emotion and passion," and how being "rational" in our society implies not the messy business of making moral choices such as resisting war or tyranny or developing empathy with the downtrodden, but "being impartial and objective, [implying] a distancing of the observer from the object of his research, or policy" (1989:199; see also the arguments concerning nuclear physics and warfare by Easlea 1983). It seems a good sign that the contemporary sciences are reminded frequently today of the shaping of the "objective" researcher's results by the politicized funding of the laboratory, the desire for personal status through the fame of discovery, or the implicit sexist assumptions that "gentlemen" agree tacitly to sustain when they ignore fully qualified female co-workers. Future historians will find puzzling just how the "sciences" — literally, "ways of knowing by dividing" — came to exclude the moral-evaluative as contrasted with the merely statistical modes of epistemology and pedagogy.

They will note how strangely we treated adolescence, the time of the greatest sexual urgency, by treating it as a never-never land isolated from both childhood and adulthood. We place before the adolescent the most explicit genitality imaginable (look at the ads and layout in any magazine aimed at the teen market), reinforce it with constant eroticized advertising and entertainment, and yet we provide no ongoing, careful

training in the erotic as a form of human relationship that is not necessarily aimed at reproduction of what is today the statistically dominant
small family unit. Imagine a parent or older sibling teaching a child how
to masturbate most enjoyably, and my point strikes home: we pile on
the statistical surveys and "how to" information, surround youth with
beckoning images of fantastic erotic satisfaction, and then expect them
to "just say no!" when it comes to satisfying the arousal the culture has
stimulated.

Cultural Constructions of Gender

My exposition of positions represented by Dellamora, Seidler, and Brittan will have clarified the approach to the gendering of masculinity
represented in this book. It is an approach that seeks imaginatively or
metaphorically to restructure gender roles, rather than checking with
some master data bank hovering in the sky or buried in a control center under the Rocky Mountains or jockstrapped beneath Rocky's boxing
shorts. The imagination, the realm of metaphor, is not the realm of the
unreal. It is the realm of the thought-through and experienced, as passed
through the metaphoric naming and symbolizing that denotes human
culture as contrasted with mere physiology. For such realms, the terms
"cultural production" and "code," as well as "cultural fiction," are used
by the classical historian David Halperin, but Halperin uses "fiction" as I
would, to emphasize the arbitrary *construction* or selection of social values. "Construction" is a term cognate in sense to "factory" — likewise
derived from *facere*, to construct or make, not from a root term implying
non-reality. The ways sexuality gets shaped and expressed, or patterns
such as homosexuality or heterosexuality are qualified, are hardly "pure
facts of life (as such things used to be called), positive and changeless features of the natural world," as objectified by the scientistic sexologists'
attempts to determine physiological roots of sexual preference. "Rather,
they are among the cultural codes which, in any society, give human
beings access to themselves as meaningful subjects of their experiences
and which are thereby objectivated — that is, realized in actuality" (see
Halperin 1990:25, 40, 43, 27).

Such objectifications become normative by means of custom and
legislation, but also because they are conveyed imaginatively through
literature and the arts. Twentieth-century researchers have developed
massive data files such as the Kinsey Report and more recently *The
Hite Report* (Hite 1981) and Nancy Friday's *Men in Love* (1980) — col-
lecting hundreds of personal anecdotes, many of which would have been

suppressed as pornographic a few decades ago. But our society has been less active in probing the more historically rooted cultural imagery that underlies social expectations and ethics, and I keep emphasizing here the need to reconsider the deep cultural images primarily transmitted through legendary and mythical models. Hence we approach masculinity and the heroic here not in the abstract, but through stories, narratives of representative human figures and beings, and their physical representation in the arts. And of course that means also through iconography and imagery that sometimes gets clarified only in retrospect. In spite of generations of analytical studies of "the nude in art," for instance, only now does contemporary society recognize that the *male* nude is as appropriate an artistic object as the female. For the ancient Greeks, on the other hand, it was the female figure that came onto the artistic scene only at a relatively late point of development.

Ours is a brave new world to which we've hardly begun to adjust. It is a world whose oppositions are more and more questionable. In canvassing what comes after the women's liberation movement, for instance, John Moore highlights just the oppositions between masculine and feminine values and perspectives that have been outlined here: "What is the difference between, or the connection between, the image of a religious woman worshipping an effigy of a near-naked, bleeding man impaled in agony on a cross and the image of a male voyeur looking lustfully at a pornographic photograph of a nude and bound woman being whipped? Why is one 'respect-able' and the other not? Why is one classified as sadistic and the other not?" (1989:154). Moore's book would be more valuable if he had attempted to answer these queries, with which he ends a chapter, but at least his aggressive questioning points both to the arbitrary nature of cultural standards and to the confusion in our own day when so many of those standards are challenged.

Anyone examining language usage carefully observes that what is meant by masculinity even in casual conversation is seldom clear: Does it refer to biological or physiological equipment? Then how can one speak about a "masculinized woman"? Does it refer purely to social roles? Then how can we compare a hulking television wrestler with a svelte gymnast and conceive of either the former or the latter as "more masculine"? Is it purely a matter of the symbolic order that certain designations apply to males, others to females, so that we have (self-evidently Freudian) "phallic" images? Or do we refer primarily to the ways one gender has traditionally exerted power over the other, in which case historical shaping of economic roles will select out one or the other gender as most "powerful" when that gender is the head of the household —

I am referring to the problem that now faces many minimum-income households where the woman may be more able than the man to remain employed.

The Hidden Power of Masculine Icons

Symbolic positions supported by our metaphors of gender are determined only partly by either self-conscious choices or physiology. They may vary enormously within any particular society, no matter how loudly that society proclaims the contours of ideal gender roles. Lynne Segal points out that while the self-consciously evoked symbolic gender representations appear to be larger than life, in fact "masculinity is never the undivided, seamless construction it becomes in its symbolic manifestation. The promise of phallic power is precisely this guarantee of total inner coherence" (1990:102). If the phallic promise is to supply what is actually lacking in real experience, its power becomes a characteristic of patriarchy — totalizing and all-encompassing on its own behalf. No wonder there is so much significance attached to phallic representations in our culture, even if they are subtly hidden by the professional conventions of glamor advertising.

And if the masculine can appear as completely self-evident, a "natural" part of the air one breathes, it will dominate discourse to the extent of suppressing questions about its own nature. According to Anthony Easthope, such suppression has taken place already: "Despite all that has been written over the past twenty years on femininity and feminism, masculinity has stayed pretty well concealed. This has always been its ruse in order to hold on to its power. Masculinity tries to stay invisible by passing itself off as normal and universal. Words such as 'man' and 'mankind,' used to signify the human species, treat masculinity as if it covered everyone" (1990:1). "If masculinity can present itself as normal it automatically makes the feminine seem deviant and different," and the dichotomizing of the fundamental understanding of gender in which the masculine and feminine categories remain totally opposed triumphs once more.

"The natural" also remains opposed to the specific socio-historical, but if one recognizes just how artificial the category of "the natural" actually is, masculinity begins to appear in a new light. It is no longer to be considered one monolithic source to be attacked or dismantled, leading the masculine power brokers to political retrenchment or to more showy wars in which to demonstrate patriarchal dominance, but as one component of the extreme social complexity of the late twentieth century. Such a deconstructive perspective will hardly be greeted with open arms by those who stand to lose inherited privilege, since it threatens the dominant view of masculinity precisely by seeking to change its definition. It will almost certainly create its own backlash as threats to traditional models of masculinity strike the paranoid as yet another blow to the absolute, divinely established social order that is already ashatter in the contemporary world. If there is no single cultural definition of maleness, conservatives might argue, the only alternative would be a chaos of alternatives that they find extremely threatening.

The overall situation surfacing here is an aspect of the postmodernist ethical open-endedness that accompanies a full cultural pluralism. Such pluralism disallows claims to transcendent, transtemporal masculine norms, as it becomes apparent that "the masculine" is in fact modeled anew within each successive historical context. Merely listing or identifying abstractly the symbolic structures through which gender is expressed ignores the fact that they are always manifested historically and materially, specifically within individual lives, and consequently "meaning" differently in each. Late twentieth-century interpretation theory emphasizes that meanings are determined and replicated within specific communities whose members implicitly agree to their significations; they are not established from the outside by applying essentialist Platonic Ideas or religious dogmas.

Two iconographic examples of such cultural relativity demonstrate the arbitrary historicity of the phallos: in the Middle Ages, Jesus' penis was not "seen" as a sexual tool but as a reminder of the Christ's symbolic subjection to circumcision and by extension to his painful suffering on behalf of humankind. In ancient Pompeii, on the other hand, penis-shaped oil lamps, door-chimes, and waterspouts were common, evidently being "seen" more in the Mediterranean custom as devices to scare away evil powers than as sexual or erotic icons in our sense, illustrated in Monick 1987 and Strage (1980:160), who notes that above one bakery shop a carved sign with an erect penis and testicles carried the legend "Here Dwells Felicity." Negotiations of meanings are not such simple or individual matters as conservative American politics and religiosity would have one think since symbolic power does not operate in splendid isolation from other social forces. Such social forces vary enormously: "many social mediators — from school, jobs, friends, family, religion and politics — effect the way fantasies may, or may not, be channelled into any active expression, and determine what form, if any, they take" (Segal 1990:91, 265).

The very material language in which we refer to gender expression is determined reciprocally by that language, so that we are always hooked into a network of significations in which decisions have been made on our behalf. So much for the rule of nature over culture! And so much for a view of the human being that stresses only radical independence and self-determination. We recognize just how strongly societies determine gendering when we confront the image of the non-heterosexual, the transvestite, the person with "gender-confusion," a man or woman who likes to cross-dress, and the like. And gay persons have been represented on television in ways that highlight gender boundaries, since boundary definition is often a titillating part of the entertainment game, much of the titillation coming from the fact that boundaries are always guarded most carefully when they appear to be threatened, as they are increasingly today (see Butters 1989).

The New Right has capitalized upon the proliferation of the changing types of experience in our century's "melting pot," and it strings together a number of supposed causes of the proliferation that can then all be attacked in the same terms. Britain had its Thatcheresque assertion of boundary claiming in the Falklands episode, the United States in the Persian Gulf nightmare and in the resurgence of political and religious right-wing groups and the well-financed "think tanks" that have produced their copious propaganda disguised as impartial news releases, scientific reports, and analyses of dangerous campus liberalism. Such groups typically oppose not only any change in traditional masculine-dominated gender hierarchies, reacting strongly to all the liberation movements begun in the 1960s, but changes with regard to many related issues such as sex education in the schools, denial of women's right to terminate forced or unwanted pregnancies, reassertion of pre-women's-liberation housewife-in-the-home roles, treatment of gays and lesbians as inferior and ill deviants, and any attempt to rethink moral values in the light of the complexity of the international situation today. Jeffrey Weeks helpfully reviews the ways members of the New Right lump together many of these issues in ideological frameworks that have forced even political liberals to talk as if they were living once again on the early American frontier (1986:12, 30, 106).

But meanwhile the languages of intellectual analysis and discussion in the humanities have echoed the technical specialization of the sciences and grown increasingly arcane and almost non-intuitive in their references to difference and the return of the same, phallogocentrism, and vaginal discourse. It doesn't take much sophisticated training in the evaluation of symbolism and the re-opening of historically and culturally produced symbolic assumptions to see how traditional phallicism finds upsetting various radical demonstrations of the socially constructed nature of gendered sexuality, with the concomitant political assertion that traditional views must now be relentlessly challenged. An example from David Halperin: "The arbitrary character of sexual acculturation is perhaps clearest in the case of heterosexuality: the production of a population of human males who are (supposedly) incapable of being sexually excited by a person of their own sex *under any circumstances* is itself a cultural event without, so far as I know, either precedent or parallel, and cries out for an explanation. No inquiry into the origins of homosexuality can therefore be divorced from an inquiry into the origins of heterosexuality" (1990:44).

Of course Halperin intends to be provocative. Of course he seizes the imaginal reins of language to make it pay out a new vision of difference, a vision of a critique that makes *heterosexuality*, not homosexuality, defend its right *to be* the phallic dominant. In our exploration of masculinity, we confront here a central problem concerning appropriate fictions or social constructions. To approach the issue as suggested, as a matter of imagining gender, leads to a recommendation to reject the conservative position in favor of the liberal, because it remains more flexible, more aware of the determinative influences of the historical and social contexts that shape our experiences of gendering and the ways we speak about gender. In this sense the metaphoric "phallos," the idealization of the masculine, is never fully possessed by anyone. As a socially determined signifier, it represents a direction rather than a realization, a goal rather than a place of arrival, even though there have been many phallos-worshiping institutions across human history. (When teaching a course on Men and Spirituality, however, I was amazed at how little the subject has been studied, perhaps because of the assumption that religion and masculinity would "naturally" be equated.[3])

Instead of representing a goal or maturation or abstraction, masculinity appears to be a propensity to develop in one or another direction. As Lynne Segal suggests, "masculinity is not some type of single essence, innate or acquired. As it is represented in our culture, 'masculinity' is a quality of being which is always incomplete, and which is equally based on a social as on a psychic reality" (1990:123). Further, masculinity is a quality we ascribe to the achievements of *human* culture, yet "it is physically tangible only as a piece of biological equipment men share with rats, bats, and every other higher vertebrate male" (181).

Now if masculinity is primarily a cultural production that will be experienced always in specific local contours, then change is possible, and books such as this are predicated upon the possibility that changes can be made, and that more useful and satisfactory gender appreciations can be developed. That development seems important in the face of suggestions such as Segal's that " 'masculinity' has replaced 'femininity' as the problem of our time — *a threat to civilization itself"* (1990:60, my emphasis). Even psychoanalyst Gregory Rochlin, speaking from a strict Freudian perspective I find otherwise very limiting, reinforces this view of masculinity as a crucial dilemma today: *"Masculinity is not a stable condition.* Again and again [we find that] in its various periods of development masculinity must be reasserted over myriad recurring doubts that just as regularly must be dispelled" (1980:4, my emphasis). No simple guides to being a man such as we hoped we'd find in the school library; not even a videotape we can watch while the person we live with is away: masculinity appears to be less an achievement than a position, an attitude that each generation — even perhaps each man — must redefine anew.

And finally we must ask about those who believe that the very physiological nature of "masculinity" — in spite of its various social symbolizations that are the ways genders are enacted — is so important that thousands of men have chosen to receive penile implants. Such an operation allows a man to perform intercourse with a fully erect penis *yet makes penile sensation impossible* (Segal 1990:219; Drummond 1987). Likewise the threat of real or imagined castration drives many men quite literally screaming onto therapists' couches, pouring out their anger and rage, but also their fear of impotence or their inability to produce anything of value that will prove their masculine productivity (Monick 1991). Do we have here just another instance of the belief in medical instant-cure? Why has the physiological become so important in our lives that we play down the psychological or emotional?

Our topic is complex in the extreme; like other global classifying concepts such as happiness, masculinity depends from both social and individual flagpoles simultaneously. Gendering is part of socialization in that it determines the parameters of what will be experienced, yet it is likewise a matter of individual experience in that the individual will realize only a few of the social meanings of the overall concept. Reflecting on interviews with men in the British men's movement, Segal argues for the need "to think in terms of 'masculinities,' rather than any single masculinity, and even then to be wary of attempts to impart to them any fixed psychological dimensions" (1990:289). Or, as we have seen in this chapter, any fixed psycho-social dimensions, or for that matter, physiological dimensions, since masculinity has become another of the elements of human experience that no longer seem self-evident, essential, or divinely given. We need new self-consciousness about genders, more complex logics for comprehending them, and greater attention to the ways genders are socially, not biologically constructed. Precisely in the context of learning to understand the social displays of gendering, the next chapter begins by looking at representations of masculinity in the mass media.

Masculinity in Media Images, Gender, and the Men's Movements

You can't look at a movie, an ad, a sitcom, or a TV weatherman nowadays without seeing men as bimbos, love tokens, pinups, video beefcake, call them what you will. From Michael Douglas parading his clenched but sagging buttocks in Basic Instinct *to the pouty pinups on "Beverly Hills 90210" to the legions of shirtless pretty boys staring from every bus shelter ad, men are being treated as, well, pieces of meat. A current ad for Wisk laundry detergent begins with a crotch shot of a guy taking off his blue jeans.*

(Stengel 1992:74)

Media Models of Masculinity

In order to encompass contemporary masculinities, one must look both backward into social history and sideways into the cultural-psychological, the "depth" or mythic dimensions that inform our culture. One must also look at the many symbolic expressions of masculinity in culture — in mass media, popular publications, iconography, and advertising. Reading in the *Boston Globe* as I write this paragraph that the movie sequel *Terminator 2: Judgment Day* capitalized out its $90 million investment after only two weeks at the cinemas, and then glancing at a copy of *Musclemag*'s "Special Commemorative Arnold Issue!," which traces Arnold's physique back to age fifteen and has a large pull-out photographic poster, I can't help but think "what else do we need to know about the representation of the masculine in our society?" But there are examples like Schwarzenegger's — complete with confessions of taking steroids, but carefully managed to mention his civic contributions and his business expertise — and then there are hundreds of other ways of representing maleness, as when we look at a figure such as Bill Cosby, himself the author of a best-selling book on father-

41

ing (1986), or at some of the homophobic representations that have been critiqued recently in works I will cite subsequently.

The study of masculine iconography and especially mass-media representations and commodifications of the masculine is in its infancy. I remember when my students in the 1970s began to discover and document subtle feminine symbols in advertising and the entertainment media, but the explicitness with respect to images of men is already at a stage of development that took twenty years with respect to images of women. I refer, for instance, to a recent advertisement for Calvin Klein's men's cologne Obsession, a full frontal nude of a male from the neck to just above the penis, and the words of the advertisement ("Obsession, for men, for the body") and the name of the cosmetics company his only adornment. The pose might seem to be directed explicitly to the gay male market, except that it appeared in a *women's* fashion magazine. I'm not so sure the obvious is all that obvious, then, and when I spoke to a fashion photographer about other Calvin Klein ads, one in which two half-dressed adolescents stare into the unbuttoned top of her jeans, another where the young woman is pulling open the crotch of her male companion's trousers, the photographer replied that, didn't I know? what was to be conveyed in fashion photography was all sex, with references to the product being sold being almost incidental.

Often when I look at advertising images or media enactments of masculinity I wonder how many people consciously puzzle through their indirect representations and social implications. What happens when *Rolling Stone*, which has been a pulpy music mag, devotes over half its pages to fashion features on scruffy males with half-grown beards and usually unbuttoned shirts, or no shirts at all? As I write this, the issue just published has on its cover three totally nude male singers staring at the camera, hands, of course, cupped carefully over their genitals and the name of the group running (hardly accidentally) in a banner just below, "Red Hot Chili Peppers." Just how the inner and the outer are related, the expressed content or purpose alongside the implied or latent, is a fascinating topic in contemporary culture. It is the basis for all sorts of interpretive and debunking enterprises, and Anthony Easthope's often-cited *What a Man's Gotta Do: The Masculine Myth in Popular Culture* (1990) provides a good example. Easthope assumes the orthodox psychoanalytical standpoint that the problem with masculinity is that of hiding the fact of non-difference; that is, the fact that physiologically, we are all initially bisexual, and hence the problem involves defending that hidden truth by aggressively covering it over with the assertion that men "should be masculine all the way through." Masculine energies are directed toward defending against any suggestion of "feminine" tenderness; "to be unified [the masculine ego] must be masculine all the way through and so the feminine will always appear as something other or different and so a security risk" (19, 42).

Furthermore "the masculine ego must master everything," and that means in particular the personal body and the body politic. The physical body becomes a kind of armored machine: "a hard body will ensure that there are no leakages across the edges between inner and outer worlds" (51–52). That theme of the hard body appears repeatedly, as in a favorite teenybopper poster of a mostly nude male hunk with the slogan "A hard man is good to find" — as well as in any of today's physical exercise magazines or advertisements (I think I first saw the Hard Man slogan on a Soloflex ad). And the personal hard body carries over to nationalism, even when, in Easthope's example, its carrier is the female prime minister, Mrs. Thatcher: the kind of overt nationalistic fervor expressed in the Falklands episode "is masculine in the way it marks . . . a hard line between inside and outside, treating the body and the ego as fixed, self-sufficient. . . . Nationalism fits perfectly with the masculine ego and the masculine body, so that each overlaps and confirms the other" (56). And the opposing side will appear, as Easthope documents from British news accounts of 1982: "(1) unstable, constantly varying in shape and outline; (2) having a false appearance; (3) as an organization made up from different bits and pieces; and (4) irrational and animal." "Our" side, the "masculine" side, displays all the opposites of these: "(1) single and undivided in body and ego; (2) true and real; (3) unified and solid, the same all the way through; [and] (4) rational, subject to reason and law" (56–57).

That the list representing normative masculinity represents just what any red-blooded contemporary would doubtless argue ought to be normative *regardless of gender* is an indication of the extent to which these "masculine" values permeate our society. But we might ask: What's wrong with changing constantly in order to move gracefully into new situations? With appearing in the best light to fit the situation? With comprising the body politic from many various interests and contributions, and allowing each to speak severally and equally? With honoring the passion and love and emotionality that often calls into question the rationally derived standards of dominating aggressor societies as they conquer others in the name of human progress? With having a soft, not a hard, body that can embrace rather than confront and conquer, enfold rather than repulse?

Such questioning is not necessarily derived from the recent men's movement, but includes attitudes fostered by the women's movement. Other recent criticism reveals more specific analysis from the perspective of the masculine. Andrew Ross (1990) and Christopher Castiglia (1990) provide examples of the sort of critical reinterpretation of popular entertainment that is already being presented at conferences, if not yet published widely. Ross points to the 1987 film *Tin Men* as having curious reflections of the early television series "Bonanza," and thence ultimately the standard Western movie, a genre that was obsessed with masculinity and its technological extensions. The side-by-side comparison of *Tin Men* and the Western brings out the problems we have with the cowboy genre today as well as with American values represented in both, in the light of what we now realize was repressed, such as the vast genocide of Native Americans (at contact they may have comprised a larger civilized population than that of Europe) and the brutalizing of small homesteaders by corporate ranchers. Furthermore, "what has been repressed, of course, is the debt of the Southwestern cowboy mythology to the *vaquero* culture of Mexican cattlemen, which it appropriated wholesale, along with the culturally specific macho codes of the *rancheros*" (88). Recent surveys of African Americans among the early frontier cowboys suggest that the standard retro-image of White Cowboys and Red Indians suppresses the accurate history of another racial group as well.

Ross points to the inability of the frontier saga to resolve "the contradiction between, on the one hand, the opportunistic brand of male self-reliance that is often referred to as 'rugged individualism' and, on the other, the communal domesticity represented by the settlement family, each threatened in different ways by the arrival from the East of technological development and government regulation" (88). Furthermore, Michael Kimmel (1987) traces the ways the cowboy image has resurfaced throughout the crisis periods of American politics, most recently in the Reagan administration, as a repressed but volatile model that has influenced not only presidents but also the very idealism of the American economy. It can hardly be accidental that Maine native George Bush found it expedient to establish his home-on-the-range credentials in Texas.

Castiglia's "Rebel without a Closet" (1990) also treats instances of repression, in this case repression of the homosexual, or possibly homosexual, friendship between the primary male characters in several motion pictures — first in *Rebel without a Cause*, 1955, and then in two television movies, *Consenting Adults*, 1985, and *Welcome Home, Bobby*, 1986. Castiglia demonstrates that the very structures of the cinematography convey disciplining perspectives on the character's sexuality; Michel Foucault's observations about the application of the dominant culture's values by means of its "disciplines" (not only the police, but social welfare programs, schooling, and medicine) are demonstrated throughout these movies. In a postscript to his essay, Castiglia demonstrates that homophobic elements abound also in *Nightmare on Elm Street 2: Freddy's Revenge*, 1985.

Both Ross and Castiglia identify ways popular materials carry gender teaching or preaching, helping us to become aware of masculinity issues conveyed as models on the movie screen, a medium treated with respect to its mythico-religious aspects by Geoffrey Hill (1992), who analyzes masculine and feminine "monsters" in thirteen movies. In addition, Easthope analyzes banter or repartee as a style of interpersonal exchange that is typical of representations of men in movies. Easthope notes with respect to *Butch Cassidy and the Sundance Kid*, 1969, for instance: "to the end [the two male protagonists, played by Paul Newman and Robert Redford] cannot admit their love for each other except through attack. In banter explicit antagonism between two masculine egos covers the implicit male bond" (1990:87). And in her extensive catalogue of representations of masculinity in film, Joan Mellen points to a series of films (*On the Waterfront, To Have and Have Not, The Big Sleep, The African Queen*) in which male figures must decide between male-male or male-female friendships. She notes that often the friendships are quasi-homosexual, "such as that between Newman and Redford," and they "proceed only when women have been eliminated" (1977:14).

Mellen notes parallels between American films in which two men travel together (Hopalong Cassidy, Roy Rogers, John Wayne, each with a faithful sidekick), on the one hand, and the "preadolescent bonding of young males who temporarily fear women and prefer each other's company, yet indulge in excessive displays of machismo to convince everyone that despite their exclusively male grouping they are really heterosexual," on the other (14). Or one might point to the elaborate insults often involved in the slap-on-the-butt put-down, or the teasing relationship formalized in "doing the dozens," a series of competitive insults: many men have been taught never to reveal overtly what they are really feeling toward other men, even if it is more positive than negative, cooperative rather than antagonistic. It is hard for American men to admit to the *erotic* aspect of a male-male friendship because of what Halperin calls our "insidious temptation to sexualize the erotics of male friendship" (1990:75) — but right there may be a helpful distinction: can we perhaps learn to distinguish the *erotic-relational* aspects from the enacted *genital-sexual* aspects? Some of the mythic models explored in this book indicate that males can have richly integrative relationships that are not dependent upon genital-sexual connections, that those connections of friendship and association may belie pathologies and demonstrate positive male-male associations at a healthy primary level indeed.

Male Objects and Desire

These examples of analysis of motion pictures indicate that stereotypes and objectifications of masculinities in popular culture are often discernible with only minimal analytical attention.[1] But regardless of how the media represent men as desiring objects or as objects of desire, "real men" get objectified and evaluated according to standard scripts the culture reserves for males.[2] Analysts within the women's movement have already documented a great deal about the objectification of women in advertising and the media. We learn that the putative subject of the advertisement, its image, may have little to do with its reference to the underlying cultural code of gender differences that become "naturalized" in a society, and that change from generation to generation, or even, in fad-driven America, from year to year. More and more frequently men are addressed directly by advertisers as they become independent consumers, either living alone or making their own purchases in the "men's departments" that have become prominent recently in many general merchandise stores (featuring expensive deodorants, hair dressings, luggage, eyeglasses), even though the new attention to male consumers has necessitated revamping some longstanding policies: "the promotion of fragrance [men's colognes, scented deodorants, etc.] to straight men, for example, involves a break with the formula that men hunt, women attract — not to mention the overcoming of homophobic resistance" (Wernick 1987:279). The "family-man" approach so familiar through the 1970s has almost vanished, as "singles" designates the hot new market, and the appeal to traditional patriarchal situations is considered out of date.

Richard Dyer (1985, 1990) observes that it is not just how explicitly the male is represented in the advertisement or movie, but how the object of the viewer's gaze is constituted that determines the relative extent of male dominance being symbolized. Consider the "heroine in jeopardy," saved by the strong silent male hero (represented in advertising by all those odd detergent/cleanser saviors who will rescue the poor maiden faced by a dirty ring around hubby's collar or grunge in the sink), or the way the hero gazes in fascination at the woman he will eventually rescue or seduce: repeatedly, the structures are the same. Both the typical dramatic sequence of the movie or ad and male sexuality are "goal-orientated: seduction and foreplay are merely the means by which one gets to the 'real thing,' an orgasm, the great single climax" (Dyer 1985:41; the Coca-Cola ads playing upon "the real thing" can hardly have been as innocent as they appeared to be on a superficial viewing: not only did they echo sexual ecstasy but the supposition that the soft drink included a form of cocaine among its ingredients).

Women and material objects are "put in their place." Men resolve problems, dominate confusing situations, and save the helpless female or child — all structural scenes easily tracked in Irving Goffman's classical critique of film and advertising images, *Gender Advertisements* (1979). But is this representation "natural"? or is it arbitrarily *selected* from *various* natural patterns? Perhaps we are no longer able to differentiate the mythic from the natural, because of our society's repetitive claim to base itself on what came aboriginally into being. The mythic, as Roland Barthes argued, is precisely what the society has decreed it will be; it is precisely what is *not* natural, but culturally defined as essential — and often that has meant *as masculine*. The process by which such definition takes place influences contemporary advertising or film, even determining the "small heterosexual family" as the only normative audience for television: John Leo (1989) notes that no gay people were represented on television programs in the 1950s and 1960s because they were considered to be a class outside the heterosexual boundaries, external to the assumed viewing family's experience. Even in the 1980s when gay figures became more familiar, they were still excluded as major figures in ongoing serial programs; and when in the 1990s gay figures are focal, they are seldom presented as individuals but rather as composite figures made up of straight stereotypes of gay life (35, 39, 42).

Surely most of us agree with psychotherapist Robert Hopcke when he emphasizes the role of popular entertainment movies in the expression of deep-reaching cultural values: "If any modern development could be credited for nearly single-handedly carrying forward the archetypal contents of the collective unconscious into modern consciousness, it would be the movies and the movie stars who populate the mythic universe of film" (1990:141). More detailed analysis of the ways masculinity is being traditionally expressed or revisioned will doubtless be forthcoming, but what is clear already is that such study will dovetail very neatly with feminist film criticism, as is clear in much of Dyer's perspective in his comprehensive catalogue of lesbian and gay films (1990) or in almost any recent study of the portrayal of gender roles in films, television, rock music, and advertising.

Analysis of the ways images of masculinity are displayed across the whole range of public communication media will most likely parallel criticism from the early years of the feminist movement that were devoted to images of women. A brief catalogue must stand in here for more detailed discussions:

- Kelly Boyd demonstrates (1991) the tensions in masculine definition in the period between the World Wars, as exhibited in magazines such as *Boy's Life* published for young men.

- Other studies are already developing close critiques of important historical and literary figures in whose public lives their masculine persona was manipulated by their own careful design or by their biographers. An example of the first will be found in Clarke's study of Thomas Carlyle (1991), and of the latter in Dawson's very strong account (1991) of the glorification of the heroic Lawrence of Arabia by Lowell Thomas, with Richard Meyer's "Rock Hudson's Body" (1991) demonstrating the collusion between the gay movie idol and his publicists.

- Richard Dellamora looks back to Victorian Britain to indicate how important the mass media can be in such situations: the punitive anti-homosexual Labouché amendment to the British Criminal Law of 1885 was introduced and enacted at the last minute in order to give one newspaper owner in Parliament a scoop over another; and without a particular muckraking press in 1889, the Cleveland Street scandal would not have occurred, since the principal figures involved would have been able to keep the wraps on the situation (1990:201, 205).

- Susan Jeffords (1990) has sought to analyze the changing American attitudes toward Vietnam through their representations in films: she finds that the post-war period saw a self-conscious "remasculinization" of national public discourse and the Stars and Stripes craze that reached across many social strata of the nation.

The traditional appeal to military and technological advances associated with masculinity and patriarchy begins to be mitigated today after Bopal, when we have seen so clearly the downside of technology, and as we learn about the destruction of the rainforests across the planet or the aftermath of oil freighter mishaps. Rather than machines conquering nature (a typical phallocentric motif), we find advertisements today emphasizing vehicles that will bring one in touch with nature; to be sure, it is a strange nature in which no one else ever seems to be present: "cars in contemporary ads are almost never shown on city streets, and often not on roads at all. Instead, they stand in fields, by the sea, or on the surface of the moon" (Wernick 1987:287). But if (culturally produced) machines are now our only access to "nature," how can we even begin to approach a biological-environmental reality that precedes cultural manipulation? Or should that pre-cultural state continue to be considered more significant than the contemporary situation? What does it take for a culture to mature to the point of social planning for a society that won't have to begin by reaching against negative, harmful models of masculinity?[3]

Contemporary Perspectives in the Men's Movement/s

It is obvious as one charts historical developments and patterns in the mass communications media or politics or in literature that the representations of masculinities vary enormously. More theoretical and critical materials also exhibit quite a wide range of ways of naming masculinity, understanding its relationship to femininity, or to gender studies as such, its relationship to the feminist movements, or to various social theories. Certainly complaints about the awkward ways in which masculinity has come to be configured within our culture reach back quite a ways. Already Myron Brenton, writing in 1966 about "the male in crisis" and "the masculinity trap," argued that it was certainly time to adjust our gender concepts to meet contemporary realities, but Segal cites an even earlier questioning in the post–World War II period when psychology turned away somewhat from the emphasis upon the female object that Freud made orthodox at the turn of the century (1990:73).

"Gender" itself wasn't central as a theoretical construction until the 1970s.[4] Within gender studies today masculinity may be nothing positive, but indeed an essentially negative identity, if we start from binary oppositions (then it becomes whatever contrasts with emotionality and connectedness, considered "feminine"), or as that which is "hard" as opposed to the "soft" when strict boundaries of the society and self are established and defended (I referred earlier to these qualities in Weeks's analysis of the British press during the Falklands episode).

The "soft" male may also be conceived in terms of lacking self-definition and assertion or aggressivity, a profile familiar recently from the excoriations of Robert Bly, who wants men to reassert their "wildman" qualities, and a highly visible segment of the men's movement convenes conferences and practices rituals to do precisely this. Bly was anticipated by observations within the psychotherapeutic communities, such as those by Andrew Samuels, who found already in Jungian publications from the 1970s a "change" in the air and "a new kind of man," who "is a loving and attentive father to his children, a sensitive and committed marital partner, concerned with world peace and the state of the environment; he may be vegetarian" (1985:2–3). But the new kind of man remains "a mother's boy because he is doing what he does to please Woman," whether his wife or his lover or his actual mother. The origins of this sort of stereotype ultimately rest in the "soft" or unmasculine male (Greek *malthakoi*, Latin *molles*) of antiquity who assumed the passive rather than the active role in sexual intercourse with another male (Halperin 1990:22–24).

Jungian social theorists see the "soft male" figure (though not necessarily the homosexual male) positively, as an indication of a powerful resurgence of the feminine in our time, a resurgence that Edward Whitmont elaborates in great detail in *Return to the Goddess*, as he proposes that "the acceptance and differentiation of emotion, feelings, and needs as a means of reality orientation and of mutual communication, will be as significant for the centuries ahead of us as was the differentiation and training of the thinking function through late antiquity and the Middle Ages. A new dimension of world orientation is in the process of development here" (1982:233; see also Tacey 1991:27).

I don't know about "world orientation," but certainly the shape of masculinities became a matter of concern due to the advent of the women's liberation movement, both in its popular-culture phase, replete with rallies and consciousness-raising groups, and in its academic phase, responsible for at least thirty-eight books directly addressing men's issues (according to Carrigan 1987:154). Carrigan and his colleagues suggest that neither phase was substantial, nor did either have a lasting impact, except as background to the contemporary movement. The parallel "men's liberation" movement of the 1970s was short-lived and had little influence whatsoever upon the social and political structures that led to the problems of masculinity in the United States and Britain. In fact the movement and the increasing political pressure of women's lib and feminism stimulated a strong backlash, with a so-called men's rights movement organized explicitly to counter the demands and claims for equal treatment made by feminist leaders.[5] Obviously, then, "the men's movement" can mean explicitly "the anti-women's movement," especially as men's or father's rights groups seek to overturn court decisions favorable to women in divorce settlements and child custody arrangements. Most of the academic literature on masculinity features sex-role studies, which Carrigan and his co-authors critique very thoroughly, arguing that many belonged to an entirely misguided enterprise, and that they produced only shoddy results: all in all, "the intellectual content of the books-about-men genre is slender" (Carrigan 1987:160–62, 156).

In contrast to the steady progress of the women's movement and subsequently gains in access to women's rights, or in contrast to the rapid growth of the gay liberation movement later, the first wave of the men's movement led at most to a partial accommodationism by which some men washed a few more dishes than before and nodded appropriately at what feminist thought was making unavoidably clear about the structures of male oppression. Overall "it is not, fundamentally, about uprooting sexism or transforming patriarchy, or even understanding masculinity in its various forms. When it comes to the crunch, what it is about is *modernizing* hegemonic masculinity. It is concerned with finding ways in which the dominant group — the white, educated, heterosexual, affluent males we know and love so well — can adapt to new circumstances without breaking down the social-structural arrangements that actually give them their power" (Carrigan 1987:164). Once again the representatives of the dominant culture agree with the opposition in a merely pro forma manner, while holding on to the reins of power, since "most men benefit from the subordination of women, and hegemonic masculinity is centrally connected with the institutionalization of men's dominance over women" — and over other men, of course, as they enforce gender boundaries by dominating youth, effeminates, and homosexual men (180, 174). The issue cannot be merely accommodation in ways that allow for continuance of the very social structures that have gotten us in the predicament of "the male crisis" itself; unavoidably "the liberation of women must mean a loss of power for most men; and given the structuring of personality by power, also a great deal of personal pain" (167).

It may be obvious from my citations of Carrigan and his Australian co-workers, as well as from quotations from works by Segal, Brittan, Seidler, and others, that British-influenced masculinity literature arises out of a context to which American sociology and political literature alike remain foreign (the essays in Snodgrass 1977 and Clatterbaugh 1990:Chapter 6 comprise some of the few North American political statements, even to this day). That context is the British-socialist politics that is fed up with polite historical and theoretical surveys that have no lasting consequences, or the sort of adjustment psychology that focuses attention upon attaining individual happiness (now labeled "well-being") in spite of a repressive culture. These writings often reflect their authors' involvement in British political movements urging social change, or they lead to specific political analysis and suggestions for implementing the social changes they advocate. Certainly they devote little space to the typical American emphasis upon the individual or even the small consciousness group, weekend programs, or sharing lectures on cassettes. These activities may have important initial impacts, but the ultimate arena has to be the political and social, or else the collectivity continues to be ruled by the inherited patriarchal institutions and values. Leaders in the men's movements have been concerned to ensure that the contemporary interest in changing men does not get sidetracked by a disproportionate emphasis upon individual personal change.

Many of the British writers on masculinity stress a much more complex social analysis, display an openness to gay liberation and feminist historiography and theory, and practice an attitude of responsible critique of what the men's movement has actually accomplished. This critique is not done in a spirit of debunking for its own sake, but of pointing to the weaknesses of the movement as it is frequently configured, for instance the manner in which the contemporary men's movements have ignored the situation and contributions of homosexuals. Not only has a rampantly ethnocentric and essentialist heterosexist bias affected most professional sociological studies, for instance, but in many parts of the men's movement today there is complete avoidance of gay issues, stemming from what seems to be a fear of acknowledging that gay men are not some sort of freaks, but men who share with male heterosexuals the major part of their gendering histories and experiences.[6] On the other hand, many of the major advances in both historiography and practical theory now derive from gay scholarship (meaning, of course, scholarship about gay perspectives, not scholarship necessarily carried out by or on gay people).

The growth of information about masculinity from all sides is exponential today. Ethnographic surveys are now available, such as David Gilmore's *Manhood in the Making* (1990), which overviews masculinities in China, Greece, India, Japan, East Africa, North America, and elsewhere, although the book's lack of theoretical perspectives eventuates in an essentializing treatment. A number of other books published within the last three or four years, many of them cited in this volume, as well as a number of popular and scholarly journals devoted to masculinity, indicate that study of masculinity has become a major interest across

Britain and North America, and I anticipate that men's groups as well as academic course offerings in men's studies, or on masculinity within gender studies and other departments, will continue to reflect this growing interest. The great splash of media attention in the early 1990s to the Bly/Wildman portion of the men's movements peaked quickly, but meanwhile long-term interest in gender studies grew even stronger and began to be influential across the academic world and within subfields of applied psychology.

Carrigan and his colleagues point to the interdisciplinary convergences across several fields as the most likely scene of real academic progress (Carrigan 1987:141). Such collaborative work will not represent only new results stemming from gay and feminist scholarship, but also from contemporary socialism, psychotherapy (although certainly not psychoanalysis of the traditional orthodox Freudian bent), the new field of culture studies, and the history and sociology of practice (another area North Americans have ignored, presumably because of the assumption that technology was not sufficiently abstract to be truly masculine, a bias that reaches back to the ancient Greek upper-class disdain for commerce and technology — see Green 1986). Most likely gender studies or men's studies departments will reflect the interdisciplinary makeup and methodologies of existing women's studies programs, hopefully without the second-class rank to which such programs have been relegated informally in some university communities.

The Men's Movement/s

The term "men's studies" has just been used to refer to one way that the academic scene may develop, but the new men's movement that burst upon the public media scene in the early 1990s has not necessarily been academic; in fact it has often been anti-intellectual or anti-academic in orientation. It is important to distinguish between the various types of interests and activities represented, since it is just as misrepresentative to speak of a single men's movement as it is to speak of a single feminism: both movements are configured distinctly according to the participants and their own interests, and we are now at the point where American writers are criticizing specific elements with which they disagree rather than simply praising or complaining about the movement as a whole. For example, in his survey of what he refers to as the new "anti-masculinist" movement, David Tacey is extremely negative toward Robert Bly and the Wildman movement associated with him, finding it dangerously romanticizing, naive, and similar at its core to

Nazi perspectives: "It is not enough simply to drag up the wildman from the unconscious and thereby imagine that progress has been made. The crucial point is how we relate to the wildman" (1991:34, 36; see also Johnson 1992, a scathing attack on Bly, and in contrast Dowden 1992, which begins "It's open season on the men's movement"). Since, according to *Esquire* magazine in October 1991, already over a hundred thousand men had participated in Wildman activities by that date, the follow-up to such activities matters considerably. Do participants subsequently connect with ongoing men's groups? Do they change their understanding of masculinity because of their participation? No data are available to answer these questions at the moment.

Others have found particular reasons for support of one or another interpretation or branch within the men's movements. James Dittes, introducing a feature section in an issue of the *Christian Century*, suggests that a religious men's movement "is about living life more abundantly and more faithfully to God's intentions"; "a men's movement guiding such discoveries becomes a prime mode of the church's mission" (1991:589). Other religious interests advocated in conjunction with men's movements tend to be more generally reflective of New Age spirituality and psychotherapy rather than Christianity, and at the conservative end of the spectrum of contemporary religiosity, churches both locally and nationally have organized conferences to counter revisionist views of male and female roles.

Nearly every one of the recent men's movement journals such as *Inroads; Wingspan; Man!: Men's Issues, Relationships, and Recovery;* or *Changing Men* has published ongoing disputes about what is or is not relevant to particular visions of what the men's movement might come to represent. Name-calling and cries of "bad faith!" fly about no less than they do in any other social movement, although in spite of a few national conferences of leaders, there have been few attempts to develop a uniform national platform or orthodoxy that would unite the various voices. Annual "Men and Masculinity" conferences sponsored by the National Organization for Changing Men (now the National Organization of Men Against Sexism) have an established history and a promotional videotape made at the 1990 meeting, *Men and Masculinity: Changing Roles, Changing Lives,* and what was billed as the first *international* men's conference, "A Journey Toward Conscious Manhood," sponsored by the Austin Men's Center, was held in October 1991. A North American Confederation of Men's Councils provides a listing of convenors who facilitate the growth of men's councils being established across the continent. At a November 1991 national meeting of leaders sponsored by the journal *Wingspan,* one could recognize agonizing signs of growth pains from groups across the country as arguments developed about the personal income of movement leaders and the difficulty of somehow maintaining a sense of community while different issues and priorities are addressed by various leaders and organizations.

An editorial by Lyman Grant in one of the men's movement publications provides a convenient listing of some of the range of interests. Grant notes that "no one ideological stance ... sums up what all men are looking for" ("MAN! What Change!," *Man!,* Fall 1991:2):

> Successful corporation executives don't need to find their warrior spirit; they might need to find their lover energy, though. Nor do sensitive New Age guys need to find magician energy; they probably need, however, to discover their inner warriors. Some men had terrible, abusive fathers and need to explore what that experience has done to them. Others must deal with overbearing or neglectful mothers. Selfish men need to move toward service for the public good; some overly selfless men must discover how to take care of themselves before they burn out. The man who abandoned his children must seek his separate peace with them. The divorcing father who wants custody of his children probably must fight a court system biased against him.

And a wide range of other issues has surfaced:

- Recovery and Twelve Step agendas: the journal *Man!* proclaims "a bias toward recovery programs," and for many men the men's movement represents a continuity of their experience of supportive communities in Alcoholics Anonymous and similar groups.

- Interest in "radical ritual," seeking to recover the sense of sacred spaces and participatory ceremonies such as group drumming and dancing.

- Dealing with war and pacifism, especially in terms of supporting those who have been deeply marked by either.

- Heterosexuality, bisexuality, homosexuality, as well as other relational issues such as sadomasochism or violence and codependence.

- Sexual abuse and violence, pornography.

- Relationship issues and gender reconciliation work; divorced men and single fathers.

- Reconnection with traditional resources such as mythic stories and folk tales that have been neglected or submerged beneath malfunctional or restrictive interpretations.

- Initiation and mentoring, especially working with young men, sometimes in connection with orientation to wilderness.

- Social change issues, especially with respect to minority and unemployed men; work with prison populations, school boards, fraternal organizations, and scouting.

- And "spirituality."

I set off "spirituality" because it has been one of the most frequently named concerns in the literature and discourse of men's groups. At least three kinds of reference can be found: (1) Some claim that *this* type of men's movement will be different, indeed superior to the ways men-in-groups have operated in the past, especially in terms of fraternal clubs and lodges. (2) Sometimes spirituality has reference to particular spiritual traditions, as in the example of Christian ethicist Dittes, cited above. Religious book publishers are now marketing a number of denominational materials that seek to reconnect contemporary masculinity concerns with the traditional teachings of particular religious bodies. (3) Fairly often a new masculine spirituality refers to a reconnection with overlooked or submerged religiosity from earlier periods, in particular with masculine earth-father figures or other figures connected directly with nature — as might be expected, this type of spirituality has a lot to do with ecological issues (see for instance Rowan 1987; Anderson 1990; Lawlor 1991; and Kipnis 1991).

Although no single spiritual tradition is elicited across the range of the men's movement, both reference to Native American teachings and appeal to the New Age or New Consciousness emphasis upon a brotherhood or family of all human beings are ubiquitous. "Spirituality" may also carry overtones of a term co-opted from religion-and-literature studies dating back to the 1940s, namely the "mythopoetic," although that term has been wrenched from its general context established by Harry Slochower's *Mythopoesis: Mythic Forms in the Literary Classics* (1970); there it refers to situations in which literal meanings of legends and myths could no longer be tolerated by a society, which then re-created the ancient stories in new guises. Mythopoesis in literature means a revision away from a literal toward a symbolic application of classical motifs: "while mythology presents its stories as if they actually took place, mythopoesis transposes them to a symbolic meaning" (1970:15). Slochower treats myths of communal harmony (Creation/Eden), homeleaving or the expulsion of the hero (Quest), and homecoming or re-creation (Destiny).

Subsequent to Slochower's book, and generally within literary circles, the term has referred to the productive creation (Greek: *poiesis*) of myth-like materials in poetry and fiction. But use of "mythopoesis" within the men's movement has been narrowed down to refer to a particular type of applied study of myth and folk tales about men that usually implicates some of the Jungian terminology concerning discovery of one's inferior or "shadow" side and learning to balance masculine and feminine aspects of one's psyche. It may likewise trail the term proposed by Erik Erikson, "generativity," the particular quality of human development that one attains when previous developmental tasks have been successfully achieved. Generativity refers to a solid sense of self-worth that enables one to care for others in mentoring and supporting fashion.

"Mythopoeic" or "mythopoetic" in the men's movement today primarily refers to the careful heeding of stories and narratives as important cultural storehouses. It has to do not only with identifying and remembering the myths, but with an attitude well captured by Graham Dowden:

> Unless there is someone to read the poems, recite the myths, tell the tales, and someone to listen to them, plus a general willingness on all sides to discuss the stories and apply them and pass them on, the great male psychic wound rots, festers and erupts in violence without end. When the myths and the poetry are kept in circulation, though, the wound becomes a womb, a place of healing, the beginning of a new life. (1992:18–19)

Other types of spirituality have been catalogued especially well in the essays in Matthews's *Choirs of the God* (1991); they include revivals of largely European practices such as Wicca, magic, shamanism, and worship of the Earth Mother, Odin, and the Wayfarer — men's mysteries to parallel those recently revived women's mysteries and magical practices.

Nine Types of Men's Movements

While there have been several attempts to canvass parts of the men's movement, such as the brief comments in Astrachan (1986) and occasional brief reflections in movement publications, only one author, Kenneth Clatterbaugh (1989, 1990) has developed a useful typology,

1. MORAL CONSERVATIVE
- traditional roles OK
- family is to control males
- feminists are the danger!

2. BIOLOGICAL CONSERVATIVE
- male counter to female is innate/natural because evolutionarily superior
- feminism irrelevant since society can't change nature
- feminism is wrong, men are the oppressed
- fight the new sexism promoted by feminists

4. ANTI-SEXIST/LIBERAL
- traditional masculinity is limiting
- men's support groups, organizes men's studies

5. MEN'S/FATHERS' RIGHTS
- preserve male privilege
- defend rights of divorcing fathers

7. NEW AGE/BLY-WILDMAN
- maintain balance between male/female perspectives
- emphasize myths, bonding with other men
- release positive aspects of inner man

9. RECOVERY
- reconstruct masculinity harmed by childhood abuse, codependency, substance abuse

3. ANTI-SEXIST/RADICAL
- must unlearn traditional roles
- sympathetic to feminists
- combat patriarchy

6. SOCIALIST
[important in Great Britain, less so in U.S.]
- change all social structures

8. PROACTIVE GAY
- homosexual male's experiences unique, homophobia the problem

although I find it somewhat problematic. I'll elaborate on Clatterbaugh's six approaches in what he names "masculinist perspectives" as he stipulates that that term is to be applied "to any point of view that offers an analysis of the social reality of American men and offers an agenda for them" — hence Clatterbaugh operates "as a social philosopher" looking at "a set of sociopolitical points of view" (1989:4, 1990:2). However, the term "masculinist" could as easily represent a pejorative substitute for "patriarchal" as a positive but male-oriented alternative to "feminist." Neat as it would be to have an all-purpose label, I don't think "masculinist" will be that term. I agree with Clatterbaugh that the various differences in masculinist perspectives "do not augur well for any ecumenical men's movement. Indeed, they point out the likelihood of ongoing sectarian battles" (1989:6), and indeed Northwest Coast men's councils witnessed such angry disagreement among factions in 1993.

Clatterbaugh's categories are expanded here in order to identify nine rather than six types, ranging them on a left-to-right schema (see figure). In his earlier essay (1989), Clatterbaugh discusses two "wings of conservative masculinism," the first, **Moral Conservatism** and the second, **Biological Conservatism** (these are conflated into "The Conservative Perspective" in his book of 1990). Essentialist representatives of both types consider customary roles for men and women perfectly comfortable and seek primarily to reinforce the traditional patriarchal values they still find satisfactory. Indeed feminist movements are treated as having threatened the natural course of development of "natural" male dominance, particularly through their threats to the prototypical heterosexual family unit. The biological conservatives seek to find behind existing cultural norms various natural laws that they claim can be identified across the biological spectrum. Both types of conservative masculinism emphasize individualistic responses to problems and adherence to the pre-feminist status quo, leaving them open to Clatterbaugh's scathing accusation: "The conservatives' ready acceptance of inequalities — between men and women, among men, or by race — opens them to the charge of being a voice for white male supremacy" (1989:4). We can understand some of his discomfort when we learn that biological conservatives "describe even rape as a reproductive strategy," or that moral conservatives consider feminism to be an anticipation of genocide and the end of the cultural family unit (1990:20, 24, with references). What makes the conservatives' positions difficult to deal with is that they are by and large the "good old boy" positions popularly represented in the large elements of American society that remain resistant to the social changes brought into prominence by the feminist movements.

Mediating the first two types somewhat, the **Men's Rights** advocates (no. 5 on my chart) likewise disagree with and oppose the feminist political analysis of patriarchal constraints, and often argue that men are the newly oppressed class, who are suffering now because of a new sexism created by the women's liberation movements. As part of what Clatterbaugh calls "the aggressive edge of a movement to preserve male privilege and destroy the movements working on the behalf of women," various subdivisions of the Men's Rights movement work toward legal changes that will more aggressively protect the husband's/father's rights in divorce settlements and child custody cases (1989:5). Their representatives argue that advances wrought by feminists, "instead of helping men or providing a model for male liberation, [have] actually made things worse" by dumping onto all males guilt for their own socialization (1990:10). Men's Rights groups have been excluded from conferences organized by the more liberal groups, at least partly because "some advocates of this perspective see the feminist movement as having evolved from a human liberation movement for both women *and* men into a women's lobby working against the interests of men" (1990:68). Men's Rights agendas have included education and legal change, although they have spanned a wide range of advocacies (Clatterbaugh subdivides them into three competing segments, 81–82).

A strong statement of a centrist position within the Men's Rights sector (he refers to himself as "a radical masculinist" and his group as focused "on recovery in a very broad sense") is found in Aaron Kipnis's *Knights without Armor* (1991), a work that documents very thoroughly just how bad the state of many men in our culture is: Kipnis deals with the physical violence of sports, the failure to integrate returning Vietnam veterans, child abuse, male-bashing by the media, and other indications of just how inadequately the nation has provided for equality between the genders. Somewhat in line with the **Recovery** type (my no. 9), Kipnis's position is that men must acknowledge their woundedness, regain their masculine self-esteem, and begin to build a supportive male community that affirms the health of the masculine while it takes seriously some of the statistics, such as that 50 percent of federal funding for AIDS care is spent on women and children who represent less than 10 percent of its victims, or that since 25 percent of children born today are born out of wedlock and 80 percent of women are awarded child custody in the 50 percent of marriages that end in divorce, "well over half of the fathers in America are now outside the home" (37, 54).

Kipnis shares some of the ways his own men's group (the Knights of the title of his book) has explored the neglected mythological figures that can be of help in developing a male-affirmative psychology. They have worked carefully on initiation and fathering, and Kipnis himself has written several brief articles on recovering mythological images other than the purely "solar" figures of traditional Western masculinity, such as the European Green Man, the Trickster, and the Earth Father. Clearly even orientations that seem initially to represent a particularly strong bias toward masculine experience have much to teach other groups within the spectrum represented by the men's movements. Kipnis provides insights about the importance of sharing men's experiences through male lodges, even *old* men's lodges, in this time that is so fascinated with youthful muscular and sexual virility.

At the left end of the spectrum I have charted, two groups work specifically *for* most of the changes advocated by the women's liberation movements. At the extreme "left," the various forms of contemporary (primarily British) socialism (no. 6, **Socialist**); it would be easy to overrate the influence of this movement because its members have been articulate writers and are represented extensively in the bibliography cited in this volume, although it is difficult to identify visible North American counterparts.[7] British men are hardly innocent of backbiting and name-calling (for instance Seidler is astonished at "the resurgence of materialist values, even on the left"), but there is clearly a dedication to working through political positions that would be unheard of in North America — this among members whose positions within British politics include consciousness raising, Trotskyist platforms, Althusserian individualism, and bourgeois capitalism!

Socialists treat "the costs of being masculine, as described by the other perspectives, [as] nothing but the alienations of men subjected to the relations of production in a capitalist society," and socialist feminists in particular note how much of the literature of the men's liberation movements has addressed only the managerial or ownership classes (Clatterbaugh 1990:11). They relate the necessity of worker control over the workplace to a pro-feminist position that recognizes that those "who wish to address the alienations of men must simultaneously address the oppression of women" (125). Perhaps for these reasons, many of the British discussions have stressed issues such as child-care and housekeeping, sexism at the work site, and co-parenting to an extent that has yet to characterize the American men's scene.

The other group at the left end of the spectrum, no. 8, **Proactive Gay**, is somewhat amorphous in that it is identified with no single activist group, but represents generally the activist gay male movement and its advocacy of rights for gay men and lesbian women. It would doubtless include many of the ongoing developments in gay studies I have named earlier, especially in the academic disciplines of history, sociology, psychology, and literary criticism. But generally the proactive component would stress that many parts of the current men's movement are simply sustaining the presumptions of white, heterosexual, middle-class men, whereas the experiences and viewpoints of gay man have been quite different: "Gay profeminists note that as homosexuals do not dominate women sexually, they do not benefit in the same ways as heterosexual men do from the oppression of women. They also point to the important role of homophobia in the formation of heterosexual masculinity" (Clatterbaugh 1990:12). Some activists advocate a separate gay culture, often because of the homophobic reactions they have experienced not so much within feminism as within other sections of the men's movement — although that would not include the National Organization of Men Against Sexism, which has historically stated a gay-affirmative position.

Clatterbaugh notes that "gay men argue convincingly that homophobia is the club that is used to keep men in their gender role" (132), and I will suggest later in this book that homophobia usually arises precisely at points where traditional gender boundaries are being challenged. Gay activists today argue against traditional heterosexist claims that homosexuals are unsuccessful, unhappy, and unable to sustain ongoing relationships; they have had to respond very strongly to the radical right-wing Christians who were quick to label the appearance of AIDS as a divine judgment upon homosexual men (not women, apparently!). And works such as *Displacing Homophobia* (Butters 1989) have begun to expose the importance of homosexual literary figures in ways that disclose just how extensively heterosexualist biases have skewed even supposedly scientific academic analysis.

Clatterbaugh names a more radical wing and a liberationist wing of the left-of-center Anti-Sexist groupings, which I have placed in the almost-far-left (no. 5, **Anti-Sexist/Radical**) and then just-left-of-center (no. 4, **Anti-Sexist/Liberal**) positions. The two positions agree on a sympathetic response to feminism that includes a condemnation of traditional patriarchal sexism and power structures, although in his book *Contemporary Perspectives on Masculinity* (1990), Clatterbaugh dumps the term "anti-sexist" for "profeminist." Members of the Anti-Sexist/Radical segment set out to attack patriarchy head-on, both in their own lives and in society. Members of the Anti-Sexist/Liberal position have worked less on attacking than on building: creating men's networks and support groups, developing men's studies programs in universities, and cooperating with feminist critics.

The two groups might differ on a specific issue such as pornography, with the more radical anti-sexists opposing it totally, those nearer the center arguing that porn, too, has to be protected by the American tradition of free speech; but such divisions can be distinguished just as readily within the positions supported within various factions within the women's movements. Pro-feminist or anti-sexist writers produced the bulk of the earlier men's liberation literature written in the 1970s and 1980s, literature that generally shared an anti-patriarchy perspective, patriarchy connoting "male domination through violence or the threat of violence for the benefit of men," and remaining in more recent publications a term that readily identifies a confessional position with regard to acknowledging males' violence against other males and against women (Clatterbaugh 1990:40). Task forces of the umbrella coalition named the National Organization for Men Against Sexism (NOMAS) still organize around program units on Ending Men's Violence, or Homophobia, and NOMAS provides "groups that counsel men who batter, homophobia awareness educators, and groups that educate the public about rape and other forms of violence" (from the announcement of the 17th National Conference on Men and Masculinity, 1992). An issue of the NOMAS publication *Changing Men* (no. 23, Fall/Winter 1991) features a review essay on recent works on pornography; this same issue focuses upon men's spirituality, a theme that has also appeared previously (no. 18, Jewishness and Masculinity issue) and that is the ongoing focus of a Spirituality group at the annual conferences. Among my nine types, nos. 3 and 4 represent the longest-term organization of reformist-perspective men, and they have mobilized a wide range of American liberals, particularly academics and health-care professionals.

The center portion of my map of types of men's movements is occupied by the group that has been most visible in the 1990s, identified by what Clatterbaugh calls **New Age Masculinism,** but which I have grouped with the Robert Bly followers to call **New Age/Bly-Wildman** (no. 7). It is typified by reacting against the most radical claims of feminism, suggesting that men have been hurt by oppressive patriarchy just as much as women, and by proposing that men can identify, discipline, and channel appropriately the wild masculine energies that the culture needs for its own progress and survival.

Regional and local retreats, campfires, and conferences across the nation have been recounted vividly in the mass media, whose reporters

find quaint and picturesque the notion of large groups of men stripping
down to undergo sweat-lodge ceremonials together, or drumming and
noise-making together with many instruments, or crying and hugging
one another as they express their own anger toward repressive masculinity and share their personal hurts and frustrations with traditional
masculine roles. Conferences emphasize releasing pent-up negative
emotions and tensions derived from anger, and for many participants
there has been little further impact. But many others go on to form or
to join long-term men's groups, either consciousness-raising groups or
mutual support groups; and still others have gathered around movement literature and media, such as the lectures, tapes, and publications
of Robert Bly, Robert Moore, Douglas Gillette, or Michael Meade. This
group, which identifies itself primarily as "mythopoetic" or "wildman-
oriented," has been the target of most of the communications media
treatment. They also engage traditional cultural materials, as in Bly's
translations and references to poetry, especially from South America, or
his repeated retelling and allegorization of the Iron John folk tale, most
skillfully in his national bestseller, *Iron John* (1990; the tale is usually
translated as "Iron Hans" in the Grimm brothers' collections). A number of materials produced from within the Jungian/Neo-Jungian camp
have followed similar allegorizing practices, focusing upon archetypal
male figures; examples include Robert Moore (1990), but are found in
articles in almost any of the various ephemeral periodicals of the men's
movement.

Finally, yet other participants among the men's groups have allied
themselves with **Recovery** programs (no. 9), which connect various
forms of psychotherapy with the New Age emphasis upon personal and
individual change. The work of John Lee and the Austin Men's Center
is representative of this approach, as are many of the city- or region-
wide men's councils (a number of them now publish ongoing journals
and newsletters and have permanent staff or facilities). The Twelve Step
process for overcoming addiction familiar from Alcoholics Anonymous
and other drug treatment programs is part of the shared experience for
many men in Recovery groups, and their activities usually include opportunities to share the pain of one's own personal life in family and
relationships. Men are encouraged to learn when they can and must
trust others and when to take on self-responsibility; issues of exerting
masculine power and controlling one's own emotional environment are
often debated.

In this charting of some nine types, I have emphasized the range
of types within the men's movements, but lacking a crystal ball to see

how they will develop, future directions are difficult to predict. For all the numerical size of Recovery-related groups, and their striking presence on the map of men's consciousness in North America, for instance, that particular type of group was not even in the picture when Kenneth Clatterbaugh published his two surveys (1989, 1990) or when earlier surveys scanned the field, even in the massive bibliography compiled by psychotherapists (in Moore 1990). What Type no. 10 might be waiting in the wings as the next focus for another group? "When the materials are all prepared and ready," wrote Walt Whitman in "A Song of the Rolling Earth," "the architects will appear." But for once it may be that men can learn some of the collaborative perspectives taught by feminist thought; maybe they can learn to let their work be paisley and patchwork and all-at-once-from-every-direction . . . cross- and inter- and multi-disciplinary . . . and feel good about such work, for all its oddness among the usual calculation strategies of straight "masculine" science and business.

Why is it so difficult for men to learn from the feminist revolution? Or from the several debunking and trashing accounts that have appeared? I think of the *Esquire* special on Wild Men and Wimps (October 1991: on the Table of Contents page the special issue is entitled "The State of Masculinity"): "To talk about the men's movement is to talk about how American men — white, educated American men — are spending money to make themselves feel good." A snippet on Bly is condescendingly titled "Robert Bly, Wild Thing," the sidebar for the last page of the article on him asking, "Are men fated to dance around for the rest of history with their weenies in their hands, trying to remember when they were swords?" And I understand that there have been put-downs in television programs, not to mention books such as Alfred Gingold's trivializing *Fire in the John: The Manly Man in the Age of Sissification* (1991), or the earlier *The Manly Handbook* by Everitt and Schechter (1982). Or *Newsweek*'s money-first judgment: "What the movement doesn't have, at least not yet, is a serious political or social agenda" (24 June 1991:49) — but this judgment particularly strikes me, since my own sympathies are with the movement toward social changes that emerge in the men's movements from time to time. Social changes happen by direct intervention in the structures of the society, and my personal experiences in that direction leave me feeling that *Newsweek* calls that shot correctly. A movement as diverse as I have sketched, with so many possible agendas, and vast disagreements across the range of types, will not be likely to have a measurable impact quickly. In that sense anti-sexist agitation will most likely have only local results, although the idealist in me recognizes that the quick change favored by American liberals is less important in the long term than fundamental change of the socio-economic base and the overall worldview of the culture.

Social change also happens by indirect intervention, and in this instance that particularly means in terms of education: education both explicitly in terms of educing roles from mythological figures that may be healthy models, and implicitly as individuals come to recognize their own malfunctioning gender perspectives and decide to change. In the rest of this book I will stress forms of education regarding many of the new perceptions of masculinities. I won't talk much about individual change in psychotherapy or recovery, and I will not focus upon social action in the activist manner that representatives of the middle period of the feminist revolution did. I have learned a great deal from working alongside feminists, and I think my restrained, realist perspective has been shaped by that experience. Before turning to the analysis of specific myths and stories, I conclude this chapter with reflections on a few more of the ongoing ways in which the new masculinities and feminisms interact.

Men and Feminism/s

We have seen that many of the various phases of the men's movements were shaped historically as responses to forms of contemporary feminism, beginning in the late 1960s when a few men's consciousness-raising groups operated in parallel to the thousands of women's CR groups. Given that history, it is important to continue to ask about the parallels between men's and women's liberation movements. What is a man to make of feminism? Well, for one thing, he has to learn to scrap the term "feminism" for "feminisms," since one strong feature of the feminist movement has been the emphasis upon importance of the specific local contexts. Each time a wo/man speaks, s/he speaks from within a particular social locale, power relation, class location, and economic status, not from within some transcendent realm of an abstract, non-material, transcendental essence. Hence feminisms, varieties of articulations arising out of particular sites and groups; no one attempts any longer to speak "for women" or "for the feminist position," but rather for some particular women or for some particular type of feminist position. I think of the analogy with what happened in the American conquest when white Euro-Americans sought to speak with the "chiefs" of the Native American nations they encountered, only to find that the typical Euro-American hierarchical presumptions had to be held in abeyance — there were seldom "chiefs" whose authority accrued from positional ranking, but rather persons whose achievements had led to their election as the first among equals, whose task it was to coordinate consensus among many equally respected but differing points of view.

Feminisms have been developed within literary criticism and critical theory, within social-equality movements, and within a number of social-change contexts. They represent nothing less than a fresh epistemological orientation to our history and environment — how we know what we know and how the process of gathering knowledge proceeds philosophically and politically. Victor Seidler's *Rediscovering Masculinity* (1989), the most sustained philosophical reflection upon the challenges of feminisms for usual ways of conceiving Western thought, is an excellent resource in gaining perspective on how earlier false linkages are now challenged: "feminism is not just a challenge to men, but an example of breaking masculine hegemony which identifies reason, masculinity, and universality" (161). Such challenges can easily be trivialized — feminism is just what a few peculiar women have developed as their means of access to the traditional male bastions of academic power — but instead I agree with Elaine Showalter (1985) when she argues that in spite of such cheap trivializing, the feminist movement will doubtless be seen historically as a fundamental alteration of Western consciousness.

I indicated in Chapter 1 some of the ways various feminisms influence my own work, and I suggest that the majority of academics today, male or female, would readily subscribe to such a list of influences from feminist work. But there are likewise many persons who recognize and reject feminist challenges that seem to implicate their whole worldview; privileged males in particular are often all too aware of the challenges to the historically specific, socially constructed, and personally embodied notions of masculinity that are the carriers of oppression and power in societies such as ours that have been ruled by patriarchal systems. That power is not easily relinquished since it is *not* just something "personal," but as Stephen Heath suggests,

> To respond to feminism is to forego mastery: "the personal is the political" tells me also that I cannot refuse to analyze my desire, that the impersonal safety of authority can no longer be mine....Feminism makes things unsafe for men, unsettles assumed positions, undoes given identities.

The personal as political means that I cannot simply refer to the personal as *my* identity, that I have to think that identity through in the social terms it carries at its center, as an *identity:* however many feminist women I know, it is not going to remove me from the structures of sexism, absolve me from the facts of male positioning, domination and so on. The oppression of women is not personal, it is social and I am involved in it as a person in this society; there is no personal guarantee against that. (1987:6, 10)

But of course the oppression of any class or gender is not experienced abstractly but in the concrete here-and-now of my own job situation or sexual relationship. And here Anthony Astrachan's *How Men Feel: Their Response to Women's Demands for Equality and Power* (1986) provides clear documentation of the ways men and women have come to terms with the women's liberation movement begun in the 1970s, in a nine-year longitudinal attempt to determine reactions from a wide range of people. Astrachan works directly from interviews rather than statistical abstractions, and he shows how many people have tried, sometimes gracefully, sometimes awkwardly, to deal with women's claims to equality. Astrachan describes those who adapt gracefully as well as those who remain sharply anti-progressive (for instance he mentions the bartender whose female co-worker was promoted to shift-manager over him, who waited in an alley to rape her as she headed home, as well as the very large number of cases in which new patterns were worked out satisfactorily). Faludi's 1991 work, *Backlash,* has demonstrated some of the more theoretical aspects of the problem of old pattern meeting new.

There can be an enormous cop-out when men appear to be sympathetic with feminist propositions only because they stand to gain thereby: when a child appears in the relationship or the woman turns her attention elsewhere, all hell may break loose as it becomes clear that the male's "feminism does not come from a conscious decision; it is only another attempt to please women and to stay in their good graces" (Corneau 1991:74–75). When it does come from a conscious decision, men may find themselves suspect nonetheless; and doubtless they will feel as I have from time to time, hurt that I would remain suspect of the nasty old patriarchial mentalities I gave up consciously a long time ago. Where men might begin to reconnoiter in such a situation implicates their abilities to be non-traditional males, that is, *to shut up* from time to time; to learn how *to respect group process* rather than individual top-down decision-making; *to regard colleagues as true part-*

ners in the discovery and portrayal of knowledge, not as merely ancillary or supportive to men (no more "I thank the lonely wife who supported my research" book dedications); and to ask *what burden it is time for men to carry* now, as women have carried for so long burdens of gender inequality and unequal opportunity in every socio-economic sphere.

But the application of what is to be re-insighted anew, re-visioned, and re-organized is not mine to stipulate. It is up to the readers of this book. Having begun to name some of the issues confronting masculinity today in these initial chapters, I turn now to the mythic resources that remain able to teach us, to cause us to re-examine where we have been and where we thought we were going, and, yes, where we may yet aim as responsibly political citizens.

Part Three

REVISIONING CLASSICAL MODELS

Chapter 4

Friendship at the Beginning: Gilgamesh and Enkidu

Background Information

Sha Nagbara Immuru, "He who saw everything," is usually referred to today as the *Epic of Gilgamesh*. Possessing as good a claim as any other to being the oldest Western myth, the story reaches back about three thousand years and represents a nightmare of textual confusion because it was copied so frequently, in several languages and dialects. While most cultures have myths about the origin of death that proclaim how death came into the world, the Gilgamesh story assumes that death is present, but deals with its inescapability. King Gilgamesh has to learn the difference between what is appropriate to the gods, for whom death is no problem, and mortals, for whom it is, even though he is himself part-god. His character graphs the way the human mind seems first to have imagined a transition from god-like to more human creatures. The acceptance of death's pain is highlighted in the story by its contrast with emphasis in the early parts upon the loving friendship between the king and Enkidu, a wild man from the steppes. The myth manages to enfold any number of additional aspects as well: the origins of culture; the relative status of deities and humans; the patriarchal separation from goddess religion; the question of theodicy, i.e., justifying the presence of evil in a mostly good universe; and life as a journey toward maturation in which humans learn humility in the face of what cannot be changed, as well as faithfulness to the beloved.

Summary

Gilgamesh, the King of Uruk in ancient Sumer, now Warka, Iraq, is one of the most powerful and handsome men ever known. However, his own aggressiveness — he is named "a goring wild bull" — has led to interference in the normal maturation of the adolescents of his city (presumably because he takes them off to war and other exploits). His control over the land is unquestionably absolute, and he has become relentless in exerting it — to the extent of enforcing regularly his royal right of de-flowering newly wed brides. The whole social fabric is in trouble as his aggressiveness gets out of hand and his subject people are worn down. But the gods devise a plan: they will cause a double to appear, a man, Enkidu, just as powerful and handsome, in his own way — initially he is "sheer nature," naked, covered with shaggy hair, and living with the wild animals. Enkidu is enculturated when a sacred prostitute-priestess treats him to six days of continual sexual intercourse and then brings him into the city of Uruk. Enkidu confronts Gilgamesh just as the lat-ter is about to enjoy the delights of yet another virgin, and they wrestle until finally Enkidu cries uncle. But Gilgamesh has found a partner, and the two celebrate their friendship; meanwhile the inhabitants sigh with relief.

When Enkidu begins to get out of shape because of the luxurious ease of city life, Gilgamesh initiates a toughening expedition to the mythical Cedar Forest, where they will first kill the terrible guardian Humbaba and then cap their fame by stealing the biggest cedar tree of them all. Although he has been fascinated by his dreams earlier, Gilgamesh has terrible, portentous dreams on the journey to the forest, but he ignores them. Enkidu cannot talk him out of the adventure, and indeed, al-though Humbaba is killed and the mighty cedar is harvested, Enkidu gets wounded in the process. The wound will turn out to be fatal, but first, back home in Uruk, Gilgamesh resists the advances of Ishtar, the goddess of love, and insults her so that she causes the Bull of Heaven to attack the two companions. Victorious again, they slay the bull, and En-kidu throws its thigh — probably, since this is a customary euphemism in the Ancient Near East, the genitals — in Ishtar's face, and that is more than she can bear. The goddess complains to the highest court of the gods, who agree that the pair of friends has exceeded propriety. Enkidu dies and Gilgamesh is totally bereft: up to this point in his life, everything has gone as he desired, but now he loses the first great friend who has fulfilled his needs for companionship.

A long trip to the underworld takes him to Utnapishtim, who is the only mortal known to have been to the underworld and back. In the course of the journey we hear the common Flood myth that will appear again in Bereshith/Genesis and elsewhere. Gilgamesh obtains a sacred plant that restores youth and heads back to resuscitate En-kidu. He pauses for a cooling swim on the sweltering day — only to have a snake devour the hard-won plant. The snake then sloughs off its old skin as a demonstration of its immortality gained from eating the magical herb. Devastated once more, Gilgamesh returns to the city and eventually overcomes his anguish at the death of his beloved Enkidu by focusing his attention upon the construction of the city walls of Uruk — which supposedly were so effective defending the inhabitants and defining civilization's boundaries that they lasted some thousand years until breached by Sargon, a later Akkadian ruler.

Transmission of the Story

Stories about a historical Gilgamesh of Uruk, in the last part of the third millennium B.C.E., circulated widely, reaching literary form across the ancient Mesopotamian world in the second millennium. Translated and copied endlessly, the epic probably influenced the myths and legends associated with Homer and Pindar, about fifteen hundred years later. It was being copied as late as the first century, but subsequently, thanks to the disdain of both the Persians and the Israelites who considered it "primitive," it mostly dropped out of sight in the West until the mid-nineteenth century. Now it has become one of the most frequently cited myth-texts, so much so that the new encyclopedia that reflects French mythographic scholarship as of 1981, *Mythologies* (Bonnefoy 1991), explicitly excludes discussion of Gilgamesh on the basis that everyone already knows what is important.

■ ■ ■ ■ ■

[*Peirithous the Lapith challenged Theseus by raiding Attic cattle*]; *when Theseus at once went in pursuit, Peirithous boldly turned about to face him; but each was filled with such admiration for the other's nobility of appearance that the cattle were forgotten, and they swore an oath of everlasting friendship.* (Graves 1955:102b, citing Strabo, the Vatican Epitome, and Plutarch)

<u>Few myths about friendship come readily to mind</u>. There are a limited number of classical friendship pairs such as David and Jonathan, Achilleus and Patroklos, or the French Amis (alternatively named Amicus) and Amile (Amiloun or Amelius) — Amis loved Amile so much that he willingly sacrificed his own children in order to cure his friend's leprosy, but <u>generally the stories are about military or revolutionary comradeship. Usually they have some external focus of attention rather than friendship itself.</u> The situation is not much different in our own time, in spite of movies like *Butch Cassidy and the Sundance Kid*. Friendship, remarks David Halperin, remains "the *anomalous* relation: it exists outside the more thoroughly codified social networks formed by

kinship and sexual ties; it is 'interstitial in the social structure' of most Western cultures" (1990:75, citing Hammond 1987). Halperin alerts us to the question of where friendship takes place, how its borders are defined, and that question seems particularly appropriate today when we move about so frequently, relate to so many different people over our lifetimes, and have to deal with the repeated emphasis upon "doing your own thing" that is especially impressed upon young persons. So much emphasis upon individualistic self-fulfillment and attaining freedom from this or that has left males little useful guidance for relating intimately; the change in ideals away from traditional communal organizations to "doing your own thing" asocially leaves many males unclear about how men are to be related to other men in other than hierarchical ways. Our society lacks anything like the earlier gentleman's handbooks of the upper class or accounts of rich and fulfilling male friendships in biography, correspondence, and fiction. About all that is clear is that now marriage has to carry much of the friendship relatedness that was earlier experienced socially, when marriage was more a matter of social obligation or arrangement and less the subsuming focus of erotic relationship.[1]

"Erotic" need not suggest "sexual" relationship here, but the companionship, the feeling of being met fully by others, the warmth of empathy, the joy of equality, and the sharing of the heart that is "erotic" in the widest sense, yet not necessarily physically sexual.[2] Halperin speaks incisively of the need to resist the "insidious temptation to sexualize the erotics of male friendship" (1990:75), distinguishing the erotic from the sexual or the genital-sexual. Reference to the erotic quality of male friendship need imply no genital-sexual component, but such a reference is increasingly problematic within the contemporary distrust of male-male relationships that has inserted the genital-sexual into *all* relationships, in the wide sense of "sexual" found in Freud. It might be possible to show that Freud also had the wider, non-genital sexuality in mind when he wrote about sexuality, but the point here is to look at the friendship of Gilgamesh and Enkidu, rather than to correct or sustain a particular interpretation of psychoanalysis.

It would be irresponsible either to pretend that an intense male-male relationship is not central to the myth, or to ignore an important interpretive orientation of our own day, in which the question of a homosexual or gay reading is no longer something forced upon literature from outside the canonical, authoritative, institutional interpretations, but represents an increasingly important interpretive lens in literary and cultural criticism. Accordingly, I begin this chapter with some remarks about the contemporary study of homosexuality before turning to the myth about Gilgamesh and Enkidu itself.

The development of a gay-affirmative, anti-homophobic scholarship has been one of the impressive academic developments of the period between 1970 and 1990. Jeffrey Weeks, Michel Foucault (especially 1985), Eve Kosofsky Sedgwick, and a number of other careful scholars have opened up perspectives on gay people in modern cultures; Walter Williams (1986) and Gilbert Herdt (1981, 1982) have revealed aspects of homosexuality that are treated as proper and healthy within several Native American and Melanesian societies. And Dover (1978), Halperin (1990), and Winkler (1990) have provided analyses with which to comprehend homosexuality in the ancient Greek framework, while Halperin, Winkler, and Zeitlin (1990) have brought together essays on "the construction of erotic experience in the Ancient Greek world" generally, and Cohen (1991) demonstrates that future studies will have to be more sensitive to the social contexts in which literary references to ideal behavior occur.

All told, the lifting of many of the traditional taboos on sexual practices has finally coincided with new socio-historical research paradigms that permit views from the expressed-ideological to the actually experienced. These representative scholars in the field of gay studies share generally the perspective of Catherine Johns, who in her *Sex or Symbol* (1982) returns repeatedly to the importance of learning not to obfuscate another culture's sexual mores because they are different from our own. "Our own" means in this instance the compulsive heterosexism that remains predominant in our post-Victorian society, a society that has continued to emphasize strict binary gendering even as it has become theoretically more liberal in stipulating who may be related to whom, but is still a strongly binarily gendered society. Foucault pointed out just how recent a term "homosexuality" is (late nineteenth century) and how it was produced defensively as a means of reinforcing compulsory heterosexuality. What had been but one of many types of sexual activity or object-choices became a matter of "identity," and laws were broadened from prohibiting individual sexual acts to include issues of one's voluntary style of life and partners, so that that great involuntary association "the closet" has been a traumatic and repressive tool ever since. Indeed, the term "homosexual," within patriarchically dominated sexology, for instance, labels people gay or straight as a means of reinforcing traditional masculinity. The fear of being gay, the threat of being labeled homosexual, comes to function as a reinforcement of the standardized male-female relationships of a select portion of Western history, although in many other societies such a male:female pattern might be augmented by any number of male-male or female-female relationships.

Several commentators have noted how intimately homophobia and misogyny are correlated politically in heterosexism; and in the face of the early Gay Pride movement, the conservative, anti-feminist, and anti-abortionist "pro-family" movement arising in the 1980s quickly reasserted the eternal "nature" of the binary male-female household and allied itself with those who consider infection with the HIV as divine punishment of gay males. The ironies of such ideological positions are always astonishing: the pro-family movement was never very concerned about lesbian relationships, and never addressed the issues of HIV spread among drug users sharing needles or through heterosexual contact; in San Francisco today it is the heterosexual, not the homosexual, population where AIDS is spreading; and in New York City, more women than men are treated for infection with what is still sometimes misnamed the "gay male" virus. Outside the United States, AIDS has never been associated primarily with gay men.

The power of what are assumed to be divinely established moral or natural norms is enormous and has been emphasized here in order to sharpen our attentiveness to the analysis of the dynamics of the myth. What Halperin states about a friendship myth parallel to that of Gilgamesh and Enkidu holds true here as well: "So long as we, too, continue to read the *Iliad* in the light of later Greek culture — to say nothing of modern sexual categories — we shall continue to have trouble bringing the friendship between Achilles and Patroclus into sharper focus" (1990:87). In hopes of developing a sharper focus in this instance, I do not turn to Gilgamesh as a model of a gay relationship, nor do I argue for or against gay relationships, but I do question and protest the standard homophobic position, and I ask what we gain from looking at the myth with that position self-consciously bracketed out.

In fact, the epic introduces a thematic of two men having an important homo*social* relationship — not necessarily a genital homo*sexual* relationship — from which women are excluded at most points (the distinction was developed by Sedgwick 1985). Gilgamesh and Enkidu are clearly thought of as enjoying sex with women, although in all versions there is a textual break after their fight at the doorway of the temple, after "They kissed each other / And formed a friendship," which may have described a homosexual union, and hence was excised. The language has to be treated carefully, but there's little point in ignoring or suppressing such homoerotic elements as the description of Gilgamesh's first dream: he is drawn to Enkidu as though to a woman, and his mother says he will rejoice as he would over a woman, interpreted by Shamhat the priestess as "The dreams mean that you will love one another." Halperin notes that the same "word that describes Gilgamesh's attraction to Enkidu is also used to describe Enkidu's anticipated attraction to the prostitute from Uruk, with whom he mates for six days and seven nights" (1990:81). Gilgamesh, when Enkidu dies, "laid a veil, as one veils a bride, over his friend."

In contemporary terms, the pair would most likely be labeled "bisexual," but such labeling is precisely what often obscures our relationship to such mythical material. Instead of asking what bisexuality means today or when it is that heterosexism itself begins to be seen from a liberal perspective as another of the chilling "-isms" of the twentieth century, what matters is how Gilgamesh and Enkidu relate to one another as friends within their own historical and cultural contexts, and not how they do or do not score on a contemporary sexual game card.

The love between them — beautifully emphasized in Herbert Mason's translation — is remarkable in its depth. Gilgamesh's slow but sure growth toward acceptance of separation and death becomes an indication of what being human means — its limitations, but also its ability to surmount pain. And in this earliest Western myth we see already the prototypical interaction between the social setting and the characters that elucidates how people ought to act in society, how they can shepherd their moral attitudes and values in the direction of concern for one another rather than merely developing further their own self-centered desires and appetites. This mythic account of how a man loves another man may or may not be a story about homosexuality — transmission of materials with such an explicit perspective is very unlikely within the taboos of Western literary conventions — but clearly it is about sharing human love and relationship within the profound depths of male friendship. It is a story about masculine feelings and about expressing them, about caring deeply for another and learning to recognize when one is loved by someone else, and finally, about going on with one's own life when the beloved (does the gender matter?) is taken away.

At the same time the language is often that of intimacy such as is usually restricted by heterosexist conventions to man-woman relationships. Mason's phrasing brings out this aspect, but it is present in all the translations: Enkidu and Gilgamesh "grasped each other to go for their nightly rest," or Enkidu "is like a groom" when he obtains clothes and goes to meet Gilgamesh. There are many passages that seem to anticipate the later biblical relationship of David and Jonathan: "your love to me was wonderful, passing the love of women" (2 Sam. 1:26).

The manner in which Gilgamesh expresses his devastation over Enkidu's death will be echoed later in that other great scene of male love, the death of Patroklos in the *Iliad* — a work most likely influenced by the Gilgamesh epic. Achilleus is beside himself there in the way Gilgamesh is beside himself here: life seems to have no meaning if the beloved is no longer present. The scene from the *Iliad* and the Gilgamesh epic both reflect ways males come to grips with their grief. To be sure, these patterns of coping are not those best taught to children — the berserker quality of both Gilgamesh and Achilleus hardly provide useful models for psychological health in our own time. But at least we comprehend that caring for another deeply is part of what is possible for humans; and we learn from the epic that one of the ways humans face the separation and finality of death is by talking about it, sharing one's pain with others, and gradually diverting the emotional excess to projects that are useful to the society (the myth indirectly undergirds the custom of memorial gifts or taking vows to complete a project in one's community in the name of the beloved).

We have become so suspicious of serving the commonweal, in a time when even presidents can be accused of delaying the release of political prisoners in order to sway an election, that it is perhaps difficult for us to appreciate the sheer ethical power of the ending of the epic. We may well suspect the psychological motivation of Gilgamesh, who attains a sort of immortality in his architecture that was not possible for Enkidu. But when at last Gilgamesh turns from his grieving to complete the city wall, we learn something of great importance about grief: that it is not the end of our existence. When one is able to turn grief into achievements beneficial to everyone in the culture, then one takes a giant stride beyond the self-aggrandizing "winner take all" attitude that Gilgamesh displays at the start of the epic, when he demands brashly the traditional ruler's right of first intercourse with all newly wed brides.

Gilgamesh transcends his solitary, bored isolation when he discovers in Enkidu his true friend, his alter ego. Their experiences together make Enkidu's death all the more tragic. But Gilgamesh overcomes his grief after he finally learns to surmount that still immature attitude of the me-first demand to mama and the gods "to fix it." He learns to accept his limitations, including the relatively limited gifts his parental deities have bestowed upon him as their servant, and through a series of moves toward compassion, sharing love, and even intuition that are enacted not so much by Gilgamesh but by Enkidu, Mr. Supermasculine Gilgamesh comes by the end of the narrative to experience the feminine in ways that transcend his earlier imperialist aggression and his domination of the first-night brides. Indeed he learns not only to admire the more soft and gentle and intuitive qualities of Enkidu, but as part of his memorial to their friendship, to incarnate them after Enkidu's death. And we can surmise that even great king Gilgamesh has learned the hard way about the definitive clout of the divine feminine — presumably he will never again mock the powers of Ishtar as Enkidu did by recounting inappropriate tales about her former lovers and slinging offensive offal in her face. Neither men nor women rule arbitrarily over Ishtar/Aphrodite/Venus, but they are *subjects* of love; true love cannot be conquered except by death.

There is more transpiring in this myth with respect to the relationship of masculinity and femininity than can be discussed here, but a few of the significant issues include: (1) Given the historical knowledge that both males and females served the goddess by granting sexual favors to worshipers, when Enkidu in the early part of the myth is cleaned up and dressed by the temple priestess, is he being groomed to become Ishtar's castrated priest or male temple prostitute? That would explain the extremity of the later insults — in the duration of the narrative he would then have turned from the feminine to the masculine for his primary relationship. (2) How is it that the initial encounter between the two men comes precisely at the point where the bed of Ishtar is laid out for the newest bride? No wonder there is trouble with Ishtar later, but does the story imply a connection between the realm of the feminine and the realm of friendship, or specifically of male friendship? Why are men's relationships so frequently configured in secondary relationships to women partners? (3) Why don't we hear, as one would expect in such a heroic epic, of Gilgamesh's family? Perhaps the smoothing-out process of transmission over such a long time has eliminated that element, yet usually friendships lead to mentoring and godparental relationships between friends and their children. (4) What is transpiring here with respect to the transition from a priestly to a more secular culture? Repeatedly we catch hints that some very important religious customs are being revised: Ishtar is threatened and so she complains, doubtless reflecting a situation in which her priesthood was being threatened somehow by the developing conventions of male friendship. She wins the round when she initiates the pun-

ishment of Enkidu, but what does she gain in the end? My suspicion
ᒿ is that we see here a matriarchal-patriarchal confrontation that hasn't
yet been resolved; certainly an earlier version may well have crowed
about the way Ishtar had conquered the upstart male pair. And finally,
(5) whereas Dilmun, the paradisal forest of the Mesopotamian mythical times, is a wonderful place, the Forest Primeval here is horrendous:
what socio-historical situation changes led to the shift in metaphoric
signification?

Perhaps the epic reflects a transition from a religious to a secular
or humanistic society, in which case the love between Gilgamesh and
Enkidu becomes important as a story of males beginning to lose their
fear of other men, of allowing other men to carry, temporarily at least,
what one can least well carry without discipline and insight, without
elaborated forms of feeling and empathic care for one another — just
what male fraternities ideally transmit. *The myth is the story of the
ideally possible male bond,* a bond that may yet be freighted with the
awful tragedy of premature endings, leaving one partner to carry on in
the painful absence of the other. That the myth stands at the beginning of Western civilization, yet still speaks freshly to us of the need to
ground sufficiently patterns of male friendship in mythico-eternal jus-
tifications, indicates just how important male friendships are, and how
significant to social well-being.

In this friendship Gilgamesh undergoes massive change, from being the pampered autocrat of the city, totally one-sided in orientation,
totally out of balance so that he had become "a tyrant to his people,"
through the process of tragic grieving, to a sort of balance, marked by
his resignation to the fact of death, which he has to come to through
his beloved Enkidu's death, and a rededication not to himself and his
own wishes, but to his society's, to Uruk's symbolic crenelated walls.
The walled city is a traditional symbol of the whole self, and through
his friendship with Enkidu, Gilgamesh comes to grips with that component of himself that is his own previously unacknowledged double;
finally he manifests a clear sense of self-recognition, gained through
Enkidu's love. Perhaps this self-recognition derives from the sort of
insight that Robert Hopcke names as resulting when a male recon-
ciles himself with the feminine elements of his personality: "to be in
relationship to oneself as a man means fundamentally to both acknowledge and celebrate a kind of homosexuality, an enjoyment of one's own
manhood as a man; this enjoyment is anathema in a patriarchal society whose dominant values and social structures are organized along

heterosexual lines" (1990:101). "A kind of homosexuality" that has little to do with the *Playboy/Playgirl* trivializing of relationships into genital performance boxes; a kind of relatedness that encompasses acceptance of the male's own countersexuality (to use a typical binary term) and recognizes intensity of feeling rather than choice of sexual object as primary.

The change in Gilgamesh that derives from the friendship strikes me as parallel to what Stuart Miller refers to as "some of the special aspects of close male friendship," in his study of the problems confronting contemporary friendships among men. Miller lists: "a willingness to take a dangerous stand for another; a special relaxation and safety; an end to competitiveness, alienation, and self-alienation; a pleasure in doing masculine justice to others, an enhancement of men's own vitality and being. Above all, a holding in the heart" (1983:15). One can imagine that Gilgamesh has learned how to hold another in the heart, how to be a friend more openly and affectionately than would have been possible previously.

Throughout these reflections upon the story of Gilgamesh and Enkidu, the important theme of the same-sex double, the twin or second self, has surfaced, a theme that will be explored further in Chapter 10. But here already it is productive to point out how Enkidu has to carry so much for Gilgamesh. It is Enkidu who recognizes the dangers of the male foray into the wilderness, Enkidu who cautions against killing Humbaba, Enkidu who encourages Gilgamesh to attend more directly to the warnings of his dreams. Gilgamesh "only half listens," reflecting the usual twinship story wherein the more divine twin remains ignorant of the limitations of his fully human brother. Remaining ignorant, he allows his twin to carry most of the emotional aspects of the relationship, just as in many marriages the wife is left with the necessity of satisfying most of the relational tasks. Within the patriarchal perspective, men consider that their god-given rights include not having to work on relationships, on wholeness — which never drops down like a bolt out of the blue, but requires patient, passive, submission to the grieving descent into the underworld that Gilgamesh finally undertakes on the chance that he can bring Enkidu back to life.

In this myth we confront a conception of male wholeness that still speaks across the span of some three thousand years. That it comes in the manner of a story of male love for another male suggests not so much that such love is a matter of "sexual identity" on the purely individual level, but that it is something transcendentally important for two such sharply differentiated males. Few of us are rulers of kingdoms or wild men from the steppes, but as we seek our own contemporary modes of wholeness, the fear of touching another man in the depths of his soul, of "getting too close for comfort," still keeps many men apart at junctures where they can least afford yet more distance and separation from others. Emotional exhibitions of hugging and chanting, important initially when one begins to learn how to recover relationships with other men, can be augmented with the honest communicating of knowledge and feeling and anger and care that appear when men face down the negative labels of our society and commit themselves to respecting each other truly and fully. The story of the love of Enkidu for Gilgamesh and of Gilgamesh for Enkidu may serve not only as a model but as a metaphoric image, a prospective symbol for what is possible within male friendships.

This legend is not only important because it is one of the oldest attempts in Western literature to share our answers to questions about the meanings of life, but also because it is one of the richest and most multiply perspected. When exposited not as just another element in the mainline masculine inheritance of Western patriarchy, or more recently in terms of a gender-neutral analysis of the nature of human finitude and suffering (a distancing analysis that takes one away from the story, not into it), various meanings of the friendship between Gilgamesh and Enkidu reward more narrowly specified points of inquiry. Such approaches ask about the ways the story helps us imagine friendship, specifically male-male friendship, or about how a man's external face to the world, his "kingship," changes when he opens himself to the second self that we are trained to suppress — although many other aspects of this Mesopotamian miracle could be explored as well.

Study of Gilgamesh and Enkidu sends one delving into the comparative literature concerning friendship (see Hammond 1987); and from there it is an easy step into the history of friendship generally, or into the representation of male friendships in recent mass media (one's scope has to broaden to include music as well: David Byrne's musical *The Forest*, 1988, a key presentation at the New York International Festival of the Arts in 1991, was inspired by the Gilgamesh epic), or into the history of the relatively restricted, primary bond models that have informed Western romantic models of "love." It is a story that touched translator Herbert Mason deeply when a dear friend was dying of Hodgkin's disease, and he found the solace to face the man's death by working on his own moving translation of the epic (1970). And it is a story that finds a poignant contemporary counterpart in Paul Monette's *Borrowed Time: An AIDS Memoir* (1988a) and his slim volume of poems (1988b), both of which honor his lover Roger Horwitz. The first line of Monette's book of elegies, given the context of those two books and the epic that has been the focus of this chapter, describes this myth perfectly: "everything extraneous has burned away" (1988b:3).

▪ ▪ ▪ ▪ ▪

Sources of the Story

There are many recent treatments of the myth, including various ways of reconstructing the hundreds of its fragments, and the choice of one or another text will be determined by one's particular interests. The most technical and up-to-date include Daley (1989), Ferry (1993), and Kovacs (1989). Sandars (1972) is widely used, but for other than technical discussion, I still prefer Mason (1970), a "verse narrative" that retells the mythic account rather than trying to reconstruct the ancient text line for line, a process that in most of the translations means reading a page that is like a crossword puzzle with random square, angle, and round brackets sprinkled on top of it. Well-polished literary-reinterpretive versions include Gardner 1984; or there is the slick historical romance by Silverberg (1984), as thoroughgoing a heterosexualization of a legend as one might imagine, and Silverberg's Hugo Award–winning account of Gilgamesh in the Afterworld (1990), published in a science fiction series.

Bibliography for Further Study

All of the translations/versions give introductions and explanatory material for the text, and usually glossaries, even maps of the relevant areas of ancient Iraq. Thompson (1981:181–205) has some useful comparisons with Goethe's *Faust*, developing a contrast between technology and the cowboys Gilgamesh and Enkidu. Dalley (1989:120–22) provides suggestions for further study. Doty 1993c is a companion essay to this chapter, dealing with problematic aspects of male-male friendships today and advocating the development of an athletics (or aesthetics or discipline) of friendship.

Chapter 5

Herakles the Heroic Trickster

Background Information

Herakles was the Greek figure most represented in the arts, especially in Athens. His stories run into the hundreds, and that complicates how to get hold of this hero. Pindar was especially fond of Herakles — "stupid is the man, whoever he be, whose lips defend not Herakles" — treating him as the ideal representative of aristocratic ethics (*Pythia 9*, Lattimore transl.). In his plays *The Madness of Herakles*, *The Children of Herakles*, and *Alkestis*, Euripides humanizes him; one can see easily how for the later Cynics Herakles became a model of unspoiled vitality, a naturally noble man. Later transformed into Hercules in the Roman tradition, however, his excessive qualities cause a certain disenchantment. In fact in Latin comedy he is just the stupid jock whose muscles instead of his mind have guided his life, and he can find employment only as a pimp for brothels. (The image devastates the herculean ideals of the muscle-building magazines. Jaws usually drop in disappointment when people hear about how *ungainly* the super-muscled body was considered to be in antiquity, because it was totally out of balance. The image of the perfect body in our culture will engage us later, especially in terms of its machine-like aspects, and in the image of *Homo faber*, the model of the engine-like producer that influences many concepts of masculinity and our ideals of "productive" life goals.[1])

Summary

At times little more than a personification of physical strength, Herakles was credited with the origins of the Olympic Games. So far as humans were concerned, Herakles was especially *Alexikakos* (The Protector), the chief helper of human beings, so that he was considered to have all sorts of curative, even medical powers, and in the Hellenistic period was addressed as *Sotēr* (Savior), as was the Christ later. Mammoth body with a small head; leaning on a massive club; draped with a lion's skin, but in such a way as to highlight his spectacular muscles: the figure is a familiar one, Herakles' pausing for a moment's rest in between the many heroic exploits, or in the famous pose in the arts where he contemplates choosing Virtue (ugly and plain, let's face it) or Vice (as always, the nasty moral position *looks wonderful!*). Important on the earthly plane of existence, he also harrows hell in his heroic labors, capturing the many-headed dog of hell, Kerberos, because resourcefully he had had himself initiated in the Eleusinian mysteries and was guided by Hermes. His mortal term came to a dreadful ending, thanks to an event much earlier in his career, when he married Deianeira. The centaur Nessos sought to rape her as he carried the bride across a river. Herakles shot the creature, but as his blood poured out, Nessos recommended it to Deianeira as a guarantee of the fidelity and love of Herakles. It certainly did that: in a later episode, Deianeira, jealous of her husband, carefully soaked a tunic in the centaur's blood and sent it to him. Putting it on, Herakles was wracked by the most intense pain ever endured on earth; it was so intense that he wrenched up pine trees to make his own funeral pyre. But as the flames rose up, Zeus intervened and took his son into Olympos, where he was married to Hera's daughter Hebe.

Transmission of the Story

The cycles of stories about the figure of Herakles were so numerous that already in antiquity there were arguments about whether or not they could all refer to the same individual. And in fact even the famous trials and tribulations for which Herakles is famous, the twelve *Athloi* (Contests or Labors) and his subsequent marvels, were differentiated according to whether they were single-handed feats, the *Praxeis*, or Exploits Proper, or those in which someone had lent a hand, the *Parerga*, or Incidental Deeds. The *athlos* (pl. *athloi*) was what an athlete did when competing for a prize, *athlon;* already in Homer it had become a technical term, while the Latin translation *labores* is the source of the English designation "the Labors of Herakles."

Recognizing the complexity and multiplicity of Herakles materials is crucial to understanding this heroic figure, and the abundance of stories is matched by the abundance of commentary; here are three examples. Robert Graves is the most restrained: "the story of Herakles is, indeed, a peg on which a great number of related, unrelated, and contradictory myths have been hung" (1955:118.2). Geoffrey Kirk comments: "in the Herakles complex . . . we see an excellent example of the diversity of myth-types: test-and-quest myths, foundation-myths, aetiological [explanatory] themes of every kind and degree, myths that reflect preoccupations over society and its relation to the natural world, myths concerned with the relation of gods to heroes and of immortality to mortality" (n.d.:296). Karl Galinsky is struck by how Herakles proved to be "surprisingly many things to surprisingly many" people. Some of these include: the great, tragic sufferer; the paragon of superhuman physical prowess and bravado; the ideal nobleman and courtier; the incarnation of rhetoric; intelligence and wisdom; the divine mediator; a comic, lecherous, gluttonous monster; a romantic lover; an exemplar of virtue (1972:1–2).

These comments by Graves, Kirk, and Galinsky may be augmented by those of Philip Slater, who gives close attention to the psychological malfunctioning of Greek society, in a book very much about Herakles, *The Glory of Hera* (1968), and who remarks that today "one would undoubtedly comment on the repetitive self-destructive behavior, the lack of impulse control" (341), and other features of this figure who was (among many other epithets) named "Mr. Hypermasculinity." Indeed, on the island of Kos Herakles was a phallic deity of marriage, which is remarkable in light of his long series of different bedpartners![2]

Slater may also give us a sense of contemporaneity and yet temporal distance from the great stacks of mythic elements packed into the materials about Herakles, and in fact into other mythic traditions as well: "all myths tolerate more coexistence of opposites than Western rationalism is comfortable with" (343:n3). But perhaps it is important to be uncomfortable, or at least to recognize that we are uncomfortable, if the alternative is to reduce the conflicts to the presentations of the overly simplified myth handbooks and storybooks. Throughout this book we will find that no mythic figure is ever "just" a cipher for some idea (Ares = War, for instance), and that it may well be appropriate to rescue myths from being treated reductively as "children's literature." All sorts of clever allegorizing techniques were developed in Hellenistic myth interpretation, but even in that literature there were few simplistic accounts such as we find repeatedly in the way most of us are taught myth today, even in the popular courses for which I overhear college students preparing frequently ("Now let's see, Ares stands for War, and Aphrodite for Love").

▪ ▪ ▪ ▪ ▪

Seeing Herakles himself or a statue of him [in dreams] is auspicious for all those who govern their lives by sound moral principles and who live in accordance with the law, especially if they have been treated unjustly by others. For when he lived among men,

the god always came to the defense of those who had been treated
unjustly and he avenged them. For those who transgress the law
and for those who do something wrong, the god is inauspicious
for the same reason. He is a good sign for those setting out on a
contest, a lawsuit, or a battle. For the god is called Kallinikos, The
Glorious Victor. (Artemidoros 1975:119)

The flashy heroic encounters seem to be possible only on the basis of the
heroic continuities of everyday activities. The hero holds up a magnify-
ing glass to the everyday, disclosing its heroic continuities. Now I begin
to comprehend what I initially found puzzling, namely, the late fifth-
century and subsequent idealization of Herakles as a model of spiritual
endeavor. We are usually inclined to see the later Greek and Hellenistic
developments as something of a muddling of the earlier (and by implication purer) Greek spirit. But perhaps we learn something of lasting
importance from, for example, Isokrates' rhetorical praise of Herakles' *psychē* — his spiritual labors, also praised by the early Cynics; his
phronēsis, or practical wisdom; his *philotimia*, ambition and search for
honor; his *diakosynē*, or righteousness; and his *philanthropia*, respect
for all humankind. The struggles within Christianity to depotentiate
the figure of Herakles should remind us that his was an image often
in direct competition with the Christ figure, and competition does not
necessarily mean opposition between two different entities.

Herakles is a boundary-crosser, a figure of the margins who constantly enters into new territories and adventures. He is a "trickster,"
to use the anthropological term, whose life is largely spent within the
"liminal" space and period. The liminal is the name for the central
space and time segment of any ritualized experience, which begins with
a preliminal period (the prelude, in Latinized English) and ends with the
postliminal phase (the postlude). The "-lude" parts of the Latinizations
prelude and *postlude* indicate "play" — not just fooling around, but sacred play, serious play, the celebration of the human being participating
in culture as a serious games-player, as *Homo ludens*. It may be healthy
periodically to recall this model of the human regarded as a player when
threatened by the dominance of the contrasting image of the technological *Homo faber*, a contrasting construct that emphasizes the human
being functioning primarily as a fabricator, maker, worker.

The trickster is certainly a player, often a playful clown, a figure like
Hermes who is always on the go and always assisting others, but seldom steadfast or consistent like Apollo or Zeus. The trickster's "tricks"
are not cheats or deceits based on muscle power, but upon cleverness,

upon using one's wits faster or better than the next person (see Doty 1993a on Hermes considered as a trickster figure). Herakles is no Hermes, but I find it striking how many of his exploits involve *his* being tricked, as well as how much of his cleverness is exhibited in the arenas the Greeks valued most: athletics, warfare, hunting, and sexuality. The focus here is upon a sort of "underground Herakles," recalling some of his aspects that already were lost when he was elevated by the Greek philosophers into a paragon of moral purity and athletic and military prowess. <u>Herakles represents a model of selfhood that goes directly against the contemporary expectation that we organize our lives to attain a cohesive personal self-identity and career.</u> The expectation often represented in New Age self-help writings as well as other pop-psych literature aims at a sort of noble maturity in which one finally becomes One Thing, One Institutionalized Person, to the exclusion of the multiple selves we imagined being when children, or when dreaming and trusting our fantasies. A Herakles figure, on the other hand, apparently keeps on crossing different borders and engaging in a wide range of exploits, some of which will be canvassed here.

In the midst of the Gigantomachia, the great civil war in which the Olympian party vanquished the Giants, Herakles fells Alkyoneus, one of the giants, with his first arrow. Unfortunately, however, the twenty-four Giants had been born directly from Mother Earth, Gaia, so that shortly after Alkyoneus fell back to his Mother's bosom, he sprang up again, fully revived (just what happens to another child of Gaia whom Herakles battles, Antaios). Wise Athene, who frequently assists Herakles, and later his alter ego, Theseus, comprehends the situation immediately and tells Herakles to carry Alkyoneus *over the border* into Boeotia. Herakles does so, and there he manages to dispatch Alkyoneus quickly with his massive club — a constant iconographic sign, like the lion pelt, throughout the many artistic representations of Herakles. Already at the dawn of Greek mythological history, then, Herakles crosses the national limen (threshold) in order effectively to carry out his projects. Repeatedly we hear of Herakles' journeys and activities at the boundaries of the known world.

Likewise he deals repeatedly with "borderline" situations. The monsters he dispatches are frequently creatures born of humans, or of gods mating with monsters. Hence they are half-human and half-bestial, and they create the sort of boundary-confusion that leads in some cultures to taboo animals. Battling the half-human/half-horse Centaurs, overcoming beastly creatures with multiple serpentine heads or tails, fins, or razor-sharp claws, Herakles functions at the borders of the Western distinctions between culture (the human) and nature (the animal). Herakles establishes a cognitive order for the environment that highlights the anomalies; apparently it takes an exceptionally strong hero to deal successfully with situations that threaten to confuse various orders of existence.

One final example of Herakles' tricksterish liminality raises echoes of David and his warriors entering the Temple and eating the sacred shewbread, or of Jesus' disciples plucking (and by strict legalistic implication, threshing) grain on the Sabbath. This story involves mobilization of the Thebans against the Minyans, who held them in thralldom, having carefully pre-empted every piece of weaponry the Theban resistance might have used. The story must have seemed shocking in its original tellings, since Herakles went to the city's religious shrines and collected all the battle gear that had been ritually dedicated and stored there, and hence was sancrosanct. Taking the sacred gifts out to the secular army, he armed the Theban warriors before leading them to victory over the Minyans. The moral seems to be similar to the Christian saying that "the human is lord over even the Sabbath," although that may not have been the original ethnic interpretation.

Such examples illuminate the many connections between Herakles and the wily Hermes, especially because they portray traits not shared with other masculine deities with whom Herakles is often in conflict, namely, Zeus, Ares, Apollon, and Poseidon. Hermes and Herakles are associated in any number of stories, beginning with the myth variant in which Hermes brings Herakles to the breast of his divine stepmother, Hera, tricking her into suckling him, and thereby assuring the baby's eventual immortality. Others said Aphrodite had persuaded Hera to take up the child, but all variants agree that because Herakles sucked so hard, Hera pulled him away abruptly, and the spilt milk formed the Milky Way. Once at my most herculean-obsessive, I charted some twenty-five parallels between Hermes and Herakles; here I will just emphasize that both of them were thought to have brought important *civilizing* elements — building highways on which the safety of travelers was secure, defending the privilege of guests to sanctuary, abolishing human sacrifice, and especially safeguarding the rights of travelers and merchants.

Tricksterish humor is a central feature of trickster stories, and the Greek and Roman comedy writers loved to present Herakles in ridiculous situations, exaggerating his muscle-bound physical appearance, playing up his stupidity and cupidity, his bumptiousness and love of drink and food. Swiss dramatist Friedrich Dürrenmatt's *Herkules und der Stall des Augias* (Hercules and the Stables of Augeias, 1985) is but the most recent in a long line of comic literary manifestations of the *Homo ludens*, the human player, that Galinsky surveys in his thematic catalogue of manifestations of Hermes in literature (1972: chapter 4; there are many examples of trickster stories in Hynes 1993).

But instead of following the herculean tricksterish hilarity at this point we may examine briefly another aspect, namely, his cleverness, a quality that Herakles shares with both Hermes and the literary figure of Odysseus — whose initial and repeated epithet in Homer is *polytropos*. This epithet is now supposed to mean much-traveled, much-diverted, a descriptor that appropriately describes the course of Odysseus' adventures in the literature ranging from Homeric epics down to Kazantzakis and Joyce. But the epithet has mostly been understood as having reference to Odysseus' clever and many-sided intelligence, or even to his "unstable, unprincipled, unscrupulous" behaviors (Stanford 1963:260 n.28; 99). Odysseus and Herakles share many traits and features: gluttony, the matronship of Athena, proficiency in archery, visits to the Underworld followed by successful returns, large physique (Odysseus is compared to a ram; Herakles is said to stand eight feet tall), skill in oratory and in warfare, and finally bravery, tenacity, and patience.

Anyone remembering the way the many facets of Odysseus are portrayed in the *Odyssey* and the *Iliad* will remember that much of the literary success of those epics derives both from their accounts of heroic exploits and perilous situations, and from the remarkable narratives of Odysseus' cleverness in resolving them. The Labors of Herakles present *Herakles* in precisely the same light: repeatedly he is faced with seemingly inhuman situations, overwhelming odds, boundless evil, only to escape without harm. His successes are partly the result of his extraordinary strength (*bia* in Greek), but they are invariably characteristic of the skill the Greeks admired even more, that of the clever manipulator who can pull the odds to his own side and win the unexpected victory. That skill was admired in commerce as in law, and indeed Hermes, similar once more to Herakles in possessing tricksterish skill, became the deity of merchants as well as of orators.

Even a few selections from the twelve heroic Labors illustrate Herakles' adaptive resourcefulness: *Killing the Nemean Lion* (Labor no. 1): Herakles soon discovers that the lion's supernatural pelt deflects even his own invincible arrows, and so, shifting the attack, Herakles quickly blocks one of the two entrances to the lion's cave and, entering the other, strangles the lion with nothing but his bare hands. Later, jealously casting his eye on the lion's pelt, he cleverly realizes that the only instrument that could dress the skin would be the lion's own sharp claws, which he uses resourcefully — the trickster turns the attack weapon into a useful tool for his own purposes.

Capture of the Deer of Keryneia (no. 3): Herakles' superb skill as a hunter is displayed in the year-long chase of the golden-horned deer that are sacred to Athene. The trickster works stealthily and steadily, stubbornly pressing on against seemingly impossible odds, and finally captures the animal as it sleeps at the utmost ends of the earth (at one significant level the story indicates Herakles' control over the borderline between life and death). *Capture of the Erymanthian Boar* (no. 4): again, tenacity in hunting pays off, but the clever trick is driving the huge beast into the immobilizing snow, where Herakles snares it with a net. The trickster resourcefully tries out unusual methods, which win the day; he experiments freely and resists surrendering to threats that overwhelm merely ordinary consciousness. In *Obtaining the Cattle of Geryon* (no. 10), Herakles masters Old Age (Geryon), by shooting an arrow through all three of his bodies simultaneously. The closing of the story cycle is foreshadowed already in this incident: when immortalized, Herakles, since he conquers Old Age and death, will be paired with Hebe, Youth.

The sort of technological skill that leads the apparently bumbling trickster permanently to alter features of the primordial landscape — as by leaving geographical tracks of his wrestling with chaos monsters — is found in *Cleansing the Stables of Augeias* (no. 5), where Herakles restores the countryside around Elis to agricultural usefulness after it has become buried beneath the accumulated manure of the many cattle of ruler Augeias. Herakles diverts a river, and the hydraulic forces scouring the flood plain carry away the excess fertilizer. He deals once more with a superabundance of manure in *Driving Off the Stymphalian Birds* (no. 6) — birds that killed people and animals by means of their sharp brass feathers. In this episode Athene aids him against Ares, to whom the birds are sacred, by providing metal noisemakers created by Hephaistos; they startle the birds into flight in order that Herakles may kill them.

A final example of Herakles' resourcefulness is the Labor of *Obtaining the Golden Apples of the Hesperides* (no. 11), where Herakles first wrestles with shape-shifter Nereus in order to locate the Tree of Life with its life-restoring golden apples, and then kills the guardian dragon. But again the story is not about force (*bia*) alone, since it also encompasses Herakles' deceitful treatment of Atlas. Before Atlas had shouldered the celestial globe, he had set out the trees and built a wall to protect them, so when the way was clear, Atlas was in the best position to obtain the Golden Apples. But when he does so, and brings them to Herakles, gloating over his success, Herakles tricks him into resuming his unprofitable work. This is by no means the only occasion where someone who helps Herakles is later deceived or killed by him. Certainly this was no god of companionship, and not even his twin brother, Iphikles, is able to get very close to Herakles, although Herakles' intimate relations with his male lovers will be mentioned below.

Other aspects of Herakles as a trickster include the long series of figures who trick him in turn, and the fact that those whom he kills or reforms are themselves deceivers or serious miscreants; it is not unusual for the trickster hero's own failings or strengths to be projected onto those against whom he struggles. Herakles usually turns the tables by repaying his tormentors in their own coin, as in the case of Lityerses, a farmer who would offer hospitality to wayfarers, then force them to compete with him in reaping. He'd always win, then decapitate the strangers; finally Herakles outreaped and then decapitated him. Or there was Pan (Faunus) who sought to seduce Queen Omphale (whom Herakles was serving) by slipping into her bed at night; but Omphale and Herakles saw this coming, and exchanged beds, so Herakles soundly trounces Pan on Omphale's behalf.

It is striking that a figure whose name has become such a byword of masculinity was so frequently associated with various feminine figures and characterized by traditionally "feminine" traits. It is almost as if Herakles' masculinity, all his symbolically masculine mountaintop activities, had to be balanced by elements of the feminine, as in his many exploits connected with symbolically feminine water elements at the boundaries of earth and the subterranean rivers. Repeatedly Herakles is associated with springs and fountains — he need only stamp his feet and water springs forth to assuage his thirst and that of his fellow Argonauts. His technology involves draining marshes, opening channels and water conduits, and digging lakes and water tunnels. The classical tradition reinforces the balancing of all that herculean maleness when it associates Herakles with seafaring and has him deal repeatedly with oceanic or riverine characters such as Okeanos, the sons of Poseidon, the sea monster Triton, the river god Acheloos, and the old man of the sea, Nereus. He is repeatedly connected with those minor *daimones* (nature spirits) who dwell in streams and springs, the fabulous Nymphs, beautiful young women whose softness and sensuality contrast to Herakles' hard muscular appearance.

The number of women with whom Herakles is connected as wife or mistress — about seventy-five — is astonishing only until we come to the tradition that he fathered at least eighty sons, or to the stories about his successive nights with forty-nine or fifty of the daughters of Thespios (some claim all of them were satisfied throughout one excessive night of lovemaking). Herakles also champions women suffering in painful situations, and hence rescues Hesione, Alkestis (fighting Thanatos, Death himself, to bring her back to Admetos), the daughters of Dexamenos, Deineira, Hermione, and Hera.

His matron Athene is his constant recourse: "And time and time again he would cry aloud to the Heavens, / and Zeus would send me down in speed from the sky to help him" (*Iliad* 8.364–65, Lattimore transl.), and Bakchylides, another ancient poet who adored Herakles, has him acknowledge Athene's help repeatedly: "but Pallas Athene, / the golden-haired, will be there to help me" (*Olympian* 1, in Lattimore 1960:72). Athene intervenes frequently in his behalf, so that it is hardly surprising that Herakles is said to have raised in Sparta a temple to Athene of the Just Rewards.

Almost always his relationship to Athene is positive, but the discords between Herakles and the goddess whose name he bore, Hera, are so consequential as to threaten to drown out entirely any positive relation between the hero and his stepmother. There is real pathology in these accounts: Hera robs Herakles of his birthright before he is born by causing Eurystheus' mother to give birth in her seventh month of pregnancy; and she sends serpents to his cradle to kill him — after all, Herakles is the biological offspring of Zeus, who had cheated on Hera! She also sends the madness that leads Herakles to kill his wife Megara and his children; she nurtures both the Nemean Lion and the Lernean Hydra as obstacles to Herakles' career; and she sends the dragon Ladon to guard the Apples of the Hesperides, which Herakles must harvest. In the end, Hera is forced to assent to Herakles' apotheosis and accept him into Olympos, but she does even that with the knowledge that she has arranged spitefully for Philoktetes (the only companion brave enough to light Herakles' funeral pyre) to be bitten by a poisonous viper.

We do not know why Hera was thought to act so oppressively toward the proto-Greek heroic figure whose name ("Hera's Glory," or "Glorious Gift of Hera") merely reflects his parents' gratitude to the goddess for having borne a child. The theophoric name emphasized that the parents' fertility was ascribed to successful supplication of Hera as the

goddess of marriage. For all of Philip Slater's socio-psychological puzzling about the construction of the Greek family and the fragility of
the mother-son relationship within it (which is usually helpful in comprehending mythical refractions of Greek social and especially sexual
patterns), we are no closer after reading his *The Glory of Hera* (1968)
to understanding why it would be Herakles, of all her stepchildren,
who was to bear the brunt of her animosity. Another critic, Nicole
Loraux, wonders if "there is some necessity that drives Herakles and requires that he receive everything, even his heroic stature, from women"
(1990:27). She regards Herakles as "one of the Greek figures representing *femininity in man*," a perspective that has interesting ramifications
even though I do not care for her argument that Herakles' feminine
side is seen *in his suffering,* "which constitutes a means of experiencing
femininity in his body" (29).

On the evidence of these accounts, the subject of heroic masculinity in contrast to femininity was important to the ancient Greeks, and
mythic materials do not replicate trivia but what seems crucial, normative. Hence all these references to *the feminine* within the almost
excessively *masculine* stories about Herakles indicate that important
issues are surfacing. Additional interpretive depth-trenches may help us
determine the significances for the ancient Greeks and for our own situations: Gregory Nagy refers to the "fundamental principle in Hellenistic
religion" that there should be an antagonism between hero and god in
myth, corresponding "to the ritual symbiosis between hero and god in
cult," and Slater provides another slant in suggesting that Hera displaces
onto Herakles some of her own hostility toward Zeus (Nagy 1979:121,
303; Slater 1968:349). Perhaps there is a greater element of complexity
here than is to be discovered in the one-sidedly masculine and warlike
Ares. Herakles' own feminine aspects appear in the mythical episodes
such as his cross-dressing, an activity not at all unusual in mythical
trickster figures, whose masculine or feminine appearance often alters
according to the specific situation. Herakles was said to have donned
female clothing at Kos in order to escape the Meropes (subsequently
his priests and every bridegroom there wore women's clothing). Loraux
stresses the iconographic representations of his womb-like belly and his
cloak — a *peplos*, or woman's dress, like that of Athene, or the *krokotos*,
or tunic, of the effeminate Dionysos (Farnell 1921:120, 169–75; Loraux
1990).

Herakles' slavery to Queen Omphale — she won his services when
he had to work off his retributive guilt for having killed his wife and

children — is a period of transvestism that has a lasting mythical trail; in the Queen's retinue, Propertius suggests, Herakles even wore a bra. In Omphale's household Herakles not only took on female dress but learned the practical arts of the Greek housewife, although at the same time he remained Omphale's lover and performed a number of heroic activities that stabilized her kingdom. Slater suggests that there was a historical parallel to this episode in early Greek marriage customs, but that the retention of the story was due to a pathological fear of the emasculating power of women. In other interpretations, Fontenrose (1959) thinks that the episode refers to one of Herakles' sojourns in the Land of the Dead. Prinz (1974) and Graves (1955) identify Omphale with the pythoness at Delphoi; hence they suggest that Herakles rendered three years of service to the priestesses there as a means of expiating his guilt caused by killing Iphitos, as well as by trying to steal the Delphic tripod in order to set up his own oracle. Whatever the historical kernel, the Herakles account has the hypermasculine hero graphically living out the feminine side of himself. Usually glossed over by myth handbooks, the episode was important enough to earn for him the epithet *Heraios*, "belong to Hera," or "the Hera-esque one."

While calling any particular personality traits "masculine" or "feminine" is more and more problematic today, our society usually refers to intuitive behavior as feminine in contrast to more objectified or long-considered behavior, and hence it is worth noting that the intuition of Herakles is such that he frequently knows instinctively and immediately what to do: no extended considering, no rational thinking-through. In fact, one of his key stories stresses that his type of masculinity was not the Greek norm: Queen Alkestis had agreed to die in place of her husband Admetos, and Herakles arrives just as the household is mourning her death, yet Admetos refuses to name who has died, insisting on feting Herakles according to the most elaborate and formal rules of *xenia*, guest-hospitality. Euripides' *Alkestis* develops the picture of Admetos as the Organization Man so utterly bound by tradition that he cannot bear the thought that people might say he had turned away a guest unsatisfied, no matter what the mitigating household circumstances.

But Herakles is shocked sober when he belatedly learns who it is who has died, and immediately, *intuitively*, he lashes out at Admetos with all the fury that Euripides' drama could marshal against the superficial rules of overly polite culture in fifth-century Athens. No; intuitive personal feelings are not to be submerged beneath social custom, even when it is the admirable Hellenic ideal of hospitality toward guests that is at issue. To drive home to Admetos just how important the issue is, Herakles confronts Thanatos, Death himself, and eventually succeeds in winning Alkestis back to life.

Not all of Herakles' intuitive, quick responses are positive: angry at his music teacher Linos, he crowns him with the lute and kills him; Eunomos and Kyathos are instantly killed when Herakles externalizes his displeasure at the way they wash his feet and serve him wine. He vents enormous berserker fury, well-captured by Apollonios in his account of Herakles' reaction to the news that his lover Hylas has been stolen from him by the nymphs of a spring where the boy had gone to fetch water:

> When Herakles heard this, the sweat poured from his forehead and the dark blood boiled within him. In his fury he threw down the pine [which he had pulled up whole in order to make a new oar for the *Argo*] and rushed off, little caring where his feet were carrying him. Picture a bull stampeded from the water-meadows by a gadfly's sting. He takes to his heels; and off he goes, sometimes pressing on without a stop, sometimes pausing to lift his mighty neck and bellow in his pain. Thus Herakles in his frenzy ran at top speed for a while without a break, then paused in his exertions to fill the distance with a ringing cry. (Apollonios of Rhodes 1959:1.1261–72)

If Homer makes Odysseus ram-like, Apollonios makes Herakles ox-like — an association that appears frequently in his epithets, five of which begin with the stem for cattle or oxen, *bou*-. It is a dedicated "oxness": Herakles gives up his role in the voyage of the *Argo* in order to remain and search for Hylas, and Herakles' relationships with his lovers subsequently became a paradigm of trust and commitment. Male lovers exchanged vows at shrines of Herakles and at the tomb of his other famous beloved, Iolaos.

Obviously this is a mythological figure who incarnates more freedom of sexual choice than we are used to having divine figures encompass, but to comprehend how Herakles could become the model for the Hellenistic Divine Man (*theios anēr*), anticipated in Pindar's earlier description of him as a Heroic God (*hērōs theos*), it is crucial to see what aspects were included. These materials indicate that the Greeks had a deep appreciation of the feeling and intuitive sides of Herakles, the *aristos andrōn* ("the best of men" in Aristophanes, Euripides, and Sophokles); that they were less likely than we to demand restraint and gentility from deities; and that they were less interested than we (or the later Romans) in defending Herakles' morality according to heterosexual standards.

Slater correctly recognizes that the survival of all the traits and stories, even contradictory ones, can be explained only on the basis that they mattered to the Greeks, that the Greek Herakles was not to be essentialized into a slot in the conventional pantheon we have made of the Greek deities. One way to approach Herakles as entailing both poles of a binary duality that is in our own social context "divine" is to look at the cumulations of traditions about his sexuality, especially since I have mentioned relationships with women and men, but discussed primarily the former. For there certainly were relationships with men — some fourteen men are named as Herakles' male lovers (technically, his beloveds, or *eromenoi*).

We do not hear enough about Herakles' relations with these men to conclude, as one usually can from the Greek materials, that they represented the standard older-man-to-younger-man relationship that was the basis for entry into society with what we now call a liberal education. We do hear about his enormous, earth-wrenching grief at the loss of Hylas (Apollonios's account was quoted earlier); and Iolaos, his brother's son and hence a fellow Theban, is reported as having been Herakles' faithful charioteer, assisting him in many of his labors. In one late legend, the charioteer restored Herakles to life after he had been killed by Typhon, by holding a herb or a quail to his nostrils, doubtless connecting up with a story about a herb of immortality that Herakles saved for the gods in the Gigantomachia (Graves 1955:133.11). Resurrections and resuscitations recur: in the traditions where Herakles does not kill his wife Megara, she is given to Iolaos, who in turn was later rejuvenated by Hebe in order to protect his dead lover's family, the Herakleidai.

Commentators are quick to assure us that the traditions about Herakles' homosexuality represent a secondary development intended to justify homosexuality within the Theban military (or some other such explanation), but Herakles' relationships with men are as determinative of his whole mytho-heroic story as are his heterosexual relationships with women. The hero who sires some eighty sons and thereby establishes a dynasty, the Herakleidai, certainly represents a different realization of masculinity than that duality of *either* homosexual *or* heterosexual familiar from our own social patterns, and we have seen sufficient evidence of a non-macho Herakles (his dressing and acting as a woman, his passivity and servitude toward others) to assert that within the Greek contexts Herakles was not appreciated solely as a solar heterosexual Super-Male. Perhaps he is more of a lunar hero (a term elaborated in a later chapter), meaning that he displays a passivity and receptivity not usually considered characteristic of the aggressive and domineering solar heroes. Emphasizing Herakles' passivity as part of his whole being helps one see that his many exploits were not performed on his own behalf, but more frequently bring about significant refinements of human culture. If his character still seems somewhat overwhelmingly aggressive, at least it is mitigated by the fact that he "suffers" his labors (as Jesus suffers his passion — *passio*, suffer). He does not use them to amass a personal fortune, but they become elements in his relationships and ongoing reputation.

Furthermore, it is often relatedness instigated by Eros: in some traditions Herakles' labors are merely the love tasks set the beloved by his lover, Eurystheus. And perhaps Plato was right in another of those odd etymologies in the *Kratylos* when he derives the term "hero" (*hērōs*) from *erōs*, on the basis that all the heroes were the product of the love of a god or goddess for a mortal, or vice versa (398.c-e). Even the conservative scholar Martin Nilsson, who seldom remarks upon the assistance of Iolaos in the Labors, describes Iolaos as "his true friend and charioteer, *without whom a hero could not be*" (1932).

In the context of asking what constitutes personal identity — the great range of exploits and relationships of Herakles cannot but drive one to the question — the clearest answer from the perspective of Herakles seems to be that the heroic being will never be singular or simple. He or she may never know a unitary maturity or a single vocation, but he or she will be discovered always contesting in the midst of labors and yet more labors. Reacting now in a more "masculine," now in a more "feminine" fashion, the true herculean figure adjusts to the contours of the immediate context — now straightforwardly, now with the deceits of the trickster. The herculean figure acts in the broad daylight (in contrast to Hades' darkness or Hermes' fondness for the shadowy half-light). Excessive size and boisterousness will mark its presence, not what has come since Nietzsche to be called Apollonian restraint (later in this book that will be treated as a misconception anyway). And as we say today, "the impossible will take just a little bit longer," because just the impossible, beyond-the-boundaries, extraordinary encounter or situation can provide the raw materials for the creative and transformative technology it needs.

Herakles continues his quests in a curious twilight of ego-differentiation: he recovers Ikarios's body from the waters and gives it a decent burial, an act that so pleases Ikarios's father, Daidalos, that the inventor honors Herakles with a marvelous life-sized statue. Life-sized and life-like, so much so that when Herakles comes upon his own statue he mistakes it for a competitor, and lays about with his mighty club, soon reducing it to a heap of metal fragments. Of course this is a comic scene. And yet Herakles' stupidity reminds us that the heroic figure will always be subject to deceptions, as well as to the temptation to worship only a single monolithic concretization of the heroic character. Allowing Herakles to lead, our own self-idols are smashed as the idealizations that others project upon any one of our strengths are rejected.

Parallels between Herakles and Homer's Odysseus were suggested above; perhaps there are parallels as well with the Odysseus of Nikos Kazantzakis, whose career begins where Homer's stories end, with the quest for spiritual realization. If that is the case, Archibald MacLeish captures perfectly the open-ended nature of the heroic spirit Herakles manifested: "Persist against impossible, unequal odds, set the world straight, staunch the horror, slaughter the enemies and then? ... and then?" (*Herakles: A Verse Play*, cited in Galinsky 1972:244). Or we may recall the herculean motto Kazantzakis had inscribed above the door to his home, in flat contradiction to the famous Delphic motto of moderation in all things (*sophrosyne*): EVERYTHING TOO MUCH!

So multifaceted a figure that his stories have evoked many others — the trickster, Hermes, Odysseus, the Divine Man who has power over death — Herakles' heroism is never simple or singular. Masculinity on his model has some stupidity to it, as in the Roman adaptations in stories about dumb Hercules, but it has as well grandeur and freshness. It manifests particularly in serving and helping capacities, and Herakles' Labors are never undertaken selfishly for his own fame and glory, although these contests do promise heroic immortality to the successful competitor. Perhaps originally told about a particular regal figure in Mycenaean times, the multitude of stories told about Herakles acted like a magnet to legends about many other heroes: looking first at Herakles in this book, then, we have an important Mr. Everyman whose masculinities are composite and representative. The apparently isolated strong man turns out to be a representative figure for traits of many others.

▪ ▪ ▪ ▪ ▪

Sources of the Myth

There is no single mythic version, although among the later collections, Apollodorus's account in *The Library* (see Simpson 1976) is the most complete. Boswell 1980:221–22 gives a useful sketch of the major treatments in classical literature.

Bibliography for Further Study

Gallinsky 1972 provides a rich compendium of the ways the Herakles figure has been treated down through the twentieth century; Loraux 1990, a contemporary study of the feminine aspects within Herakles. Rose 1959 is good on the series of heroic Labors; Nilsson 1932 is a bit technical, but neatly focused on the background and development of the cycle of Herakles stories.

Chapter 6

Narcissus and the Narcotic
of the Self/Body Image

Background Information

There are many ways to interpret the significance of the story of Narcissus (Greek: Narkissos). Analysts stress the problem of self-love (breaking the vanity taboo), finding self-love too late, Narcissus's inability to relate to Echo, his frigidity toward any other love objects, a lack of paternal acceptance that led him to seek from outside the affirmation he should have had from within, and so forth. The figure of Narcissus appears sparingly in Greek sources, and it was the Roman poet Ovid who developed the canonical version, in his *Metamorphoses*. But an interpreter can stress the early part of the story or the later, or pick up a point of departure from some of the subsequent retellings, so having one normative version does not help us much. Even Freud contrasted a primitive type and a mature type of the psychological problem that came to be called narcissism (thanks to a German translation of the term "Narcissus-like" used by Havelock Ellis in 1898; Freud first used it in 1910), and post-Freudian thought rewrites Freud's teachings on narcissism (especially in the work of Otto Kernberg, Jacques Lacan, and Heinz Kohut).

My own view of Narcissus includes both positive and negative elements, respecting the many-sidedness of mythical figures. While the common preference today is for singularity and clarity, myths and legends help us remember that life is never singular or clear; they offer us ways of integrating the mirrored insights of others into the package of events we come to call the self or personality. The Echo and Narcissus story has to do with fantasy and projection and impossible dreams, but it also challenges the normative patterns by which construction of the self takes place, even today: What are the limits of self-identity? How does our self-image comport with what others project onto us? When do we feel comfortable in responding to another's call to love? — comfortable in the sense that the perceptions of others are not inordinately

103

puffed up, nor is our own self-perception skewed by impossible visions of who we might be. Narcissus mythology is *self* mythology. It brings to a crisis what every human has always faced, the relationship of the solitary individual to the other human beings whose lives give one's own existence meanings that transcend particularity and individuality. In the Narcissus legends we confront the ultimate ethical issue of the legitimacy of being singularly "I" in the context of the social "we."

Summary

A gorgeous boy child from birth, the beauty of the sixteen-year-old Narcissus was such that both males and females sought his love, but he was so prideful that he refused all comers. A nymph named Echo fell totally in love with him, but ate her heart out when Narcissus would only reply: "Keep your hands off me! I'll die before I give you power over me." She suffered so much that eventually she was reduced to a mere bodiless shred of a human voice. Other young people were likewise rejected by the pretty lad, until an unrequited male suitor cursed Narcissus to love only himself, and Nemesis, the goddess of retribution for evil deeds, agreed that the curse was appropriate. So one day when Narcissus, all hot from hunting, came to a perfectly still pool of silvan water to bathe, he caught a reflection of his own handsome body — and at once fell fatefully in love with it.

Now *he* became the frustrated one, because he never could seize the body of the mirrored reflection. He was deluded, Ovid tells us, just the way any of us are when we go after the mere illusion rather than the real-world, flesh-and-blood reality — just what Narcissus rejected initially when he refused to pair off with any of those who had desired him. Nor does he remain quite so stupid for long: he soon realizes that he's in love *solely with himself*, and of course that's the part of the myth that contributed the diagnostic term "narcissism" to psychological literature. The young lad finally wasted away as Echo had earlier, so that the well-developed, statuesque body melted like the watery images that surround his character throughout the narrative. When mourners came to bury him, nothing was left of that much-admired male form, but in its place was a flower with white petals surrounding a yellow center (the narcissus flower was famous in antiquity for fading quickly). The Greek name implies becoming stiff, non-feeling, as seen yet in "narcotic" or "narcolepsy"; and remember that it was a narcissus that lured Persephone to the underground, into submission to Hades' realm, so that it was planted at gravesides (on the technical aspects of the plant see Spotnitz 1954).

Transmission of the Story

There are a few traditions about Narkissos in Greek literature, but primarily the West came to know about Narcissus through Ovid's *Metamorphoses*, a long retelling of a wide miscellany of mythic stories from Greece and Rome that was an early expression of the philosophy of cultural evolution. He sets the story in a section that as usual humanizes the deities and shows them to have all-too-human foibles. Arguing over whether men or women had the greater experience in sex, the instance of Tiresias is introduced; he had experienced life from the perspective of both sexes, and Ovid uses his name as a literary frame for two only slightly related stories, that of Echo and Narcissus, and that of Bacchus (Dionysos). Ovid was always self-conscious about his stories of transformation and change, and here he may not have felt that his point got across satisfactorily, because in the next book of the *Metamorphoses* he relates the story of Salmacis and Hermaphroditus, a story that has so many parallels with the Narcissus story that it is essentially a literary doublet with different characters. Photius transmits a Greek fragment by Konon in which Ameinias, the man who loved Narkissos, is given a beautifully decorated sword by Narkissos, with which he killed himself dramatically in front of Narkissos's own dwelling, calling out for vengeance on the arrogant lad who rejected all suitors. Another Greek variant relates the conceit that Narkissos was in love with yet another boy, and pined away because his own love was not returned.

▪ ▪ ▪ ▪ ▪

The opposite pole of love is not so much hate as indifference.
(Whitmont 1982:25).

[The beloved doesn't realize] that his lover is as it were a mirror in which he beholds himself.
(Plato, *Phaidros* 255d; Hamilton-Cairns ed. 1961:501)

Narcissus' tragedy ... is that he is not narcissistic enough, or rather that he does not reflect long enough to effect a transformation from identity to identity with a difference. (Babcock 1980:2)

How about "vanning" as the perfect image for a narcissistic society? The people inside the van are completely enclosed. The Rock music inside is so loud they can't hear anything else and the walls have little windows so that they can see out, but no one can see in ... and I question how much they do try to see out. By cutting their lives off from the rest of the world they're, if not actually,

then existentially killing themselves, because they're not living
connected to any real world. The van certainly strikes me as a
good 20th century equivalent of Narcissus looking into the pool.

("A Conversation with Dr. Shirley Sugerman,"
Drew University *Reporter* Nov./Dec. 1978:6)

Although I planned for some time to write more about Narcissus, and
hence had explored the myth from a number of directions, Agustín
Cárdenas's sculpture, "Narcissus," 1989, which I saw reproduced in an
art magazine, first drove home to me how the Narkissos motif is related
directly to a discussion of masculinity. According to a long tradition in
art, Narcissus lies languidly on a stream bank glancing at the reflection which he takes to be either some other beautiful young adolescent,
unattainable to Narcissus, or himself, absorbed in the self-scrutiny that
has caused Narcissus to lose interest in the rest of the world outside the
self. But as can be seen from the reproduction on p. 107, Cárdenas's figure is not lying flacidly on a stream bank but seated and staring into his
own crotch. The "gaze," the fascination, is such that essentially Narcissus and his penis have become one: his whole person, his "face" to
the world, has become one with his genitals, and nothing can break the
concentrated circuit of that gaze. If the realm of Eros consists of reciprocal circuits in which we give and receive love, here Narcissus has pulled
the circuit breaker. Appropriately in this context, Freud saw Eros and
Narcissus as antipodes.

Cárdenas might provide a very different explanation for his sculpture, but I suggest that it speaks of the entrapment of sex, the way in
which the genitality that ought to be a part of a sexual relation to another can become the sole self-reality, a sort of playboy-forever motif
that counts "scores" the way hunters supposedly notch their gunstocks
to record kills, yet remains entirely self-reflective and self-absorbed. Narcissus becomes so enamored of *phallos*, of the male principle, of his own
maleness, that he excludes every other relationship; he rejects every
challenge to his own self-sufficiency.

To be sure, there is a religious aspect to phallos, which Eugene Monick treats in *Phallos: Sacred Image of the Masculine* (1987; see also
Elder 1987). But the way many of us know Narcissus today is not
through any sort of spiritual phallicism, but through our own or another's phallic self-absorption. Cárdenas's sculpture seems a powerful
comment on the fantasy of the ten-inch dick that rules contemporary
culture — one men's magazine advertises a $5,000 reward for finding a
man with a larger penis than that of its own champion. Likewise I take

Cárdenas's sculpture to represent a critique of the cult of the beautiful body, the outstanding genitals, the superb sexual technique — and right there we recognize the motivating energies behind a very large portion of the investiture of monetary capital in our society.

Masculinity becomes problematic when it is less a matter of reciprocal relationships with others than of whom we can engage in mutual intercourse, when being male is judged by the duration of one's physical or symbolic erection.[1] The atmosphere that surrounds so much contemporary masculinity restricts its very complex nature and reduces gender and personality to sex. Such reduction in focus is not just contemporary, but can be identified throughout this century: I've felt something of the same visual message I find in Cárdenas in several of Aubrey Beardsley's prints. His illustrations for Aristophanes' *Lysistrata* frequently center on messengers with enormous sexual members, or on worship of the phallos as such: it is stroked and caressed, light streams from it as from a sacred object, and most of his figures are preternaturally endowed. But in others of Beardsley's work, one senses that Beardsley's own relationship to Phallos may have had problematic aspects, as in the illustration on p. 109, where the artist is attached by an elegant silk rope to an ithyphallic Priapos off to the side. The illustration raises the questions of how the phallic is "tied to" the individual male, where masculinity in the overall framework of a male's life becomes explicitly phallic or sexual, and how narcissistic self-regard is sited appropriately or inappropriately.

Erich Neumann, one of the first generation of Jungian theorists, argued that narcissism was necessarily and normally part of the movement toward "centroversion," in which there is a magical relationship to one's own body, a body that is to be adorned and developed (1962:122). According to Neumann's pattern of male development, narcissism precedes first *phallicism*, where there is "an aroused and actively desiring masculinity," and then *ego-consciousness*. Hermaphroditic imagery often makes its appearance during the narcissistic stage, so for Neumann there is good reason for Ovid to move on to the story of the hermaphrodite immediately after the story of Narcissus (307). Whether one operates from such a Jungian developmental model or a more Freudian one, it is clear that within its perspective what is being masculinized is *the body*. Not only *physiological* gendering and the pubescent shaping of the secondary physical characteristics, but also the *relational* physical body and the person relating self-consciously in terms of ideas and politics and occupational contexts — just what seem lacking in the "health" or "body" magazines or the widespread promotion and commercialization of the handsome young male body today.

The faces of male models in clothing ads, in men's health magazines, or in *Playgirl* all seem bored and lifeless. When interviews are included, the models seldom discuss ideas or issues or life goals, but instead state how pleased they are *to be seen* in the publication. Appearance seems to have taken the place of personality, physical beauty to have become the ultimate ideal for masculine development.

So can a real man be muscular and handsome? What a question! If the answer is no, a sizeable portion of the muscle-building empire crumbles overnight, and that does not seem very likely. But what happens when the handsome muscular body joins sexuality as the primary focus of masculinity, when it becomes a replacement for a mature personality inside? Well, the result is a narcissism of the culture, a fascination with the artificially produced image that Christopher Lasch (1979) analyzes as it sweeps across contemporary culture. He and others such as Neil Postman (1985) point out some of the tyrannies of the artificially structured image, of the carefully machined Soloflex body. We recognize image instead of value or depth as the organizing element in many significant arenas in our society. Particularly our political economies (politics in short, but we forget that it still refers to something of significance) are organized according to what *appears* best, regardless of the actual facts. My reference is not just to blow-dried hairstyles and smiling poster photos of political candidates who can hardly articulate a party platform, but, for example, to President Bush saying that his aide John Sununu had "an appearance problem" — implying that we onlookers were falsifying the messy situation in which a member of his Cabinet was apparently bilking citizen tax monies for personal gain. When Sununu was forced to resign in December 1991, it became obvious that he was forced out by his unwillingness to play the same political, unreal word games that other Bush staffers considered entirely normal and, by extension, "masculine."

When all that matters is *appearing* to be this or that, the word games and the pseudorealities strike close to home because they are not sufficient to ground real constructions of identity and mobilizations of gendering. Feminists were alert to such issues a long time ago: for years, critics have discussed how women have been manipulated and controlled by the idealizing "gaze" of males. But now a shift in the object of the gaze begins to be obvious: Peter Watrous writes in the *New York Times* Arts and Leisure section (1991) that today "men in pop [music] are getting the treatment that used to be reserved for women — tight clothes, obsessional camera angles, fetishization." Illustrated by a half-nude photo of scratchy-chested singer Jon Bon Jovi, the article suggests that "today, men are using their bodies to storm a position formerly occupied by women"; "where women were once the focus of an audience's unresolved desire, now men have joined the action" (27). The hard-body gym-culture of the 1980s, plus the wide exposure of flesh in MTV, lead now to a fetishization of the male body as well as the female. "Until now, few men in rock felt a need to hone their bodies into the ideal expected of women," and a sidebar to the article by Watrous traces the recent history of "The Male Animal, Androgyny to Muscle."

The festishization is complete when the appearance of the body rather than the music becomes central: Watrous cites the instance of two male "front bodies" who stood in to be photographed in place of singer Milli Vanilli in an MTV production, and the author of a subsequent article on MTV refers to another guitarist, Tad, whose video "Woodgobling" was rejected by the MTV channel "in part because Tad was too ugly" — hence, the author concludes, "performers' appearance, fashion sense, and dance moves" *may now be more important than their musical ability* (Pareles 1991:19). Just as, one is tempted to add, the politician's appearance on videotape counts for more than her or his historical achievements or ability to lead the country in political matters.

In *Deeper Shade of Soul*, situated in California, a videotape narcissizes the male musicians and skateboarders in "a closed world that posits a type of joy and community without female interruption" (Watrous 27). It is likewise a *mechanized* narcissistic world, as can be seen from so many of the men's exercise and health magazines that began to appear in the late 1980s. Issues feature articles on how to have the most efficient workout in the shortest amount of time, or how to develop one particular ripple of muscles. Watrous's conclusion about MTV carries over: "the excessive athletic control of a body can seem militaristic, a sign of power and force. <u>The perfect male body, glorified and venerated, ends up representing discipline instead of freedom and may just be a symbol for these bellicose, male-dominated times</u>" (27). Or, following an insight of Guy Corneau, the male body may represent something else: "the more fragile a man feels internally, the more likely he is to try building an outer shell to hide this fragility. This shell may take the form of bulging muscles or a bulging belly" (1991:38). Likewise Stengel notes that "primping and pumping... are false answers to real problems. The real problem is that men don't feel powerful in their lives ... bodybuilding may be an elaborate compensation for sexual anxiety; men pumping up every muscle but the one they can't pump up" (1992:77).

Mishkind and others, in an extensive study (1987), warn strongly against the current emphasis upon the armored soldier's body with the unrealistic muscle-man body, the "well-developed chest and arm muscles and wide shoulders tapering down to a narrow waist," because it embodies a contemporary ideal of the mesomorphic body shape that gets equated with ideals of sexual prowess, yet is achievable by very few individuals, and hence contributes generally to a lowered acceptance of one's appropriate masculinity.

The muscular men featured in the magazines are of course *young* men, with practically missing waistlines, and well-defined pectorals, and by not so subtle implication, genital perfection. Sexual performance is treated repeatedly, alongside general dietary issues, including which candy/snack bars provide the best nutrition for the price. Shopping has become one of the major segments of American "leisure" time, so it is not all that remarkable that men's magazines regularly evaluate the relative merits of designer waters or health food brands, or space age workout attire.

The periodical *Men's Health* features articles on avoiding heart problems, improving one's sleeping pattern, and dealing with anger or stress. In this magazine, relatively few articles are narcissistic, in contrast to the great number of "how to take control" stories in much of the popular press; we may hear about nurturing relationships, sex within and outside of marriage, and even everyday heroes other than musicians, film stars, or sports people. But a self-aware attempt to balance what I have termed the mechanistic approach to the male body ("Pecsercises for YOU!") appears in only a small part of the market in occasional treatments of fathering or relating to a former spouse. In general, the bulk of the glitzy mags has been devoted to a very narrow spectrum of the male experience, namely, his physical appearance, and that leads me to ask just what is being narcotized, made narcoleptic, pushed below the threshold of awareness and worry. When an advertisement for a new magazine entitled *Men's Journal* indicates that men's experience will be represented only in terms of travel, adventure, sports (including "Attack Tennis," sea kayaking, and race car driving), and fitness, one's anticipation can only be that once again the purely external world will entirely fill the existential frames of The American Man.

As pointed out in the introductory material to this chapter, there is quite a cluster of words around the name of Narcissus: narcotics, narcolepsy, narceia (or narceine, an alkaloid substitute for morphine), narcosis, narcotism. The direct association with the mythic account is the reference to Narcissus's languorous torpor after he catches sight of his beautiful image, falls in love with it, and pines away physically, having recognized that it is not attainable, at least in an ordinary lifetime. Tradition suggests that Narcissus finds a quiet glade to stare into along the hypnotic Styx, the river of Hades. But quite apart from any literal connection with narcotics, we may ask what is being narcotized here, why the physical component so overwhelms the mind-body balance that the Greeks and later Romans idealized and that has been the slogan of so many educational institutions: "a sound mind in a sound body."

The narcissus-narcotic flower was produced mythically by Hades to entrap the Kore — the generic young Greek woman, personified as Persephone. One sniff of the sweet-smelling flower and instantly Hades is able to abduct her into the underworld. Her disappearance leads to The Mother's (Demeter's) search and grieving, and finally to the gods' intervention. But suppose we look at the Narcissus story as the entrapment not of the Kore but of the Kouros, the generic young man of Greek sculpture. Does maleness get trapped by a specious overemphasis upon the physical body? Upon sexuality? Upon phallos? How is Narcissus's body — usually represented as kouros-like, slender and barely pubescent — comparable to or different from that of Herakles — represented as bulging with grown-up muscles and hair on his body?[2] Are these male images quantitatively different from corresponding female images such as those of Artemis, Psyche, the Kore, Aphrodite? It is remarkable that we have just begun to develop sophisticated ways of answering such questions about the male, as compared with the female, figures within our mythic iconographies. Books such as this one can at best point out where we need additional study and interpretation, and in this instance contemporary scholarship is only beginning to develop, as in the work of the French scholar Pierre Vidal-Naquet, whose studies of the young Greek adolescent hunter or warrior (1986), along with those of Bernard Sergent (1986), have begun to clarify just how the Greek models that had such decisive influences upon Western culture were shaped around images of exclusively *male* beauty and virility.

The young male Narcissus comes to be regarded negatively because of his *superbia* and *vanitas*, his pridefulness about his own beauty. These features seem most problematic not in terms of his own self-image, as the problem in the myth is usually exposited in terms of individual psychology, but in terms of *relationships*. After all, you cannot have a very satisfying relationship if all your energy goes into crowing about your own beautiful body or powerful phallus. Ovid's fussy preaching has been replicated for centuries: taking the appearance for the (sole) reality, placing the corporeal beauty above the moral, developing the manly frame rather than the wisdom and ethical rigor that enables one to avoid narcosis or death. But instead of pursuing the narcotic aspect, asking what about males gets deadened by exclusive focus upon male self, body, or appearance, we might inquire about what gets opened up if we look slantwise against the traditional stories. In particular the issue of relationships can be insighted afresh through the recurrent theme of mirroring and reflectivity, of the echoing aspects that are crucial in ongoing relationships.

I like Thomas Moore's suggestion that the narcissist has to learn how to recognize the components of himself that are transcendental, elements of the soul that are gifts of the gods and not "earned," in order to escape the purely introverted focus upon the unique self (1992:63). Likewise Lewis Hyde notes (1983:53) that when one learns to honor properly one's daimon or genius (the source of creativity and insight that comes from spiritual beings), it becomes in Roman terms, a Lar (protective household god) rather than a Larva or Lemur! Narcissism in such a context means claiming all the praise for one's own creativity rather than respecting the genuinely creative elements that happen upon one, come to one out of the blue as something other than one's own production. Bringing the self up from that unconscious state of being stuck on one's own predilections and tastes enables one to recognize the common experiences shared with others, and so opens the way to sharing, fully interpersonal relationships.

The association of Echo and Narcissus is puzzling yet significant, as Ovid builds up his many narrative tensions.[3] The action is entirely within the realm of the social-sexual, not only because the story turns on Narcissus's inability to keep erotic power in motion within a relationship, but because Echo, we learn right away, suffers the loss of her voice[4] precisely because Hera, the goddess of marriage, is punishing her. Echo had kept Hera *talking* long enough for Zeus (actually, Jove, since this is a Roman version) to have his way with a clutch of sexy young nymphs. So Hera takes back that which has been Echo's strong point, her voice,[5] just as at the end of the tale, Narcissus's strongest feature, his body, is "taken back" as he suffers a male sort of anorexic waning away and then death. Failing to develop even the faint echo she has provided, Narcissus remains stuck on certain entirely familiar images of self that leave him isolated and alone.

Might not the paralleling of Echo and Narcissus, and the context of relationship, even though it is not a marital relationship, remind us to ask what it might have been like had Narcissus and Echo become a pair? Wouldn't Echo as a permanent partner have been dreadful? Yet who doesn't overhear such people: "I don't care. Whatever you'd like, Dear!" No, no merely echoic partner, thank you: show me people who can argue well and fairly, who have their own ideas and intuitions, and I'll be interested. As Louise Vinge notes (1967), Echo reflects or mirrors Narcissus, the voice, at the beginning of the narrative, just as the quiet pool later echoes the body — and both are quite *deadly*. Reflectivity is useful, helpful, crucial: but if does not manage a smooth transit of the mirror stage; the strong sense of *who I am* never counterbalances the attraction of the overpowering force of everything outside oneself. The narcissist is afraid constantly, never sure whether or not his meager self-assurance, so painfully scrabbled together, will be taken back, or whether the appealing Other will suddenly overwhelm, bringing physical or psychic death.

Negatively seen, narcissism is the narcotizing of the expressive self that might reach out toward others and allow them to touch oneself in turn. Strabo called Narcissus "The Taciturn," explaining that Narcissus's withdrawal from others was experienced as a sort of hostility, and well might it be, especially if one observes that persons experiencing withdrawal often consider themselves superior to everyone around them. Such anti-social hostility is the basis for Freud's general distrust of introversion, the turning inward toward one's inmost being; as he saw it (negatively), the introverted person's interests and libido are concentrated entirely upon one's own self. Echo would be the exact opposite, the classic extravert who has no inner life of her own and can only find it outside, in others.[6]

Ovid's contemporary, the Greek writer Konon, considered Narkissos to be guilty of a crime against Eros: Narcissus was too proud to be a mere mortal, obediently accepting the apportioned lot when it came to lovers (there are echoes of the Gilgamesh story here). No, Narcissus wanted total control — displaying the sort of hybris that flashes red lights warning of the message of divine retribution such as, of course, Narcissus gets when he kills himself. Konon tells us that having heard the story, Thespians living in Boeotia heeded the message quickly, and were stimulated both to fear and to honor Eros more fully in their public services and in private sacrifices (Vinge 1967:19–21; Stein 1976:43).

I am hardly the first to suggest new readings for some of the classical figures, and in particular Thomas Moore's positive revisioning of Narcissus needs to be mentioned. But first it is important to highlight a feature of the story of Narcissus that goes back to the sequence of psychological developmental issues mentioned earlier, which have to do with *timing* within the normal progress toward maturation. All that gets puzzled through and temporarily resolved in a body of mythology can never be simply listed, and we need to return to interpretations of such materials repeatedly, sometimes taking an insight from study of one myth and applying it to another. In this case the insight that helped me clarify the Narcissus story came as I studied the story of Kastor and Polydeukes (Castor and Pollux, the divine young men or *Dios kouroi*, Latinized as Dioscuri, the Twins I will have more to say about in Chapter 10).

Clearly, had Polydeukes been aware of his own immortality sooner, he might well have avoided Kastor's merely mortal death: that's the insight. It translates here to: Perhaps Narcissus's problem is not that he discovers what everyone else knows all along, that he is beautiful, but that he internalizes that discovery-knowledge *too late* — too late in the sequence of development, so that he gets stranded at that awful level of adolescence wherein one never knows from moment to moment who one is going to be, of which gender (it feels like), or in what relationships. Probably everyone gets stuck there from time to time — not just during pimply adolescence, but repeatedly, as we deal with personal change and all sorts of human relationships. Perhaps Narcissus reminds us to keep our own "beauty" always securely in mind, less we get blown off our course, finding that beauty out there somewhere in a manner that we can never conceive of as being our own. Why, one wonders, are we so terrified of loving ourselves appropriately?

Thomas Moore reads the Narcissus story positively, as an account of the "mysteries of self-discovery" that Ovid emphasizes in his repeated concentration upon change and metamorphosis. The myth, states Moore, "describes with sensitivity and insight the feelings and ideas which surround and constitute the human experience of change" (1976:50). Subsequently, in Moore's symbolic reading against the usual interpretation, "the transition from the body to the flower is a death and resurrection; the story of Narcissus is a symbol of transformation" (1976:52). Bernard Sergent likewise stresses the rebirth aspects and notes the tradition in Konon that "it is from the blood of Narcissus, which flows along the banks of the river, that narcissuses grow" (1986:82–89). I am reminded of Salvador Dali's painting, "The Metamorphosis of Narcissus," in which the flower breaks out of an egg, drawn as a visual parallel to Narcissus's head.

Given such positive readings, the narcissistic experience can be revalued as one of discovering an aspect of oneself, a new image of oneself, not previously recognized. Such discovery is possible if one does not get caught in the nemetic-necessity, the knell of fate, that ruins Narcissus, but Moore's reading assumes that Narcissus, having found the appropriate level of self-love, will now move to other-love. Moore also sees Narcissus as rediscovering the beauty that the myth says he has at birth: a sixteen-year wait, but then some of us never get to that point. Narcissus has begun to seem less a figure of the psychologists or myth handbooks and more a projective cipher for self-recognition of our own importance and our own personal orienting of the meanings that determine personal and social worth.

In whatever manner we choose to read the myth of Narcissus and Echo for now (presumably we'll read it differently another time), it stimulates discussion of many of the aspects of masculinity that seem especially problematic, including the role of appearances in contrast to depth values, the shaping of the physical body, the expression of one's sexuality in relationships, the coming to self-appreciation of one's own beauty, and the need to move toward acceptance of one's own inner worth by accepting the admiration and affection of others. This mirroring shatters false self-worth; it kills just as surely as Perseus's mirror (his polished brass shield) killed the Medusa with her multi-hydra-heads of deceit and falsehood. To learn who we are truly, at the wrong time, without the sense of our own inner worth, or the sense of how to value and interpret our experiences as they are mirrored back to us, can indeed activate the blocking, shielding introversion that seems like death.

Within that introversion in which only the individual self has significance, within that narcissistic retreat — if it doesn't continue for too long — lies the sort of insight that was evidently lacking in Ovid's Narcissus. We do not go stupidly into that scene if we have examined life through many different mythic windows and learned to face the dark sides of our selves and our culture. We are perhaps ready to be Narcissus again, but this time self-consciously. I like Murray Stein's statement of Narcissus's situation: "psychologically, his love is purely projective, in that what he loves is a reflection of an aspect of himself of which he is unconscious" (1976:40). The business of education into the values of a particular culture, and mythically that means leaving self-adoring adolescence behind, is to make that unconscious conscious. My attempt in this book is to do something of the same for aspects of masculinity.

Or masculin*ities*, I keep arguing. And *selves* rather than a single identity or self. Mirroring-back is native and natural, and yet we learn how to retrieve those mirroring images only as we learn to double-sight figures such as Narcissus. Here is no stable self, but a plethora of selves, a plenitude such as we also find in the Hermes stories in Chapter 7. But the reader will be aware by now that I regard such multiplicity less as a threat than as a promise. In fact the many mythological manifestations help us to see at least some of the ways a postmodern masculinity begins to shape itself. The issue is: with or without our help? Will we merely be passively acted upon, or can we contribute politically to positive new shapings that escape many of the problematics of the past?

In this respect the image of Pygmalion and Galatea is another Narcissus-like story to re-examine. The sculptor Pygmalion was a first-rate narcissist who claimed that no woman could ever be as beautiful as the idealized statues he sculpted. In order to create his most beautiful statue to date, he modeled Galatea as a glancing reflection *of his own appearance,* and before he falls hopelessly in love with her, he displays the true narcissist's response of rejecting her because she is now "other" to him and not merely a narcissistic extension of The Same, of himself. No wonder the story has remained so relevant for so long: like the story of Narcissus and Echo, it portrays the malfunction of the self, its inability to reach outside itself to achieve a self-regard properly developed in a sort of dialogue with the inner self and the relational others whose attitudes toward us are essential components in escaping the merely narcissistic trap.

Masculinities will doubtless be different in the future. Some of the signs of that change belatedly strike men across the planet, with at least some of the power that the women's movement conveyed earlier. Where we have come from is interlocked with where our culture is headed, in our language, metaphor, imagery, narratives, psychological attitudes and values. Patterns of masculinity in this book are not models that derive solely from any individual store of experience, but reach back in some cases at least three millennia. They would not have lasted so long had they not been meaningful models of various aspects of masculinity across more than one cultural continuum.

Opening ourselves to some of these age-old materials as an imaginal, mythic exercise, we begin to see Pygmalion and Narcissus differently. We begin to see *ourselves* differently, and the world around us. We begin to ask new questions: picking up a beautifully produced volume of early portraits of Native Americans at a bookstore, my first thought as I opened it was "I wonder if they are all male?" That question wouldn't have arisen for persons living earlier who shared the assumption that of course "portraits" would include males exclusively! But then Havelock

Ellis and other early sexologists were almost totally preoccupied with women because they thought masculinity was a seamless entity void of any of the troubles we've come to recognize recently. As Jeffrey Weeks notes, "Male sexuality was not a problem, Ellis suggested, because it was direct and forthright. It was female sexuality that needed to be understood because through it the race was reproduced" (Weeks 1986:23).[7] The same author cites Richard Dyer, who suggests that "male sexuality is a bit like air — you breathe it in all the time, but you aren't aware of it much."

What we ought to look for is perhaps not primarily a matter of what we already recognize and feel comfortable with, "the air we breathe in" that is nothing but the narcotizing path of Narcissus's self-absorption in The Same. Not more of the same, in a self-worshiping closed circuit of admiration, but learning to flex our imaginal muscles, our psychic pectorals, in the hopes that we can recognize both the negative and harmful, and the positive and eutropic shapes of the masculinities that are taking shape today. Masculinities that, because we are aware and concerned, we help to shape; and because we care, masculinities that we engage to influence as our culture grows out of its adolescent self-/phallos-worship and fascination with the phallic phalanx of wars — an issue that will be on the agenda with respect to Ares in Chapter 8.

The Narcissus story models less the danger of self-regard than that of remaining only at the adolescent level of staring into our masculine center (as in Cárdenas's sculpture) and ignoring the others who enable us to transcend ourselves. The self is not evil — nowhere is it stated that Narcissus rejects his own beauty and worth as Nietzsche suggests that Christianity admonishes one to do, and loving the self is not problematic except when such self-love excludes the amplified self one can become in relationships with others. Thomas Moore catches the cycle of the story perfectly: "It is a true re-cognition, a remembering, since Narcissus from the very beginning of his life was lovable. The Narcissus experience, then, has the aspect of remembering, of recovering, a lost self-concept, of seeing again, even though the vision may never have been a conscious one, one's own true nature" (1976:55).

Cárdenas's sculpture begins to have less phallic meanings than I thought at first. Or we might say, "phallic" comes to mean less "genital" than "self." Self-disciplined reflection includes the phallic self, but goes well beyond genital self-identity. The gaze into the self that our culture currently sponsors may lead beyond the singular orgasmic self-sexuality into a transcultural *eros* of relatedness. Narcissistic images represent the narrowing onto the singular, individualistic self, just those same images that make one question the values of the solitary, self-reflexive focus upon one's own attitudes.

Narcissus legends focus upon the dangers of self-absorption while they clarify the fruitful self-regard that lets one recognize the multiplicity of self elements that might comprise contemporary masculinity. A story about an individual, Narcissus, becomes a story about the eternal importance of the transindividual, the societal context within which individual stories become archetypal legends of communal coherence. Precisely the individualistic Narcissus shocks us into consciousness of supraindividualistic values, into recognition that the Narcissus myth is only a myth of *adolescence,* a myth that must be superseded by myths of the social collectivity.

■ ■ ■ ■ ■

Sources of the Story

Ovid, *The Metamorphoses,* Book 3.339–510, Echo and Narcissus. Vinge 1967 conveniently supplies the Latin of Ovid and the Greek texts of Konon and Pausanias, with English translations.

Bibliography for Further Study

Stuart 1957 emphasizes psychological aspects; Vinge 1967 recounts various ways the myth was retold and interpreted in antiquity and subsequently; Moore 1976 and Stein 1976 provide contemporary and positive revisions of the myth. Lasch 1979 is a remarkable work of cultural criticism, demonstrating how contemporary society inculcates narcissistic values through its mass communications and education, even through its therapeutic and bureaucratic-managerial skills.

Phallic Hermes between the Realms

Background Information

One of the primary Indo-European deities, Hermes is an Enlightened
One born of the virgin Maia, just as the Buddha, whose name means
Enlightened One, was born of the moon goddess, Maya. The range of
Hermes' manifestations is almost overwhelming — once I charted some
357 descriptive epithets, and worked from there to twenty master categories ranging from athletics to law, crafts and commerce, to magic,
oracles, and dreams, from guardian and savior to deceitful thief, and
above all messenger and interpreter (Doty 1980). Hermes was assimilated by the Romans to the figure of Mercury and in the Hellenistic
period connected with a secret mystical figure, *Hermēs trismegistos*, or
Thrice-Great Hermes, who remains important down into the Middle
Ages.

Summary

Child of the nymph Maia and Zeus, Hermes is a typical heroic wun-
derkind in that at twilight on the day of his birth he slips from his cradle
and steals his brother Apollo's cattle. He claims to be innocent when
Apollo brings him before Zeus, noting that he never "stepped over the
threshold" because literally he *slipped through the keyhole:* deception
and fraud carried out on the first day of his life — one can imagine
why he was the patron of thieves! But he was also the patron of orators and those who deal with language (he was already warping *literal*
meanings when an infant), and of those who combat thieves: this is a
rampantly phallic god, and the phallos in antiquity was apotropaic (protective) against evil and thought to repel negative influences (hence tiny
reproductions of the male genitalia were often worn as jewelry). Baby
Hermes knows how to get the cattle under control (subsequently he is
represented as something of a pastoral deity) and how to make his way
by deception and stealth.

On the way out of the birthing cave, he stumbles over a tortoise
shell and, being luck-bringing Hermes, does not just pitch it aside, but

121

invents from it the musical lyre, the shell becoming the sounding box (later Apollo likes it so much he trades Hermes a type of divination oracle for it). Anyone who can get around as easily as Hermes ought to be able to help others to do so, and hence Hermes became the patron of travelers, his statues modified into milestones along the roadways, and furthermore the god of athletes and merchants who performed at the boundary-crossings of society, athletic activities in conjunction with the religio-civic ritual of the Greek city-state, and mercantile activities that were usually restricted to the public plaza or the edges of towns or countries. Herms, columns dedicated to Hermes topped with his head and openly fronting male genitals, often appeared as boundary markers (they were later replaced by Christian crosses or images of the Virgin), but he also marked the metaphorical boundaries of discourse: when a conversation resumed after an awkward pause, it was said that Hermes must have passed by.

This is seldom a boundary-deity of clear daylight rationality, a position more frequently occupied by Apollo. Hermes is most likely to appear in the twilight darkness, in mysterious hints and urges, in instances where one recognizes only afterward that one has been accompanied by a god. No wonder then that he is the deity to whom one dedicates the last libation before going to sleep, or that he is the male god who communicates through dreams. One doesn't *reason* with a hermetic insight; one has an intuition or feeling about something. Hermes always leaves the interpretation of the insight up to the dreamer, whose task it is to find good or bad luck within the message. Already we pick up indications that the hermetic figure will not model the direct exertion of authority often associated with masculinity: his images are almost excessively masculine, yet he *acts* in ways that hint of more "feminine" qualities, inspiring, making something useful from obstacles and detria, stressing emotions rather than intellect, and so on.

The message he brings will most likely come as one strikes out from the familiar — Hermes' oppositional pairing is with the goddess Hestia, whose very name means Hearth in Greek. She is the central fire of the household; he the flashing fires of inspiration that shape the artwork or the moving public oration. He, always on the go (his iconography includes winged cap and boots), stirs up and incites and stimulates; she, never budging, warms and calms and draws everyone toward a shared center. She remains virginal in the ancient sense of being in conscious control of her body; his close association with Aphrodite indicates an eroticism that is not single or confined any more than was Aphrodite's. Hence we learn of multiple sons of Hermes, including, in some versions,

Eros, the personified principle of erotic connectivity; and of countless liaisons, even more than for other Greek deities.

Transmission of the Story

My earlier attention to the epithets of Hermes (1980) was a sample of an approach to complex divine figures that builds upon both statistics — the number of times, in particular contexts, the figures are cited in the surviving literature — and typological interpretation, organizing the citations into thematic blocs. Some such an approach is useful when looking at mythic heroes whose many stories do not have any single "canonical" version. Even though there are many versions of the Gilgamesh epic, for instance, there is a central core of events to the narrative; but for figures like Hermes who are so variously interwoven into a whole culture's mythology, the selection of incidents in any reconstruction of a core narrative depends upon one's particular interests. In this chapter I recognize the problem and deal with it not by attempting to organize a biographical sketch of Hermes, but by selecting out key mythic elements that concern masculinity.

The Fourth Homeric Hymn, "To Hermes," is focused upon Hermes' childhood encounters with Apollo; it anticipates many of the characteristics of Hermes that will appear in subsequent accounts, but there is no other primary narrative or poetic account, and this fact in itself seems characteristic of this male hero, who appears and disappears on the margins and boundaries of scenes, connecting people, bringing interpretive messages, and getting involved in incidents across the range of Greek mythology (and later, as Mercurius, in Roman mythology as well). It also characterizes the diversity of mythical materials, a diversity often forgotten when working only from myth summaries or handbooks rather than from the wide range of the mythic literature itself. Another hymn to Hermes, for instance, by Alkaios, a sixth-century lyric poet, reads "TO HERMES. All glory to the Kyllenian Ruler! My very soul praises him, born on the crown of the mountain after Maia mated with Zeus" (my translation of Diehls fragment 73.2). Not in the cave stipulated by the Homeric Hymn to Hermes, but on a mountaintop! The ancient Greeks considered such diversity of mythic narratives and details to be primarily a matter of where one lived; they assumed that various parts of the country would tell the sacred stories differently, with no assumption that there might be one absolutely correct prototype. Perhaps we will find the same situation with respect to masculinities, but certainly Hermes models a more ambivalent masculinity than is to be found in Herakles or Ares. He is not so much the administrator or chief executive officer as the aide-de-camp, the assistant who gets things done even though his superior gets all the credit.

■ ■ ■ ■ ■

The thief, the lie, the deception of magic, the surreptitious border-line areas fall into shadow and can but return (opportunistically) to attention through tricks and theft.

In the sunlight world, the artful dodger is an opportunist. Psychology calls him shadow. But Hermes is not shadow cast off by light, not Lucifer. He is dark to begin with. He belongs to the night. From the hermetic perspective and the serpentine eye, it is rather the hero, sunfixed and immovably centered, who is the benighted one. His is the consciousness that sees in terms of black and white, and points to evil to justify the enormous destruction which we always find in his myths. (Hillman 1979 [1972]:159)

Whatever may have been thought of Hermes in primitive times, a splendour out of the depths must once have so struck the eye that it perceived a world in the god and the god in the whole world.
(Otto 1954:124)

The multiplicity of the Hermes figure has amazed me ever since I began tracking his many manifestations. A book project was set aside when I could not figure out how to reduce such a multiform hero into manageable contours. Even sketching this chapter, I soon had two pages of points I wanted to treat — enough to expand the chapter to about triple the size of most of the others. But then I caught myself saying under my breath as I made tea, "Hermes, be with me now!" — or some equally awkward equivalent — and as I realized what I'd done, the hackles on my neck rose. One does not invoke a deific figure lightly, even if one is as nonreligious as I am. But then I remembered one of my first experiences of this deity, in a dream that came shortly after I'd decided I had done enough research on Hermes, and was about to turn to another of the Greek gods. In the dream I was invoking Hermes, all right, although I have no notion of how such invocation may have happened in antiquity. No, but I was chanting (in Greek) "Hermes! Hermes! O come, Hermes!" And when I woke up I was aware that my hackles had risen that time as well; but I also realized that in spite of the awkward stance and situation, my invocation had been made in a favorite retreat in Vermont, and that my action was periodically to raise and lower the U-shaped top section of a bottomless aluminum porch chair, held out in front of me.

I get nervous in making direct connections, and I try to be cautious toward the use of allegory throughout this book. But reflecting on this dream of almost twenty-five years ago led me to know exactly where to begin: with the element of *communication*, of connection — in this case connecting a strangely modern evocation of a Greek god from antiquity with some of the ancient characteristics of the mythical Hermes figure. And the cheap porch chair (originally I was most upset that my dream self did not have the sense to use something more elegant) seemed a clue of some importance: at least on the psychic level, the archetypal figures do not remain just "back there" in antiquity, but have transformations appropriate to our own discount-store era.

There are connections also in terms of relating the mythological figures to one another; tracking mythological siblings and parentage and children is an important part of obtaining profiles of such figures. And connections in terms of the interactive network of psychological and behavioral features that they represent, or in terms of analogues in other cultures: parallels to Hermes are easily sighted in masculine deities in Egypt, Africa, the ancient Americas, Haiti, Japan, Northern Europe, and elsewhere. And finally connections with associated mythic figures: to comprehend Hermes fully one needs to know a good bit about his brother Apollo, about the many characteristics shared with Herakles (especially in athletic contexts), about the long string of progeny Hermes either generates (Eros, Priapos, Pan) or nurses (Dionysos; Hermes is generally regarded as the god of the adolescent transition to adulthood), and about his relationship to Hestia and to Aphrodite, even to Zeus and Iris (the feminine counterpart to his role as messenger), and to the Muses (his connection to the world of the arts he shared with Apollo is so important that sculpting might be referred to as releasing "the Hermes in the stone").

The roles of Hermes as a connector are particularly of interest in a period of increasing attention to modes of communication and access to information. And given popular gender stereotypes that suggest that it is primarily women who are empathetic and able to relate to others, it is of note that this is a *masculine* figure, that an important part of this heroic masculine figure is that he brings people into intimate relationships — by ferrying them physically from one to another love relationship, by carrying messages, or even, in his role as the guide of souls to the underworld, by easing their final transition from life. Hermes was patron of servants, even cooks (developed from the duties of the herald-messenger, which included slaughtering and preparing the sacrificial meat offerings), and likewise patron of lawyers — both *serving* occupations in which an individual supports someone else. Evidently Greek masculinity was not threatened by servant roles, roles in which caring for others rather than only for Mr. Number One predominated. This point balances somewhat the historical evidence that Greek society was sharply divided into rulers and ruled, haves and have-nots, and that Greek masculinity had everything positive to say about being aggressive, dominating, nothing positive about being receptive, passive.

Hermes was the helpful guide on the road; indeed, he was the primal *traveler*, to the extent that his iconographic attributes include the broad-brimmed hat and the duster or cloak of the wayfarer, to which were added wings on his shoulders and/or ankles. He was able to skip across distances quickly, and could appear now here and now there at will. Now that feminine Hestias are no longer simply waiting at the hearth, but travel about as much as masculine Hermes figures do, the traditional role of protecting travelers and keeping them from getting lost may need to be reconceived, just as the present century has recognized the inappropriateness of gender restraints upon so many traditionally male professions (police, physicians, pilots). When in one famous incident in antiquity, the phalli were knocked off all the roadside herms, the social reaction was immediate chaos — the threat to one's ability to find one's way came out clearly. Masculine roles have often included guiding and leading persons to their destinations, but again it seems appropriate to question why women as well as men might not perform such functions equally well today. The hermetic figure of connections models few clearly male or clearly female traits; the hermetic role seems, like many others, to have been assigned only arbitrarily to one or the other specific gender.

Hermes' statues often appeared at doorways and gateways: points of connection but also points of transition. Like the two-headed Janus figures with one head looking backward and one forward, some of the herms had two, three, or even four faces, and Hermes' epithets reflect the understanding that his herms were guardians against harm from any direction. This seems a logical reason for other epithets he bore that indicated that he was the "most well-disposed" toward mortals, or "the one who frees us from care," or *Philanthrōpotatos*, "most loving of human beings." Not only did he guard against evil, and hence like his brother Apollo was named *Alexikakos*, "evil-averter" or "savior," but he is downright beneficent in the positive sense of providing the lucky find, the best option in the deal, and hence was addressed as "the giver of riches." Not, like the Roman Fortuna, a goddess, but a

masculine, openhanded deity, Hermes in his generosity may represent
a particular manner that men have of sharing by giving in such a way
that the gift must be fulfilled by the skills or attitudes of the recipient.
The "trade" involves not a maternal gifting but a cooperative venturing
into something not yet tried or completed.

We are not accustomed to thinking of deities in the context of the
marketplace, but the Greeks and Romans were somewhat more realistic than we and did not suffer the centuries in which Christianity
systematically preached against earthly treasures. Hermes was patron
of merchants, who worked in the Greek *agora*, and hence was *Hermēs
agoraios*, named for the emporium or sales arena. In the Roman context there is a connection between the *merc*antile world and *Merc*ury,
and his attribute in the arts is often a money bag.[1] No namby-pamby,
unworldly deity, then, Hermes/Mercury was fully involved in the day-to-
day male world of economics, whether in terms of traveling, marketing,
merchandising, or making deals. The study of finance in antiquity discloses that women were more active in economic affairs than the literary
representations of an all-male business world would suggest. One wonders if particularly hermetic men may not have specialized in brokering
women's affairs along with their own negotiations in what classical
society chose to represent as a primarily male preserve.

Hermes is involved with commerce, law, communications (he's famously the *keryx*, or herald): just in this context, rather than some
pious realm of make-believe, is where we discover a masculine figure
who has a great deal to do with the sphere that has been relegated to
the psychological or the religious in our culture, namely, the sphere of
the soul, or psyche. Hermes appears as the boundary-setter and border-
crosser in his role as the traveler's friend, and then also as the patron of
businesspeople and merchants, since business takes place in the market place (*agora*) located in the border areas between homes and temples
and schools. This deity influences social intercourse by sheltering the
intuitive insight that makes great deals or keeps one's perspective open
toward the new and untried source of profit. Perhaps when I had my
initiatory dream about invoking Hermes, I needed to move in a new direction; perhaps when the Greeks invoked Hermes it was because they
needed something more than the goddess of the hearth; they needed
change and excitement toward different viewpoints. In such a perspective, the psychological, the arena of the psyche, or soul, is not unrelated
to the world of business; there is a masculine realism about the hermetic
that I have come to appreciate more and more.

Hermes was a god of the *palaistra* and the *gymnasion*, both terms for the sites where young Greek males gained a comprehensive liberal arts education as well as a network of fraternal relationships that would pay off later in the adult business context (teaching at a university strongly influenced by Greek sororities and fraternities, I recognize parallels immediately). The terms refer to racing and wrestling in the first instance and to physical athletics (practiced in the nude — *gymnas;* hence the Latinization as gymnasium) in the second, although both involved a wide spectrum of education beyond what has come to be associated with the modern sports gymnasium, since it included music/poetry, philosophy, and mathematics.[2] Hermes was often considered the ideal judge of games and was involved not only with athletic contests, but simultaneously with the contesting of wits in oratory and the law.

Of course the messenger will be a good speaker, but the sorts of skills attributed to Hermes go beyond merely repeating information that might be sent by electronic facsimile transmission: he is called "loquacious," "skilled in words," a "persuader of the mind," a "bringer of good news" (angel or evangelist — these closely related words are used in New Testament Greek). Above all he is a *hermeneus*, or interpreter, a title associated in folk etymology with the verb *hermeneuein*, to signify or interpret, which later became the source of the modern noun "hermeneutics," identifying the theory or disciplined methodology of interpretation generally. For much of the history of Western culture, interpretation has indeed meant *male* significations, a tendency now increasingly questioned, and certainly qualified by the highly complex vocabulary of contemporary feminist critical theory.

One pays heed when Hermes brings the message, because of his tricksterish aspects: playfulness can go in that direction, as well as toward the frolicsome diversions of games, and Hermes shares with Herakles, among the other Greek deities, a love of tripping up people and solemn assemblies (for treatment of Hermes in the context of other trickster figures, see Doty 1993a). As we saw, he slips through the keyhole as a baby, before he becomes the deity of entryways; but even so he is said to enter the house *aproidēs*, invisibly, from an unforeseen direction. A number of epithets mark him as clever, as an intriguer, furtive, full of various wiles, a sharp-tongued mocker, devious-minded, even deceitful — traits often assigned culturally to *women*, not men, yet obviously allied to the functions of the professional communicator. No wonder Hermes could be a nuisance to gods and humans, and no wonder the flip side of the respectable merchant is Hermes the thief, a characteristic that reappears throughout his legends, beginning already with the artfully disguised theft of Apollo's cattle.

Obviously the boundary-crossing border person will be suspected of thievery or deceit. Human societies always assume that their values are ultimately correct, that any word of disagreement represents an attack by the stranger at the gates. But Hermes teaches one to expect that any change will be met with suspicion; he supplies our rhetoric with persuasive skills just as he helps the merchant choose the best advertisements for selling products. Coming most typically at twilight, he makes visible the darker side of finance, of public life. He is not the god of the high noon shootout, but he inculcates the importance of expanding our logical, scientific capacities by encountering all the arts of our cultural heritage: in hundreds of Greek vase paintings, Hermes leads the Muses in dance. What, one wonders, would an artistic sort of business look like? How might it operate? On which boundaries of our own culture? How many geniuses such as Stephen Wozniak, the Apple computer wizard, operate just outside the profitable centers of corporate America?

Hermes leads more to questions than to answers: in no single narrative but in a whole patchwork of ways in which the deity was approached in antiquity in literature and the arts, he is uniquely allied with what is frequently named the postmodern condition. A scene of endless openness, with all the attendant chaos that a fully normless society brings, postmodernism is a stage of cultural change that leaves behind the sureties of the twentieth century as we face the twenty-first. Perhaps many males are conservative, monotrack workers who worship only the status quo, but Hermes as Mr. Postmodernist seems appropriate in several respects: his many-sidedness, his heteronomy or polynomy, models the self not as that single carefully produced entity familiar from standard pop-psychology books, but as a multiplex combination of selves. In fact the Hermes I find most interesting is the exact opposite of the simplified single-trait character of the myth handbooks. He is a figure for a complex, transitional time, and he may well model a means of breaking through the restrictive logic of binary gender oppositions identified in Chapter 2. Hermes may likewise be a model for encompassing the wide range of men's movements surveyed earlier: not a singular masculinity, but a number of masculinities; no orthodox challenges of "You do not belong to the men's movement I follow," but "Thanks for helping me recognize that perspective in addition to my own."

Such modeling begins already in the characteristics of the deity himself. It follows a mythographic perspective according to which the inclusive range of characteristics include those of his progeny — which in this case include Hermaphroditos, a figure whose very name reflects the combining influences of Aphrodite and Hermes. Indeed if we think backward to the manner in which the father is refracted in the son, Hermaphroditos brings to bear a particularly feminine aspect of Hermes' own characteristics.[3] Hermes' cunning intelligence or intuition, his preference for the twilight rather than the bright light of noon (what has come in the West to be considered "enlightenment"), and his sensitivity to the needs of each particular situation — he is always serving others at the particular point of their needs, often arriving on the scene before they realize they have those needs — marks a feminine aspect that is not found, for instance, in Herakles or Apollo, certainly not in Ares or Hephaistos.

Ginette Paris, speaking of "the feminine intelligence of Hermes," calls Hermes "a god who is male by sex but feminine in spirit" (1990:84, 85). Such a spirit plans how to win through intrigue rather than force; it seeks a way around obstacles rather than plowing through their midst; it incorporates the found object, revisioning it as part of a new whole not previously envisioned. And it remains in awe of the complexity of human and divine being, seeking not an Apollonian simplification but the hermetic mysteries that will develop from the manifold legends of the mercurial messenger himself.

The hermetic hermeneutics remains subservient to the message; it listens before herding its words about like so many steers being branded. Like the baby Hermes attempting to seduce Daddy Zeus into believing that he was innocent of stealing his brother's cattle, the hermetic messages insinuate themselves just under the skin, just under self-consciousness, like a perfume; we know they are there, but not what they are or what they mean. They keep us unsatisfied with any particular achievement since there is always a sense that *something more* hovers in the hermetic twilight, and we can only learn by being more receptive, not by bringing up the high voltage searchlights. Hermes sometimes appears to be the faithful secretary providing reminders to the boss that something remains to be done, that another aspect needs to be dealt with, that half-way is not the whole way. Hermes' wisdom is allied with that of Athene: the two of them frequently *accompany* heroes on Greek vase paintings, Hermes initiating, giving impetus, Athena supplying the connective knowledge and the experiential aspects of what must be learned. Cicero sees the conjunction quite clearly when he reverences the *Hermathēnē*, the herm topped with a bust not of Hermes but of Athene (Atticus 1.1.5, 1.4.3).

Can masculinity encompass what have come to be considered such "feminine" traits as I have modeled in this chapter? Perhaps a statue of a hermaphrodite in a bathhouse provides an answer. Its inscription begins "To men, I am Hermes, but to women, I appear as Cypris [an epithet of Aphrodite]" (Greek Anthology, A.P. 9:783). Perhaps the positive:negative, good:evil, masculine:feminine judgment calls made everyday are primarily matters of social and personal projections. "Beauty lies in the eye of the beholder," yes; but in other situations a category such as "beauty" is not figured solely on the basis of the Western, masculinist, logos-oriented aesthetics. Here the phallic deity par excellence — who else but Hermes could be adequately represented by an erect penis alone? — appears to be modeled by means of a much more complex aesthetics and ethics and psychological combinations than those to which we are accustomed.

Already as a baby such a figure is praised for his *kratos*, his male strength, in the Homeric Hymn "To Hermes" (4:407), and in the myths all characters are clear about the caution needed in approaching him. He is also the technological god, in the sense of the Greek *technē*, which is closer to "arts" than to contemporary mechanistic concepts of technology (the Hymn has an impressive chain of *tech-* words, indicating ancient fascination with the fabricating of meaning as well as objects), and technology itself begins to appear as a realm that must be entered cautiously, as the last century has made evident, especially as technology and warfare have been so fatefully linked.

But this artist-technologist does not just lead the culture to war; he brings (according to the Hymn, 4:449) "good cheer, love, and sweet sleep." Perhaps we all, like persons in antiquity, ought to arrange our beds so that they faced the statue of Hermes, the *Oneiropompos* /Guide of Dreams! Learning from the dreams, presumably one learns something about Hermes as *Psychopompos* / Guide of Souls (into Hades) as well.[4] The psychopomp's role is that of the shamanistic guide to the underworld, and it fits Hermes perfectly since he accompanies so many souls across the eternal divide between the living and the dead. "Everywhere that Hermes appears," suggests Karl Kerényi, "there is an influx and invasion from the underground" (1976:84–85).

Kerényi's mentor Carl Jung sensed the inherent opposition between Christianity and shamanic intercourse with the underworld and recognized just how poorly Christianity deals with the dark, deadly side of culture generally. Hence Christian-influenced contemporary societies have trouble facing the dark aspects of the goddesses and gods, especially those of Hermes, "Lord of all those who do their business by night" (Euripides), just as we have trouble admitting to the depressed, "inferior," dark aspects of culture as a whole. Typically the masculinized West expects that the rest of the world will "catch up with us" and have deodorized bodies, cosmeticized teeth, liposuction, and face-lifts just like we do. But I wonder if the West does not cut itself off from significant guidance about the human position when applying the American Smile as the upbeat conclusion to any problem. Even the television news program must, according to this anticipation, independently of whatever tragedy has just been reported, end on a positive note with something comical. Our sights are set on simplicity and singularity on the one hand, and on forgetting the daimonic on the other — orientations that can be extremely limiting.

The road to Hades is "neither straightforward nor single," Plato notes in the *Phaido* (108): "If it were, there would be no need for a guide, because surely nobody could lose his way anywhere if there were only one road. In fact, it seems likely that it contains many forkings and crossroads, to judge from the ceremonies and observances of this world." The West seems to have ignored such a realistic perspective: but then if the period of *transition* or the physical passageway to the other world is the great danger, as it is in many of the world's mythological narratives, then the Guide of Souls will be primary. When on the other hand the danger is the Final Judgment upon *arrival* at the Heaven:Hell switching point, as in Christian teaching, there will be less need for a figure who eases the transition, and consequently more emphasis upon the arbitrator-gatekeeper (St. Peter) — hence, perhaps, the psychopompic, shamanistic aspects to Hermes were ignored for so long.

Figures native to the passageway, the tenuous realm between life and death, this world and the next, have come to be conflated to the demonic in general, as the Christian opposition between positive:negative god images produced the God:Satan dichotomy, and as a male-dominated culture frequently conflated the demonic and the feminine, or at least came to fear "female" traits sullying male behaviors. But there are other connotations to the demonic, especially if we refer to the original Greek *daimones*, supernatural beings who were considered to have specifically localized spheres of influence and thought to be the elementary spirits out of which goddesses and gods are developed in formal religions. Hermes certainly has associations with such elemental spirits, the daimonic encompassing (again citing Plato 1961, this time the *Symposion*, 202.e–203.a):

They are the envoys and interpreters that ply between heaven and earth, flying upward with our worship and our prayers, and descending with the heavenly answers and commandments, and since they are between the two estates they weld both sides together and merge them into one great whole. They form the medium of the prophetic arts, of the priestly rites of sacrifice, initiation, and incantation, of divination and sorcery, for the divine will not mingle directly with the human, and it is only through the mediation of the spirit world that man can have any intercourse, whether waking or sleeping, with the gods. And the man who is versed in such matters is said to have spiritual powers [*daimonios anēr*], as opposed to the mechanical powers of the man who is expert in the more mundane arts.

We begin to see that the daimonic is multiple and changeable and adaptable; it is changeable and transitional and connective; and it is both capricious and inspirational — in other words it is much like the hermetic mode of action, and it has few gender-specific characteristics — important to remember as the male-identified sciences come to recognize their limitations and seek to recover the recreative insights of the positively daimonic/inspiring aspects of human culture. A hermetic science would demand gender freedoms in all endeavors or workplaces, just as it would recognize that the dark realm of the past, of death, and, traditionally, of women can again be resources for inspiration and renewal.

One last aspect of the hermetic remains to be discussed here, that in which Hermes is not only guide of souls between this and the next world, but of souls within the immediate context of everyday human lives. This context is one of infinite multiplicity, and it is one that is often resisted strenuously as being inferior to a more simplified, abstract, idealized realm quite apart from daily affairs, as many mainline thinkers have mapped onto gender distinctions various totally extraneous matters, as the realm of the abstract and ideal has come to be considered the realm of the masculine, the embodied, material, social, the realm of the feminine. In a generally male-dominant culture, the latter realm has been ignored if not suppressed, and it has only been since the beginning of the current century that the bias in Western culture against the multiplex, the non-singular divine, has been revered. Characteristic traits of the long dominance of the masculine, the logical, rationalistic perspective, surface in our continued reluctance to confront the mythic theme

of the darkness, the in-between realms where the bright rational consciousness is suppressed by the soul-infused twilight realms of feelings
and emotions. Those are the realms avoided as the culture stipulates
the contours of masculinity or maturity or the high points of intellectual
and scientific evolution today; yet they are also the realms confronted
in private terrors and nightmares and socially in the anguishes of the
misguided Teutonic genocide of the Nazi period, or the consistent treatment of persons of color, whether indigenous or from Asia or Africa,
across our own continent.

So proud of our logos-scientifical achievements, of the rationality of
our intellectual academies, we seem nonetheless unable to ignore the
seam-y (boundary-like) junctures of life, even while the entertainment
media's talk shows *appear* to leave nothing hidden, yet remain consistently shallow, superficial, ungrounded. In real life, however, one finds
persons working with their dream imagery, encountering few simplistic
Johnny Carsons, and many dark, Hermes-like figures. The "darkening
of the soul" comes out repeatedly, and the Hermes images repeatedly
enforce descents into personal and social underworlds of great power,
into realms where one is lost without a hermetic guide who can recognize the importance of going into the darkness willingly, the importance
of hearing the significances of the deathly side of things even while the
culture's labile salespersons tout escapes into idylls of sensory pleasure.

If the only recognized deity is the high god of illumination who
speaks to Moses or Jesus "on the mountaintop," her/his predominant
model for us will be one of seeking isolation from the material, embodied aspects of society (from the maternal, the feminine; Hillman's 1979
essay emphasizing how the West segregated the masculine, abstract,
intellectual from the feminine, material, embodied, remains crucial in
the twentieth-century recovery of the importance of the soul and the
feminine in contrast to Enlightenment emphasis upon intellect and abstract spirit). Encountering the shapes that the dark forms may assume
then becomes a genuine threat to what are understood to be the transcendent social values. From such a perspective, one finds it normal
that nineteenth-century Germans would respond affirmatively to a radically reinterpreted natural mythology that would later prop up the Nazi
enterprise, but "WE? . . . Never!"

And so contemporary spiritual movements that emphasize the physical body, acting out, and meditation and devotion (again: "WE? . . .
Never!") seem foreign, just the way the Dionysian emphasis upon an experiential dimension to Greek religion threatened the men of the Greek
society represented in Euripides' *Bakchai*. If masculinity is pure spirit,

the traditional modes of feminine religiosity will seem embarrassing, and the embodied, phallic Hermes obscene. But the representation of the male in contemporary culture, with its progressively greater uncovering of the body, might argue that on the surface there remains a denial of the physical even while powerful erotic currents underneath call out the animal in each of us. The rapidity of change is remarkable: a few years ago a relative could not take us to his tennis club because we did not have white linen outfits to wear; last year a local club ruled that thong swimming suits were permissible, but not completely backless models.

Spirits and daimones seem far from the erotic appeal of the nylon swimming thong, yet one learns from antiquity that the erotic is never far away after all, that it is a constituent part of all our experiences, including those of the dark, of the deathly. There is something to be learned from adolescents' fascination with the death-dealing and tragic, even from the surfeit of symbols of death printed on the covers of rock albums and worn by band members. There were representations of the genitals on tombstones and memorial markers: Hermes teaches that the phallic, the erotic, is no stranger to the deathly, perhaps especially by indirect reference to generations, generativity, the continuing link of soul between the living and the dead. The after-this-life continuity of significance is represented by the very spirits or daimones who bring masculinity and femininity into prominence not just as genitally exciting, but as fundamental to the human condition in terms of assuring its replication. Hence out of death, life, no matter how much death rites emphasize the departure of the particular soul, and not the human family that remains and turns once again to the propagation of its race, or to the memorialization represented in the Gilgamesh epic.

Entering the remnants of a catacomb in Rome, or the smoke-filled air of a Southwest-American kiva, or spending an hour with a soul-endangered person skirting a permanent entering of the realm of darkness, any sentient being will perceive that there are spirits present, elements of life that scientific and medical rationality cannot address. Not the pleasant logos spirits of light and happiness, but powerful nonetheless, spirits whose birthing has taken place within the dark chambers ignored at the peril of remaining ignorant and helpless before spirits who threaten to pull soul back there forever if they are not properly recognized and honored. Hence the importance of knowing about shamanism and death rituals and soul-traveling. Hence the need for gods of transition, for Hermes figures whose very biworldly complexity promises sustenance in dealing with our manifold human crises.

Not so much Hermes and Hestia, who are addressed together in Homeric Hymn 29, but Hermes and Hekate: both fertility-bringers who aid and bless their favorites, who assist the judge and the public speaker, the athlete and the sailor (Hesiod, *Theogony* 7:420–52). And Hermes and Hades-Pluton: their statues stood together at the foot of the Acropolis of Athens (Pausanias 1:28.6). And Hermes *chthonios* /the underworld deity, regularly conducting heroes to the underworld in so many memorial vases, as well as mythologically fetching Persephone and Eurydice back from Hades' realm.

The ferrying back and forth is always *atremas*, without trembling, calmly, quietly, as Hermes leads one into the realm of forgetfulness and eternity. There are appropriate times, surely, when the soul is ready to relinquish its daylight preoccupations in order to regain the All, the continuity with all that has gone before and all that is to come. Sappho's fragment 97 (1958) speaks volumes about the readiness to die, the appropriateness of finishing this round, that Hermes teaches us:

> I have often asked you
> not to come now
>
> Hermes, Lord, you
> who lead the ghosts
> home:
>
> But this time
> I am not happy; I
> want to die, to see
> the moist lotus open
> along Acheron.

Hermes' way into the underworld is one that makes return possible; he guides us to an underworld experience that is not limited to death, but makes everyday life more satisfyingly complex. Through his guidance one comes to view even the termination of life as but another of the terminal points he is famous for sponsoring. Hermes' lesson is that cessation of a particular form of being, or, in this context, of being masculine, may be the ending of but one or another particular interpretation of life's meanings. Like the countless science fiction imaginings of alternative worlds upon which any given lifeline has ever so many alternative possible enactments, Hermes' realms multiply endlessly, and enlist our imaginations in wondering just how contemporary world representations and engenderings may be altered in the process of facing a twenty-first-century postmodernism that is only beginning to come into view as we relinquish non-functional models of gendering and especially of masculine privilege. Ever a transitional figure, Hermes divinizes transition. He calls eternally into question any simplistic gendering, any reductionist separation between this world and another, any other. Hermetically one opens out endlessly, never closing down nor attaining the point of stasis, but always evincing anticipations of futures all the stories of the past have only begun to intimate.

▪ ▪ ▪ ▪

Sources of the Story

When "Homer" became the name for the central cluster of Greek epic traditions, it became such an important carrier for the Greek narrative impulse that it drew around it many materials that had little connection with a historical bard named Homer. In most of the Homeric materials we meet "literature" shaped initially by oral and musical repetition over a very long period of time. Such materials are seldom the same twice, since a clever narrator will adapt the dialect and interests of the local audience and she or he will take care to connect closely with local events and characters. Although Hermes has several functions in the *Iliad* and the *Odyssey* that will remain characteristic — he's already a messenger and connector — it is in the Fourth Homeric Hymn that we come closest to having a canonical account (the thirteenth hymn, only a stanza long, is also dedicated to the god). The Alexandrian chronicle of Nonnos (1940) is a mishmash of materials from several centuries, but it provides a useful checklist for epithets and characteristic episodes in Hermes' career. Pausanias reports many descriptions of herms and where they were located.

Bibliography for Further Study

There are many translations of the Hymns, although I prefer Athanassakis 1976; I have surveyed six types of references and resources for further study of Hermes in Doty 1980:132–33. Barbara Walker's *Woman's Encyclopedia* entry stresses the post-Greek multiforms, 1983:395–99. Although a posthumous work that remains sketchy, Kerényi 1976 is full of insights (see Doty 1978), as is Brown 1947, a work that stresses the commercial and social contexts of the mythic stories.

Chapter 8

Ares the Aggressive Militarist

Background Information

An extensive encyclopedic source such as Robert Graves's *The Greek Myths* (1955) must be consulted in order to find out much about Ares, since most myth handbooks pass him off as "the god of war" with a side mention of his love affair with Aphrodite (her husband, Hephaistos, caught the two of them in bed with a magical net) or an indication that Ares is not very popular with the other deities themselves, let alone mortals. That is certainly true of Athene, who comes to represent a more civilized approach to warfare, and who already in the *Iliad* refers to him as "violent Ares, that thing of fury, evil-wrought, that double-faced liar" (5.830–31, Lattimore trans.) He is also a foreigner, constantly associated with Thrace, and hence perhaps inserted into the Olympian tradition (which really did not need another goddess or god of war!) because of vested interests of immigrants; his sites of worship were primarily outside the bounds of Greece proper.

Summary

The son of Zeus and Hera, Ares bears many children through liaisons with goddesses and mortal women. These children included Argonauts and various provincial kings who claimed descent from the god, and the Amazons, born from Ares and his daughter Harmonia. A hell-bent-for-leather war god, nonetheless Ares himself gets flattened or defeated in several stories, most famously when Otos and Ephialtes put him in fetters and stuff him in a brass jar; thirteen months later he is rescued by Hermes. Astrologically the figure signifies stirring up, growth; probably the motif is derived from the stories about his ability to incite warriors, as in the instance where Perithus forgets to invite Ares to his wedding, and outraged Ares consequently leads the Centaurs in attacking them. His signature animal is a wild boar, but few iconographic characteristics identify him in vase paintings: this was not a richly conceived deity but almost an allegorical abstraction, and at times an embarrassment because of his excessive anger and lack of control. That the famous hill in

Athens, the Areiopagos, was named for Ares by no means indicates that the Athenians respected him — actually, their matron, Athene, constantly trashed him — but instead the hill was traditionally the place where he was tried for the first murder in history.[1]

Transmission of the Story

I find it curious that the Greeks had such a low opinion of Ares, yet continued to tell his stories. It makes sense that his assimilation into the important native Roman figure of Mars would ensure that Ares' own materials would be carried along, but even before that, they are repeated, even though their subject is described as performing "the murderous work of manslaughtering Ares" (*Iliad* 5.909). My perspective here will be partly guided by puzzling through this contrast between the apparently repulsive aspects of the deity, and the way in which warfare is treated later as an important part of the noble male career.

▪ ▪ ▪ ▪ ▪

Mars, when he is honored, gives a deep red hue to everything we do, quickening our lives with intensity, passion, forcefulness, and courage. When he is neglected, we suffer the onslaughts of uncontained violence. It is important, then, to reverse the Marsian spirit and to let the soul burst into life — in creativity, individuality, iconoclasm, and imagination. (Moore 1992:136)

Mars represents confrontations, insults, blows that define limits and trigger hostilities. He is also one who can decide things, cut through them, and slam the door as he leaves. There is much more to Mars than just that, though: Mars is also a very important psychological activator. He gets things moving; he provokes confrontations and jolts us out of our stagnation. Mars is a vital force, a thunderbolt, an awakener. He is the springtime that shakes the world out of its torpor. (Corneau 1991:132)

The possibility of a strong connection with a deity whose very name (Ares) means *warfare* or *slaughter* (*arēs*) is difficult for those whose moral and historical scope isn't limited to modern American triumphs. Modern wars will never again have the sort of clear ethical sanctioning that previous conflicts did, but neither are they reversions to archaic, pre-civilized types of conflict. Waged increasingly by a semi-professional military class, warfare drives an inordinately large segment of national economies, yet in our specialized, compartmentalized society, war has become so little a part of our direct involvement that within a decade of the Vietnam debacle students could not recall which side we supported, nor did the populace protest the extraordinary press censorship exerted by the Bush administration during the Persian Gulf invasion.[2]

But American battlefields are not just military but also commercial and corporate as well: "Recent biographies of robber barons such as John D. Rockefeller, Andrew Carnegie, Andrew Mellon, Henry Ford, and Leland Stanford reveal a startlingly common preoccupation with masculinity, in which their supremacy was proved daily on the corporate battlefield" (Kimmel 1987:244). And the battlefields are political as well, with both Johnson and Reagan, among recent presidents, famous for their high-testosterone challenges to competitors and their sharp rebuffs of critics. Michael Kimmel suggests that Johnson "was so deeply insecure about" being considered more of a man than Kennedy that "his political rhetoric resonated with metaphors of aggressive masculinity; affairs of state appeared to be conducted as much with his genitals as with political genius" (247). And of course there was LBJ's famous slashing comment about a member of his administration said to be turning against American involvement in the war, "Hell, he has to squat to piss!"

A very different model of warfare and fighting confronts us when we look to ancient Greece. There war had formal social functions and divine sanctions and was part of a whole complex of male communal activities that included politics and socializing, athletics, and sexual contact, as well as the hunt and the battle — all of which were occasions in which one's masculine dominance of others (so important to the Greek concept of virtuous masculinity) would be demonstrated. A connection between masculinity and warfare is especially clear in Greek, where "male," *arsēn*, and war, slaughter, *arēs*, are closely related etymologically, and in Latin, where *Mars* is related to *mas*, a stem of "masculine." An important component of the Greek worldview is found in the derivation of another concept from the same word group, namely, *aretē*, the excellence that is the very first quality of masculinity.[3]

Already within the Greek tradition Ares is losing ground before the "higher warfare" pursued intellectually and administratively by Zeus and Athene, and in fact in spite of his name and its associations, we hear little about his actual successes in battle, much about his innate bloodthirstiness. In the *Odyssey* he is the butcher; in the *Iliad* he is lord of fighting, violent, a thing of fury, evil-wrought, blood-stained, manslaughtering, the brazen, battle-insatiate, most hateful of gods, forever quarrelling, the bane of mortals, and the blood-stained stormer of walls. A fragment attributed to Sophokles complains: "Ares is blind, and with unseeing eyes / Set in a swine's face stirs up all to evil" (fr. 754 Nauck, trans. Bowra). Wounded by Diomedes, Ares runs speedily to Olympos, where he complains loudly to his father. But Zeus himself responds with little sympathy: "Do not sit beside me and whine, you double-faced liar. / To me you are most hateful of all gods who hold Olympos. / Forever quarrelling is dear to your heart, wars and battles," and Zeus goes on to lambast Ares as replicating the excessive anger of his mother, Hera (*Odyssey* 5.889–94, trans. Lattimore).

Zeus's rejection of Ares may indicate that Ares represents the *negative* side of warfare and aggressivity, and that there was a more positive. But the question we have to place before the Greek materials today is: <u>Why did he remain an Olympian? Was he an imported figure before whom one felt awkward?</u> — his foreign origins in Thrace were constantly emphasized. His later Roman assimilation to Mars, a figure so important that Mars was second only to Jupiter, meant that a whole raft of qualities associated with Mars, such as being a fructifying vegetation deity, got grafted onto Ares' death-dealing genes. And the warlike functions of Zeus and Athene would seem to make the Ares-figure unnecessary in a sophisticated society such as Athens became — or was there something represented in Ares that simply could not be set aside?

We have less trouble comprehending how Mars's fertility aspects might excuse *his* martial excesses, and he also fathered the civic founders, Romulus and Remus, but there must be something here in Ares/Mars we are not yet aware of. How is it that he is one of the only two sons fathered by Zeus and Hera (the lame Hephaistos was the other)? How come he never married, yet begets a large progeny? How could he be associated primarily with Aphrodite, and with the birth of Harmonia: Is the experience of Love the same as the experience of War? Is the experience of Harmony only an apparent value of wartime, when even pacifists must shut up before the militant majorities? His sister Eris/Strife stirs up occasions for war by spreading rumor and causing jealousy, and his companions or progeny are even more objectionable: Deimos/Rout, Phobos/Fear, Anteros/Terror, and a series of individuals known for their brutality and unconventional warfare, namely, Diomedes, Oenomaus, Evenus, Molos, Meleager, and the Amazons.

Otherwise we have few associations with other Olympians. Ares has no importance in the social, moral, or theological realms, nor is he even connected with the concepts of divine vengeance as is true of Mars Ultor/ Mars the Avenger. In fact, there are fewer myths about Ares than about any other of the Greek deities. Is this the case because he is left to carry the negative side of human aggressivity for the other gods? <u>Or is it because the Greeks recognized the positive side of the military experience, the feeling of group bonding in war, the friendships formed, even the aesthetic side displayed in the orderly rows of marching bodies and neatly laid out battleworks</u>?

Or is it perhaps because of the intoxications of war, "the intoxicating fever . . . of actual combat, like a sexual or drug rush, an unstoppable transport to another condition that makes humans passionate about physical combat, addicts them to it, for they are then, during these moments of battle rage, in the embrace of a divine energy" (Hillman 1991:11; cf. Hillman 1987:122–23). Intoxication, not the strategic planning that looks so interesting decades later, or the mobilization of the commonwealth in support; in fact, not even the victory, but the immediate sensation — that may explain how the horrors of war can get transfigured into the delights of military experience and the feeling that at least in battle, one knows how to act like a man, right now. As Jean Shinoda Bolen puts it, "The Ares archetype, like the god, is present in passionate, intense reactions. With Ares, a surge of emotion is likely to evoke an immediate physical action. This is a reactive, here-and-now archetype" (1989:196). She finds exemplars such as Rambo to be "taken over by mindless aggression," to be motivated by loyalty, outrage, and retaliation," driven by "battle lust" at the necessary moment of engaging with the enemy (196–97).

But I think such a perspective misses the pleasure experienced by practitioners of the martial arts, most of which (in contrast to the outrageous kick boxers in Saturday morning flicks for children) stress learning how to get out of the way, learning how to discipline one's own body so well that one exudes a self-confidence from within that is like a protective shell against outside aggression. Both women and men acquaintances have shared with me their great pleasure in the *discipline* of these *arts*, their confidence stemming from knowing that they *could* defend themselves if called upon, and in today's cities, they may well have to. Except for his "a man" language at the start, I like Corneau's phrasing of this point:

A man is not a man until he has accessed his raw, untamed energy and taken pleasure in his capacity to fight and defend himself. Only then can he transform his blind rage into the power to commit himself, to handle tensions, and to make difficult decisions. A feeling of inner security also develops; it is based on his realization that, whatever happens to go wrong, he can get help from his inner resources, from the basic energy of his aggression. (1991:131)

A "warrior" in this sense is also one who knows and protects his own: Bolen reviews myths in which Ares as a father protected and requited his children (1989:195).

By and large the modern world is unprepared ideologically to deal with human aggressivity; in *Men in Groups* (1969), Lionel Tiger astonished many people with his socio-biological conclusions that stressed the "natural" aggressiveness of men in groups, and such claims recur in the conservative or essentialist posture identified in Chapter 3. But healthy ego-functioning requires a balance of both receptivity and aggressivity, as Edward Whitmont emphasizes. Our own culture has demonized aggressivity, casting it onto figures we can easily hate (such as, I'm arguing here, Ares), yet we must remember that mythically and psychologically Ares and Eros are brothers, and we need to recall that power itself is not evil; it is its manifestations that take on evil or benign aspects (Whitmont 1982:17, 245). Again we have individualized something that other societies have understood as normal *communal* functions and have contained within socially sanctioned channels such as athletics and hunting — both communal activities, traditionally, rather than arenas of contest between individuals isolated from the collectivity, as frequently experienced today. And such activities are disciplined in hierarchical ways, in highly ordered, aesthetically pleasing fashion: perhaps Hillman is correct is suggesting that much of our aversion to the Martian spirit lies in the fact that we regularly see only one side of Mars, the battle spirit (1991:12), whereas we now miss the disciplined hierarchical expenditure of energy and power that kept restraints effective so that one did not overindulge or overextend the boundaries of what one could honestly expect to accomplish. Soldiers who now return to our open-ended, anything-goes society often experience severe adjustment problems. They may have distinguished themselves within the carefully disciplined hierarchical military arena, but are not prepared adequately to re-enter daily social indeterminacy and absence of explicit chains of command and responsibility.

There's a positional justification of Ares, of the "aretic" spirit within Greek society: it is the stimulating, arousing militaristic enthusiasm that causes one to ignore the poor food and lack of comfort on the battlefront because one's patriotism has been stirred utterly and one must respond. As Aischylos puts it in *Seven against Thebes*, "The madness of Ares masters men in masses" (l. 342, trans. Vellacott). Furthermore the sort of characteristics represented by Ares are integral to the Greek system, in ways that no longer apply in our own, in several respects. The Greek hero partly obtains his defining qualities by manifesting that driving force toward victory, toward achieving dominance over others, that Greek males admired above all else. Having been free to play at the borders as an ephebe (adolescent, boy scout), once one became a hoplite (soldier), one was to turn toward defense of the centers, the inner part of the homeland. The proper hero makes the transition from playing to defending, but perhaps some of the problem with Ares is that he (or "the Ares type") wants to continue to celebrate, to revel in the high-energy passions and the psychological unanimity of the war camp, rather than accommodate his personality to the more settled virtues of the husband-citizen. A famous political cartoon from World War II portrays a group of exhausted, slouched-over soldiers watching a scowling youngster with aggressively clenched fists. One remarks: "You can tell he's never seen action, or he wouldn't be spoiling for a fight." The realities of warfare can only highlight the peaceful family ideal, by contrast.

The Greek warfare literature, such as the Homeric epics, glorifies certain ideological positions as all great epic literature does, making the aretic passion seem crucial and necessary with respect to any particular moment. But the ideological representations in the Homeric folk epics dominate only initially the ethical worldviews that the philosophers were to develop later. Certainly not many philosophers thought much of Ares! Indeed, already the mythical system suggested counterbalances: a brief but especially helpful essay on Ares and Athena by Jean-Pierre Darmon (1991) develops the antinomies and outright contradictions between the values assigned to Ares and to Athena.

Repeatedly Ares is lack of control, riotous fury, the one who often loses. Athena is moderation and rationality, "substituting the ordered combat of hoplites for the wild melees of heroes" as a function of her role as matron of Athens. Here, then, is some of the reason Ares can be regarded so negatively: he is *not the only way* Greeks understand warfare. His boisterous late-adolescent lack of control, his fury and excess, are cooly countered by the supreme embodiment of Mētis/Cunning Intelligence (Zeus swallows her mother, Mētis, then gives birth to Athena through his forehead): "Through Athena, war is domesticated, subjugated to the ruling power, and made available both to the macrocosmic order of the City of the gods and to the microcosmic order of the city of men. To the city's benefit, Athena tames the forces deriving from Ares as well as Ares himself, just as in other realms she subdues the savage energies in the orbit of Poseidon" (Darmon 1991:415).[4]

I extrapolate from the comparison of Ares and Athena that war as such does not have to be imaged as negatively as it is in the figure of Ares, a figure so excessive that "all the gods hated him." War can be elevated from the raw rule of force Ares represents to the Athenian self-protection of the community. Hence although Ares/Mars is divinized, it is only so within a pantheon of figures who map various ways of bringing brute force under the control of the political community. One wonders about all the modern myth handbooks blithely treating Ares/Mars as "the god of war." One wonders as well about aspects of his story that are so aggressively individualistic (and elitist, if we realize that only upper-class boys had the opportunity to be ephebes and then hoplites, officers), in terms of the associations of the warrior and masculinity as such.

But other connections also remain troublesome, such as that with rationality, frequently cited as a "masculine" value. Brian Easlea (1983) argues that precisely such a connection is what has led to the climate of threatening nuclear horror that we face. The scientific communities have largely grown powerful while stressing the imagery of warfare over nature — a warfare made possible, of course, only by initially positing a bifurcation of nature, assimilated to the feminine, and science, as the "naturally" dominating masculine. Science becomes yet another battlefield in which males "penetrate" the feminine, nature, or "bring it around." Men learn to repress, even mutilate, the parts of themselves that innately protest such dominance, until in the context of atomic weaponry we see the results of the gendering of science in ultimate terms: "the principal driving force of the nuclear arms race is not the brute fact of scarce material resources, important though it is, but masculine motivation — in essence, the compulsive desire to lord it over other people and non-human nature, and then manfully to confront a dangerous world" (165).

A curious circuit of imagery, in Easlea's portrayal of the masculine sciences of nuclear war, and in antiquity: the very-male Ares also was associated with death, and even considered by some Greeks to be the Death God. His sons Phobos/Fear and Deimos/Panic and his sister Eris/Strife appear among the demons of both the battlefield, as we have seen, and of the underworld.[5] Hades was said to be one of the few fellow immortals who appreciated Ares — because the latter sent him so many warriors! (Graves 1955:§19a).

Modern experiences have made unavoidably clear some of the connections between science and death, as well as those between war and erotic sexuality. As several historians have noted, the World Wars created all sorts of post-war behavioral problems. Carrying a gun had seemed a sort of continual hard-on; but what does one do when turning back to home, if the opposite is constant tumescence? Entire contingents of rest and recuperation personnel proclaimed the hero's military — and, by implication, sexual — prowess, but back home the soldier is just another over-his-prime male whose sexual perquisites are soon exhausted. And soon enough, the pumped up muscles relax, and the body softens.

Naturally enough, yet so symbolically significant in our society that masculinity may be threatened when the stomach begins its inexorable sag. The soldierly body becomes the ideal to the extent that it echoes the conservative militaristic trends in society. The manufacturers of diet pills profit, as do the exercise machine companies, but by locking a single image of the soldierly body into the American ideal, the slender yet muscular physique may represent the narcissistic ideals of a masculinity defined by power, strength, dominance, aggressiveness, even destructiveness: armored against the outside world, expressive only of powerful exertions against others, and utterly unable to accept care from others or relate to others non-aggressively.

Strongly concerned about such a male-body image now widely entrenched, Marc Mishkind and colleagues propose that it, "and various pressures for men to conform to it, may be producing psychological and physical ill effects at the present time" (1987:38). Ninety-five percent of men they studied were dissatisfied with their bodies, and 70 percent felt that they did not come close to their ideal of body type, which was precisely the trim mesomorphic soldier's. Since body type is *not* largely under voluntary control by dieting or weightlifting, Mishkind and colleagues suggest that the future portends widespread trouble with male eating and dieting patterns such as are now frequent among women (45).

Richard Stengel notes that pectoral and calf implants on males, as well as surgery to produce more shapely buttocks, already accounts for 60 percent of the business at the Beverly Hills Institute of Body Sculpting (1992:77), and he also worries about the anxiety produced by the search for the svelte, muscular, youthful male body displayed across contemporary media. For most men, such a physique is as unattainable as the Marilyn Monroe body is for most women.

Although one argument for homosexuality was that it created a ferocious core of fighting men who would gladly die to protect their lovers, today the Ares body is definitely a heterosexist body, and corresponding heterosexism comes to *embody*

> personal characteristics such as success and status, toughness and independence, aggressiveness and dominance. These are manifested by adult males through exclusively social relationships with men and primarily sexual relationships with women. Heterosexual masculinity is also defined according to what it is not — that is, not feminine and not homosexual. Being a man requires not being compliant, dependent, or submissive; not being effeminate (a "sissy") in physical appearance or mannerisms; not having relationships with men that are sexual or overly intimate; and not failing in sexual relationships with women. (Herek 1987:72–73)

Insofar as such heterosexist models of masculinity dominate politics and international relations, notes Gregory Herek, they may "increase the likelihood of interstate warfare and thereby be maladaptive for the entire human species" — in fact they may now represent little more today than "an outmoded identity seriously in need of transformation" (73). With respect not to warfare but daily life, such a position merely reinforces the extension of imperialist regimes across the planet: "Imperialism is the ultimate form of machismo: aggressive; possessive; fearful of appearing impotent; its malign reality covered with the language of chivalry, talk of duty, honor, and courage" (Hamill 1978:399).

The civilian becomes a soldier by identifying with especially masculinized symbols and turning his back on other symbols of the home, the family, the community, friendship, loving relationships, nurturing, parenting, and so forth. The old symbols have to be turned aside so that the sole reality of the new position in life can be articulated, and new identifications confirmed. Such is the identification of the Rifle and the Marine, as seen in the Parris Island training code:

> This is my rifle. . . . My rifle is my best friend. It is my life. I must master it as I master my life.
> My rifle, without me, is useless. Without my rifle I am useless. I must fire my rifle true. I must shoot straighter than my enemy who is trying to kill me. I must shoot him before he shoots me. . . .
> My rifle is human, even as I, because it is my life. Thus, I will learn it as a brother. . . . I will keep my rifle clean and ready, even as I am clean and ready. We will become part of each other.

> ... My rifle and myself are the defenders of my country. We are
> the masters of our enemy. We are the saviors of my life.
>
> (Cited by Cafferata 1975:235)

The phallic association needs no Freudian crib sheet to be identified, but
I wonder how often we remember the close associations of manliness
and the savior-soldier. Gendering will be stressed most strongly in times
of attack from without, or when a populace is told that it is in danger
of attack.

Susan Jeffords (1989) analyzes the relationship between American
representations of gender and the Vietnam war. Reviewing many of the
post-war films, she discloses a pattern that she finds generally throughout the culture, namely, the movement away from the sort of gender-role
liberalization that had become established in the period before the
United States went to the Southeast Asian jungles. It is a movement
that could use representations of the war — and her account of the role
of Rambo as reinstating a sense of aretic masculinity is very well developed — to "remasculinize" American culture by layering a monosexual
gender portrayal (did no women serve?) on top of or as a displacement
for an adequate long-term and democratically conceived foreign policy.

Femininity and masculinity got all confused as veterans returned
not to a proud and receptive homeland but to a situation in which the
(mostly male) veterans were femininized as they became "the poor misguided vets" who needed taking care of. This time even the frequently
cited male-bonding of warfare did not count for much, since another
aspect of the Vietnam experience was that the younger generation
tended to withdraw its trust from the older generation, who consistently misrepresented political motivations and thought up garbage-can
euphemisms such as "pacification" and "body count." Rambo? Yes, and
Ronald Reagan, Oliver North, even J. R. Ewing: figures who trumpet
male privilege, winning at any cost, returning to traditional wifey-
hubby relationships, yet can only propose the most simplistic political
conservatism in the public arena.

Robert Hopcke notes how frequently images of police or other strong
authority figures appear in dream materials when the individual has
trouble with dependency-independence issues (1990:56); Hopcke tries
to move clients away from projecting authority on such external figures and toward finding an internal self-affirming authority that is
realistically constructed on the basis of "an individual's own creativity, generativity, and achievement" (59). To be sure, frequent viewers
of television are never far from images of the police, and Andrew Ross

echoes Jeffords's attention to Vietnam as well as Hopcke's treatment of police imagery:

> *Miami Vice* and its moment in American TV history comes at the end of a decade of attempts to reconstruct the credibility of male institutional authority from the vacuum created by Vietnam — a process of reconstruction that has, in a sense, been concomitant with the rewriting of the history of that war. That a third of all new network programming is now made up of law enforcement shows is testimony to the privileged capacity of this genre not only to secure the franchise of authority but also to accommodate almost any and every form and manifestation of social conflict.
> (1986:150)

But perhaps our martiality got satiated in the Persian Gulf, nor does one hear the old "law 'n order" cries in the political arena. The main topic of discussion in the aftermath of the Los Angeles riots of 1992 was not how to have more stringent control measures, but how to rescue financially and politically the urban centers of our country. Perhaps the Ares figure changes, evolves: let's hope so. There are battlegrounds now in ecology as in the abortion controversy; opportunities for discipline and the physical arts in many locations of our careers and leisure. Like other types of hero figures, Ares can be re-insighted and reconfigured repeatedly, and so perhaps even I can become more comfortable with him if Ares is thought of as a soldier for peace. But that's also an old story we forget, that he who controls war also controls peace. The author of the ending lines of the Eighth Homeric Hymn "To Ares" already knew that it was the peace of the hearth, not the battlefield, that provided the true opportunity to be manly:

> But, O blessed one,
> give me courage to stay within the secure laws of peace
> and to escape the enemy's charge and a violent death.
> (Athanassakis 1976:58)

Many of the themes surrounding the figure of Ares explored here — the militant attitude, the military body, the skirting of issues about sexuality — surround the figure of Arnold Schwarzenegger, the weightlifter, politician, and movie star who is so phenomenally successful that he is said to be recognized by a billion people who cannot recognize a photograph of George Bush. Very much an appropriate representative for the recent turn toward the political right (he is described in an issue of *Musclemag International* as "the epitome of the self-made man, a conservative Republican who loves his life, America, his friends and family"), Schwarzenegger's devotion to order and discipline have been evident in his life-long body-shaping training as well as in his admiration for the figure who can hide his emotions under muscles (cited in *The Village Voice*, 12 February 1987; 36/7:58) and whose public statements often echo Friedrich Nietzsche's admiration for the superhuman representative of the Will to Power.

His media image spans both the military (through roles in the *Conan* and *Terminator* movies, *Commando*, *Raw Deal*, and *Predator*) and the body-beautiful (books and films: *Pumping Iron*, other books and many magazine features on bodybuilding). In each occasion the image represented is not only the "hard" machine-like body, but the sculpting of it in a manner almost detached from the personality itself. Perhaps not surprisingly, such a personality refused to take time off from pumping up two months before a contest to attend his father's funeral (Goldberg 1992:174). Jonathan Goldberg's essay in "The Phallus Issue" of *Differences: A Journal of Feminist Cultural Studies* examines various aspects of the self-detachment from the armored body represented in such a figure, and its relationship to an anonymous yet pervasive phallicism, dominating by always comparing "whose is biggest" and substituting "the pump" (in which the posed muscle is engorged with blood) for intercourse with another person. Goldberg also notes how the bodybuilder is the object of the gaze of others, including gay males, although homosexual aspects of the sport are rarely discussed.

Finally, Goldberg remarks how analogous Schwarzenegger as a hunk is to the cyborg roles he has played. Both are beyond human capacity, just as the swollen muscles of the bodybuilder are beyond usual masculine norms. And the aggressive masculinity of the Terminator roles, in which the cyborg just keeps coming back for more punishment, seems oddly echoed in muscle magazines with their advertisements for "Testosterone 6X" tablets, articles on the size of one's penis ("did I get the short end of the stick?," one asks), and "a user's guide" to making deposits in sperm banks. There is a sort of narcissism here, an air of unreal surpassing of the male norms that smacks of the dangers of hypermasculinity, of the too-easy transference between the military imagery and the hypermuscular body.

I am not inclined to interpret Schwarzenegger's personal values from his many public appearances and pronouncements, since anything said in public by a multi-millionaire such as Arnold will certainly be carefully managed. But obviously his media *image* has been widely heeded, and even there one imagines that a movie such as *Kindergarten Cop* must have been tailored to soften an otherwise too-macho image. Arnold Schwarzenegger as the contemporary Ares? Not entirely. But then that role does not fit completely with General Norman Schwarzkopf, either, whose utterly patrician coolness had about it an air of unreality. Perhaps if Ares/Mars "stirs up," as suggested in the epigraphs to this chapter, what he stirs up today is the questionableness of the figure itself, in a time that despairs of military solutions to any dilemma and looks instead to the reshaping of global economic markets as the new scene of militancy and aretic endeavor.

▪ ▪ ▪ ▪ ▪

Sources of the Story

There is no single canonical mythic account. See the brief Homeric Hymn no. 8, *To Ares*, and the *Iliad*, throughout, but especially 5.821–63. Mars is prominent in Virgil's *Aeneid*.

Bibliography for Further Study

Bolen 1989: Chapter 8 is good at drawing contemporary parallels with the classical figure. As usual Graves 1955 has the most thorough compilation of legends and variants; start from his index in vol. 2.

Part Four

TOWARD NEW HEROES
AND HEROINES

Connecting the Active and the Passive: Monster Slayer and Child Born of Water

Background Information

Seldom featured in anthologies, twin brother or sister myths are actually quite universal; and universally they map out polarity or duality such as good:evil, light:dark, masculine:feminine. The focus here is not upon twin myths as a whole, but upon those from native North America, where one twin or sibling is more outward-going and aggressive, the other more inner-directed and passive, as is true in the Navajo myth we will examine, and in several Seneca stories.

Although they are not major figures in Greek mythology, the *Dios kouroi* ("God's-boys," Latinized as Castor and Pollux, the Dioscuri) appear fairly frequently, especially in the story of the Argonauts. Kastor was mortal, and after his mortal death would have spent eternity in Hades, except that his divine twin Polydeukes persuaded Zeus to allow him to share in his own immortality; consequently they spent alternate days on Olympos and in Hades. In Roman transformation as the Castores or the Gemini (Twins), they are the guardians of the city of Rome and the protectors of sailors; in astrological contexts Pollux is the morning, Castor the evening star.

Summary

In the southwestern United States where the Navajo live (Utah, Arizona, and New Mexico), a portion of the myth of primal beginnings includes an episode in which the goddess Changing Woman bears to Father Sun a light twin son named Monster Slayer, and then to Water, a dark twin named Child Born of Water. (For this Navajo scripture, *Where the Two Came to Their Father*, see King 1969.) Typical hero children, they careen around the place when only four days old, and at twelve, set off to find their all-powerful Sun father. They are aided by Spider

Woman, who teaches them how to survive the dangers of their journey to the sky. Locating the awesome Sun's House, the Twins magically
surmount the several trials that he sets to see if they are really his own.
After they satisfy him that they are indeed, the Twins are given their
sacred names and are equipped with solar armor and weapons made of
flint, so that they can destroy the Monsters who are plaguing humans on
the earth. The story of their overcoming evil and gaining divine power
is replicated today in the ritual derived from the myth that is performed
to benefit persons going off to war. The rest of us remember their path
every time we see the rainbow upon which they traveled back and forth
to the sky, and when on the mesas we pick up pieces of flint rock —
which are chips from their magically protective knives and armor.

▪▪▪▪▪

*Although [the Navajo Twins] possess tremendous power — that of
their respected mother, Changing Woman, that of their dynamic
father, and the combined powers of all earth and sky creatures,
deific and humble, even the power of the subdued evils — they
walk with men and are sometimes called "Earth People." They
belong, therefore, in every realm; they are the personification of
all conceivable power of the universe.* (Reichard 1950:482)

*The twins make everything possible; they are, in Heidegger's
terms, "the rift of difference" itself. That rift... "makes the limpid
brightness shine."* (Tedlock 1983:245)

Since I have emphasized repeatedly that masculinities are products of
complex social, historical, and economic settings, it ought to come as
no surprise that I begin this chapter by discussing one of the specific
ways in which historical perspectives are shaped, and that means in
this case with respect to the work of mythographers, that is, serious
students of myths and their various interpretations. Mythographic analysis can form a useful part of the study of issues such as how gender
is understood and conveyed in any particular period, since myths and
heroic figures serve both to shape values and to reflect those already
established.

Writing at the middle of the twentieth century, hence at a period
within modern scholarship when it seems he should have known better,
Paul Radin, an influential scholar of Native American materials, refers
in "The Basic Myth of the North American Indians" (1950) to what he

terms "a specific American Indian myth, The Twins." He then proceeds to discuss not only a number of variants, but indeed three fundamentally different versions of the story, spread from the northwest coast of Canada to southern South America, as all representing one underlying narrative. Such procedure is suspect today, as Radin's globalizing claim would be: "I feel it is not an exaggeration to designate [The Twins] as *the basic myth* of aboriginal America" (359, my emphasis), although some Americanists do refer yet to the myth of the dying twin as being characteristic across a more limited area, the Midwest.

To be sure, scholars in Radin's time were more comfortable with sweeping summaries of the psychological meanings of basic myth patterns than we are today. He could write, for instance, that "few, if any, ethnologists exist today who do not believe in the psychical unity of mankind, who do not, that is, believe, in some form or other, in the existence of certain basic and fundamental ideas, relatively small in number, which repeat themselves over and over again among all peoples" (1950:360). Such a claim — just like many of the traditional claims about what elements comprise masculinity — sounds ridiculous just forty years later, although recently the revival of interest in the writings of Joseph Campbell has refurbished some of the culture-transcending approaches such as Adolf Bastian's *Elementargedanken* (fundamental ideas), or Jungian archetypal analysis.

Reference to Radin is not included merely in order to crow about contemporary mythographic superiority, but to indicate distance from some of the positions of former generations of scholars — and from much of what has transpired in the name of gender research — even while we appreciate and utilize some of the findings of each. If one can tolerate a few of the more grandiose claims, such as that "the theme of the gradual unfolding of the powers of the Twins" symbolizes "the evolution of man's sense of reality from the unconscious to the . . . conscious" (Radin 1950:405–6), there are useful analytical insights with respect to gender issues faced in Radin's book. We can usefully explore the question of the Navajo Twins' outright confrontation with their father, one of the steps in relationships between parents and children that is perhaps not avoidable; or we can reflect upon the extent of psychological complementarity necessary for human progress and change, which the Twins model powerfully.

Radin sees the Twin mythologem providing externalizations of internal psychic issues, and it is possible to discern how mythic and heroic materials perform such a function, without buying fully into his unclarified psychological presuppositions. Since his essay appeared in the yearbook devoted to the transactions of the discussion circle at Eranos, on Lago Maggiore, which was dominated by Jungian interpretation until it closed in 1988, and Radin was associated with Jungian interpretations in a later book on tricksters (1955), one assumes the presence of at least vaguely Jungian contours. But again, we can learn from his work without necessarily adopting his psychological positions, or those of Freud or of object-relations or any other school. Radin's comments about the Winnebago version of the twin brothers myth are in fact quite remarkable:

> each Twin constitutes only half an individual psychically. It is because the two are only complementary halves that they have always to be forced into action, be forced into wandering. This coercion takes the form of a defiance of the father's command, that is, of a command from an authority outside themselves. It is likewise because they are complementary halves that one twin has to coerce the other either by persuasion, as here in the Winnebago version, or by force. . . . Each alone can do nothing positively. . . . For constructive and integrated activity . . . the two halves must be united (1950:387–88).

Initiatory collaboration against the father, complementarity of the dual psyche, coercion of one another, the necessity of cooperation with others: Radin at his best could always develop very rich interpretations, even if his accuracy as an ethnographer is sometimes challenged today.

The immense body of Navajo mythology is an interconnected, branching tree, but our attention here is solely upon some details of the Holy Twins narrative that follow the Emergence from the underworlds and the creation of *Asdzaa nadleehe*, Changing Woman, who is the feminine complement to the masculine *Johonaa'ei*, The Sun. The discussion of the Twins myth is bracketed by beginning with a look at the wider context in Navajo mythology and by ending with the extra-Navajo trail of the twin sibling pair that might well lead us eventually to Cain and Abel, Esau and Jacob, Gilgamesh and Enkidu.[1]

While Navajo religious ritual ought to be exactly repeated and correctly performed, the Navajo stress upon personal individualism ensures that every priest-chanter develops idiosyncratic retellings, and so there are no normative texts or versions, and the Twins themselves multiply in manifestations both in mythic narratives and in the religious arts in which they are imaged. Multiplication of representations and epithets is one sign that the Twins belong to the highest rank of powerful deities. The accompanying chart of some comparative epithets and characteristics of the Twins will help distinguish their names and traits.

Ethkay-nah-ashi, The Two Who Go Together
(also called The Twins, The Brothers, The Twelve People,
The War Gods, The Holy People)

Naayee neezghani, Monster Slayer	*To bajish chini*, Child Born for Water
Slayer of the Alien Gods	Changing Grandchild
Reared in the Earth	
Holy Man, Holy Young Man	Holy Boy
The Man Who Killed Fear	
Firstborn, Older Brother	Secondborn, Younger Brother
Dwarf Boy, Disgusting Eyes	
One who repeatedly slew monsters	One who cuts around it [i.e., makes trophies from what his brother slays]
One starting out for slaughter	One who gazes on the enemy
With zigzag lightning he came down	Born in Yellow Mountain
Came down on a sunbeam	
white, black, pink	blue, yellow
mother: Changing Woman	Whiteshell Woman, Salt Woman
father: The Sun	Water (=the Sun's semen)
the warlike, destructive potential of the black north	the benign, blue south
a bully, impulsive aggression	reserve, caution, thoughtful preparation
takes initiative, kills, enacts	stays behind, follows, ritualizes
right	left

While the War Twins are not featured in every Navajo religious ceremonial, their characteristic male-hero exploits are usually mentioned at some point. In the basic sequence of the Navajo sacred legends, The Emergence is followed by the The Settlement of the Land, stories that explain the geographical ranges and racial types of peoples living throughout the Southwest, and then the cycle concerning the Twins. Radin's statements have alerted us to the psychomythical "place" or function of the Hero Twins episodes: they seem to precede "civilization" in the manner that the hero pair of Gilgamesh and Enkidu precede the establishment of the walls of Uruk. There is a dimension to the stories about the Twins that is not easily assimilated to Western myth handbooks reflecting "macho" exploits of the hero as something belonging to mature grownups.[2] And the Twins provide a balancing and complementing of an initial gender-related imbalance that is present across the contours of Navajo mythology. It is a mythology quite explicit about sexual and gender relationships, although it has taken contemporary revisions of the basic materials (as by Paul Zolbrod 1984) to understand that explicitness, since earlier ethnographers shied away almost totally from such explicit episodes as that in which the penis made of turquoise and the vagina made of white shell learn to shout to one another in ecstasy.

The Twins correct the imbalance of the hell on earth caused by the presence of innumerable primordial Monsters who make life miserable for earth-surface people and impede civilizational development. The list of these terrible creatures omits few terrors known from the lore of other national groups: the rocks that clash together and smash the passerby, stabbing reeds that attack as one walks through a marsh, sand dunes that pull victims into their suffocating depths, and even a cliff-dweller named Rock Monster Who Kicks People Off, who, just like the Greek Skiron, kicks travelers over the side of the cliff. The War Twins manage to demolish the Monsters with the help of their Sun Father, thus performing a human adjustment to the initial order divinely established during the long process of emergence onto this fifth world.

The *source* of the Monsters is important because it reflects a common problem in Navajo morality: they result not only from the evil side of Johonaa'ei's philandering, a motif very familiar from stories of the philandering of the Greek Zeus, but also from the inability of the Navajo First Man and First Woman to get along with one another. So we have a state of social imbalance caused first by the implied discord between the Divine Father, the Sun, and the Divine Mother, Changing Woman, and then by that between First Man and First Woman. In a subsequent segment of the Emergence myth the sexes separate, men on one side and women on the other of a large river. In one highly misogynist episode, when the women cannot stand their loneliness any longer, they masturbate with phallic stones and cacti, both of which cause them to give birth to the Monsters. By the end of *Where the Two Came to Their Father*, however, Changing Woman has agreed to accept the new home that Johonaa'ei has made for her — implying that they are reconciled — and the worst of the Monsters have been killed off, implying that men and women henceforth will heed their "proper" contrasexual roles in Navajo society. As a finishing touch, in some variants the Twins themselves obtain marriage partners.

Along the path of their many exploits, the Twins learn a great deal about brothering and male companionship as well as about the inescapable coexistence of good and evil within each of us.[3] In the many Native American twin stories, and specifically within the Navajo stories, it is important to remember that the Zoroastrian-Christian dualism by which one deity represents total good, another total evil, is exceptional in religious belief systems. Most religions anticipate that deities will manifest both evil and good, and hence ritual means are devised to assure that one will be in the benign rather than the malign path of divine activity. In the Navajo Emergence Myth, First Man is accused of being malignant, and he does not shirk the fact that he can be, but treats it as *positional:* "It is true, my grandchildren. I am filled with evil; yet there is a time to employ it and another to withhold it" (Moon 1970:82). Sexuality must be balanced; the relative amount of evil or good must be balanced. We are picking up the consistent Navajo teaching about reaching the blessed state of *hózhó,* about attaining a beautiful, peaceful, harmonious-holistic environment that is entirely comparable to the Hebrew *shalom,* and hence means also peacefulness, health, and wholeness.

In his commentary to *Where the Two Came to Their Father,* Joseph Campbell summarizes many of the points I have made here. His summary provides an apt conclusion to this section, before we look more closely at the two heroes of the Navajo myth itself.

> Everything in the world represents the interworking of [the male and the female principles, the aspects of the one male-female path]. In all Navajo rites it is male corn and female corn, male prayerstick and female prayerstick, male feathers and female feathers; the two are everywhere present, the two are in all things. A Navajo singer told Miss Oakes [who recorded the paintings of the ritual] he had been taught that both the sun and the moon were both male and female. And the brother heroes, though they are spoken of as masculine, are really both male and female; they are of both the male and the female colors. It is a powerful trait of Southwest mythology, this recognition in everything of the equal interplay of the two. One thinks of the Chinese Yang and Yin (Campbell in King 1969:44).

Clarifying the names of the two hero Twins will illustrate additional features of their Navajo context and significance. *Naayee neezghani,* Monster Slayer (or Slayer of the Alien Gods), is so named because his primary function is the forceful elimination of the Monsters. *To bajish chini,* Child Born for Water, is his twin, by convention, although literally the two children are only cousins, or at the most half brothers, since Navajo biology (like Greek biology earlier) understands twins to be produced by the semen of two successive fathers. Anything good can duplicate at will in Navajo religious thought, and hence the Twins themselves can be represented in ritual paintings duplicated and then later quadrupled by their own complementary figures.[4] So too, Changing

Woman is also White Shell Woman; and — but here the Euro-American mind boggles — the Sun impregnates her both as sunrays *and* as the dripping of water, since in one respect the water is considered his semen. Clearly customary oppositions can recombine mythically in ways seldom anticipated; some of the complex Jaina logic discussed in Chapter 2 may be appropriate here.

Throughout the sequence of their hero escapades, First Born and Second Born are learning how to be a team, so that it is as a complementary pair that they are able finally to rid the world of destructive monsters. They learn how to relate properly to their powerful parents, in the process bringing the two parents into a newly complementary relationship of their own. The ending of the exploits of the Twins fulfills the expectations of all Navajo mythical progenitors: they teach the ritual details necessary to reclaim the armoring power of the myth itself by ritualistic enactment, including the designs for the drypaintings (made in this case on buckskin). The pigments become powerful prophylactic medicines, touched to the patient who is being healed of war-sickness or being strengthened to avert it.

And when they have finished their heroic exploits, the twin brothers settle down to become parents in their own right, the flint armor provided by their sky father no longer an uncomfortable daily garment but now back on the shelves in the House of the Sun. Once the fantastic provisioning has helped attain the heroic boon, in this case changes in the social-sexual context, the hero does not expect to remain "merely" a hero for the rest of his life. While the Hero Twins episodes are central to Navajo upbringing,[5] it is clear that the Twins are considered to be models for adolescents, not grown-ups. They undergo an initiatory ritual themselves, even as their own encounters become the basis for young Navajos going off to war (the ritual was revived when many Navajo youths were conscripted in World War II). Works such as Leslie Marmon Silko's novel about a Laguna soldier, *Ceremony* (1977), portray the existential significance of such rituals, as well as the psychological chaos that can result when they are not performed at the appropriate time.

Looking at this myth this way alerts us to the need for adolescent rituals in our own culture. Robert Bly (1987) lays a major portion of the blame for our crisis of masculinity upon the lack of appropriate initiatory rites by which the older generations demonstrate their care for the younger and pass along the vital survival wisdom they have accrued. Bly notes how the Vietnam war was a point of great crisis, as young men came to distrust their elders who led them into such a senseless, no-win conflict and then developed euphemisms to cloak its horrors.

Since Western heroes are so important in our own ways of rearing children and in our extended childhood that now extends to the scripts enacted by Charles Bronson or Clint Eastwood as well as to Arnold Schwarzenegger's technoavenger roles, it is curious to note how the Navajo pair makes that familiar model seem only half-mythed: as we have seen, the traditional Navajo model of "heroism" does not just stress machismo but includes characteristic, complex, "feminine" features that we do not hear about very much in stories of Ares or John Wayne. The primary vocation of the younger Child Born of Water is that of cooperating with his twin, Monster Slayer; *together* they perform many of the Monster-eliminating heroics. That Child Born of Water primarily remains in the vicinity of the home hogan (the eight-sided traditional Navajo housing unit) is emphasized repeatedly: "older brother is identical with courage and heroism while younger brother, the stay-at-home, receives and domesticates the new power" (Zolbrod 1984:399 n. 65). The tasks at home are not specified except for that of ascertaining that Monster Slayer is not in trouble; Child Born of Water knows that because he keeps before him a warning prayerstick that glows, burns, or turns blood-red when Monster Slayer is in danger and needs help (Reichard 1950:449).

In one characteristic instance, when Monster Slayer relies on his flint armor in an attempt to destroy the Rock Swallow Monsters, the swallows attack so swiftly and fiercely that even the hero's arrows made of lightning cannot deal with them. His warning prayerstick begins to burn, and so Child Born of Water summons onto a white cloud Cyclone, Hail, and Thunder, and these beings kill the evil birds, permitting Monster Slayer's survival. In another incident Monster Slayer gets into trouble by drawing incorrectly a sacred figure on a ritual instrument (a bullroarer), and Child Born of Water has to enlist the Holy People and Big Fly to restore his strength and teach him how to make the bullroarer properly.

Not the extroverted warrior type, Child Born of Water nonetheless possesses many savior-type abilities: once even before they have left the hogan together, Child Born of Water hears singing that he thinks must come from his mother, but then he realizes that the songs are the dark night itself speaking to him. When, at the end of the narrative, Changing Woman finally agrees to move to her new hogan, she first sends Monster Slayer on ahead, and then, by means of that same Darkness — now fully a substantial being — Child Born of Water. At another point, when the boys are learning how to master use of the Sun's power, Monster Slayer (in the personage of Holy Man) goes to the doorway and hears nothing, but Child Born of Water (now Holy Boy) hears Big Fly coming from the sky; at that point Big Fly whispers into Child Born of Water's ear how they can take down the flashing disk of the sun at the precise moment of midday and so avert disaster. Later it is the same Big Fly who tracks down the missing younger brother (Child Born of Water) when he has been swallowed by a large fish.

Typically, Child Born of Water sights the problem or monster that must be confronted, and then Monster Slayer deals with it. Or Child Born of Water grasps the overall situation, and Monster Slayer treats the problem: from the skyland of the Sun, Elder Brother is not able to recognize their homeland (the episode forms one of the Father's tests of the Twins), but Younger Brother knows how to get the necessary information from Wind. Child Born of Water has a ritual or priestly role in the pair, because he knows how to deal with Holy People more effectively, a situation represented in one episode where Monster Slayer's excessive aggressiveness also comes out: urine-scented Coyote is ejected by the Night Chant dancers, but when they try to begin chanting, they find that in revenge he has taken away their power to sing. Monster Slayer sends out Talking God to reason with Coyote, who is still offended, but to no avail, and Monster Slayer then reacts angrily (inappropriately):

> "Bring him in if you have to use force. When we did not want him in the hogan [for the ceremonial], he came; now we want him in the Dark-circle-of-branches [the ceremonial site of this segment of the rite], he won't come!"
>
> Changing Grandchild [=Child Born of Water] spoke up: "It is no use to be angry with him; angry words and shouting will not influence him. Offer him some gift and perhaps he will come in and help you."
>
> Monster Slayer replied, "You are right. We will do as you say. Let us make him the god of darkness, daylight, male rain, corn and all vegetation, of thunder and of rainbow." As soon as Coyote heard about the gifts, he consented to enter and restore the dancers' voices. (Reichard 1950:406)

The balancing between the two approaches to the world could not be more evident, and of course the myth simultaneously indicates how important it is for brothers to work out disagreements amicably.

Monster Slayer is characterized as having the rougher temperament, as at the end of another of the Hero Twins segments, when the Sun is seeking to convince Changing Woman to move into the new hogan he has made for her in the west in order to regain her affection. When

Changing Woman continues to resist, Monster Slayer speaks *angrily* and *disrespectfully* to her: "You certainly have little sense," he says. In a variant, Monster Slayer thinks himself equivalent to any task and tells his Father that he'll just force his mother to move, but Child Born of Water remarks: "No, Changing Woman is subject to no one; we cannot make promises for her. She must speak for herself; she is her own mistress. But I shall tell her your wishes and plead for you" (Reichard 1950:450). Repeatedly Child Born of Water is closer to his mother; he is her darling, and again we see him as an intermediary, not afraid to serve as go-between for the two powerful divine parents.

In another instance Monster Slayer is impatient and forgets a sacred totem (a talking prayerstick), and as a result he gets pulled under the water by the Water Ox People. His impatience sets in motion the journey already mentioned during which his separated brother gets swallowed up by a fish. Although generally Monster Slayer is credited with saving Child Born of Water from the fish, we also hear that Child Born of Water remembers just in time that he has a sacred necklace of flints, and uses one to cut his way out of the fish's belly — the passive twin may not move aggressively toward the Monsters, but he has taken steps to provide for his own defense, all the same.

Once Child Born of Water silently accompanies Monster Slayer to the home of the dangerous White Weasel and watches from a distance as his brother is maimed. If he enters the fray directly, he will be disabled as well, but since he doesn't, he is able to carry his brother to some Cactus People who heal him. Here as usual, the adventures of Older Brother lead him to learn ceremonial rites, paraphernalia, and songs on the field of action, and then he returns to teach them to Younger Brother (Spencer 1947:69–70). The ritualist Child Born of Water is the one who records and preserves, in contrast to Monster Slayer's initiating and inventing. His type of "heroism" is not that of the outwardly brash and adventuresome hero-conqueror, but a sort of empathic, reconnective, and commemorative learning and knowing. Child Born of Water is a heroic prototype of some importance — not a prototype of the muscled, aggressive storm trooper, but the model of the conservator hero who supports others, records sacred materials, and transmits messages between people.

Even this brief summary of the Navajo Twins makes evident that they represent a different perspective on the masculine hero from that which surfaces in so many of what our culture terms "hero accounts." I want in particular to broaden the heroic perspective by looking further at the more passive of the paired brothers. Several recent discussions of the personal and social relevance of same-sex-siblings patterns such as that of the Twins provide resources for such reconstruction. The first is Mitchell Walker's provocative essay (1976) on the same-sex double in which Walker seeks to surmount the traditional Jungian opposition between anima and animus.

Jung's anima, or female principle, and the animus, or male principle, have been reinterpreted recently by Hopcke (1989, 1990) and others (e.g., Hillman 1985) in ways that transcend the usual sexist genderings initially set forth by Jung. The "principles" are reimagined in terms of figures that do not just represent the negative "shadow," the negative or inferior parts of ourselves that we tend to project onto others. Walker suggests that males do not always need to find a female counterpart, nor females a masculine; he locates a mythical figure appropriate to the same sex of the male in what he calls the masculine double, which contains the archetypal images of father, son, brother, and/or lover (165). Walker cites mythological examples of hero-pairs such as David and Jonathan, Achilleus and Patroklos, and Gilgamesh and Enkidu (see also Walker 1991).

The same-sex double, who represents "a powerful helper, full of magic to aid in an individual's struggles . . . often appears with an aura of beauty, youth, and perfection or near-perfection" (1976:168), and "is one's deeper support, one's partner, leading on, helping," "a soul-mate of intense warmth and closeness" (169). It "is not necessarily a homosexual archetype," but it "embodies the *spirit* of love between those of the same sex." The double is particularly "facilitative of *rapport*. It creates an atmosphere between the friends of profound equality and deep familiarity, a mysterious, joyful sharing of feelings and needs, a dynamic, intuitive understanding. . . . Such a pleasureable camaraderie easily extends to a sharing of purpose or goal through which difficult tasks are undertaken and fulfilled" (169–70). This aspect of Walker's proposal strikes me as useful for exploring literary same-sex friendships, including those such as the duplicated twins of Navajo mythology we have just examined, and for developing our own categories of sex or gender roles, since it develops a same-sex model that does not necessarily imply a genital relationship in its focus upon the sharing interaction of males.

Several revisionist studies of male-male relationships stress the particular ways heterosexist values support homophobia and gay-bashing, the incidence of which reached alarming proportions in the early 1990s, and seek to elucidate the ways our models of masculinity contribute to such social pathology. Walter Williams's history of European and American models of male relational roles, a section of his important recovery of the Native American berdache traditions (1986), provides an example of the recent revisionist historiography that identifies relational patterns in specific areas and historical periods rather than in an essentialist paradigm that treats all homosexuals alike.

The first type of male-male relationship Williams identifies was mostly derived from the ancient Greek type of adult male:adolescent male bonding by which younger upper-class males were socialized and educated. Later lower- and middle-class Christians derided that pattern as sexual "sodomy," and after about 1250 associated it primarily with the Islamic enemy (269). The second type was institutionalized more recently in gender-bending entertainment figures such as the castrato and drag queen; partly the extreme behavior was what led to the Stalinist and Nazi purges as well as to the American stereotyping of homosexuals as child molesters on the one hand or sissies on the other (269–70). Finally a third model derives from the necessity for male bonding on the female-sparse American frontier, and later in the "buddy system" developed during World War II: "This new masculine erotic bonding was different from the man-boy pattern and the gender-mixing patterns which had earlier existed. The new image that emerged out of World War II was the army buddy pair, masculine to the core, and above age eighteen" (270). Just this historical setting was an important context in which paired male friends began to appear in contemporary literature, and it is analyzed in terms of the decline of the male hero in American literature in a very important comprehensive study by Leslie Fiedler (1962), and more recently in an essay by John McIntyre, S.J. (1978).

McIntyre points to a series of references in recent criticism to the "loss of heroes" in American literature and culture in the late 1970s, indicating "a dissatisfaction with the American male character" itself (1978:75). He emphasizes the problems that attend the Adamic and Edenic presuppositions of many of the American literary heroes: these literary transformations of Adam never grow old; never learn to deal adequately with evil, either projected or internal; and never gain the wisdom of experience. Finally, the Edenic scene "simply does not allow for a social mythology" because of its focus upon purely personal development (77–78). Once again in this book problems constituted by the excessive individualism of the American hero, his one-sidedness, come to the fore. Perhaps cooperative rather than competitive hero models, such as the Hero Twins, will come to be recognized as helpful alternatives.

Another significant analysis of an aspect of American heroes, Robert Jewett and John Shelton Lawrence's *The American Monomyth*, suggests that the development of the frontier hero, as late as 1940 or so, is a clear sign of the abandonment of earlier communal hopes. Indeed, the uniquely American hero is a loner from elsewhere who sweeps into the frontier situation, clears out evil rustlers or gamblers, forms no long-lasting relationships, and then vanishes off the distant horizon. Such an escapist fantasy engenders little hope for communal problem-solving: it "betrays the ideals of democratic responsibility and denies the reliance on human intelligence that is basic to the democratic hope" (1989:210). When the community does act, it is as a vigilante group that acts outside the social structure rather than within it, the situation reflecting an extremely pessimistic view of public responsibilities and actions that echoes news reports about the large number of members of Congress who have found serving the public too onerous to bear, and hence are withdrawing from politics.

The authors of *The American Monomyth* pull no punches in labeling the debilitating aspects of American hero worship. The book leaves one feeling bereft of positive models that might replace the idealized frontier saviors who were a kind of secularization of the Christian savior motif. In *Habits of the Heart* Robert Bellah and his coauthors (1985) agree that we have attained little progress beyond the vigilante approach, and that unless we attend more carefully to corporate ethical responsibilities in the nation, we risk being adrift in a very rickety raft on a very stormy contemporary sea.

John McIntyre looks at another feature of the American literary representation of male relationships, namely, the brotherly relationship. Here the individualism is tempered by fraternity, by immediate friendship with another male, in ways that American society sometimes overcomes its individualistic me-first biases. The brothers motif McIntyre charts is not, he clarifies, a homosexual relationship, but a structuring principle applicable across a wide range of American literature (80).[6] While the dark-vs.-light tension structures classical romance, McIntyre finds our American Brothers relationships figured more along the lines of what Nathaniel Hawthorne called the sun-man and the moon-man:

> Generally the sun-man represents the establishment; he has achieved the economic and political resources necessary to consolidate power. Using logic and religion, he maintains his social

status usually at the expense of others. Often Hawthorne describes his Puritan forebears and their descendants as men of iron who carry the Bible in one hand and a sword in the other. The moon-man, however, dissembles by day and creates by night. Because he cultivates a visionary sense, he threatens the power-elite, who either forces him underground or into exile. (81)

I am taken with MacIntyre's suggestions that the male relationship in our fiction often "acts like a metaphor for the formed or the unformed life," that it often serves as an indicator of the making of the social ego, as we learn to relate to the friend or neighbor, and that when just that relationship is troubled, our social fabric is imperiled. The relationship of such cautionary observations to the accounts of Child Born of Water and Monster Slayer will be clear: <u>if we cannot find important and affective mythic models that reach beyond the stereotypical American hero models, the effective years of our culture may be shorter than we ever have anticipated.</u>

Over the last several decades, our national literature has been treated repeatedly in essays entitled something like "Where Has the American Hero Gone?" There have been so many that one might ask whether the title names a new genre, "the plaint of the vanished hero." But if McIntyre is right, the problem may be that of looking only at an inappropriately restricted inherited model. Recent concern for the vanished *traditional* hero may well indicate that we are now giving more proper attention to the building of community and ethical sociability, rather than merely continuing a dysfunctional macho heritage of individual rights, with few supportive brothers surfacing to advocate the caring, sheltering, sponsoring generativity of Child Born of Water.

One theme found in much of the contemporary literature about masculinity, namely, the necessity today to cultivate the *softer* masculine side, the moon or feminine phase, leads one to reconceive or revision inherited masculine models. To the extent that the heroic image carries our projections of the self, it is doubtless of great significance that real men do eat quiche; certainly it is often crucial for males in therapy or men's groups to learn how to express the moon-side. But the issue is potentially important across the range of approaches to gendered behaviors, as well as of concepts of the healthy self.

I am struck in Hillman's rich "Peaks and Vales" essay (1979) by the importance of re-examining our past assumptions about the supposedly feminine *soul* and the supposedly masculine *spirit*, that has shaped Western philosophy and historiography. Hillman attributes to the influence of Plato and neo-Platonic thought the Christian theological views that so determine Western understandings of the relative differences between masculine and feminine. The first great schism, the separation of the Eastern Orthodox Catholic Church from the Western Roman Catholic Church in the tenth century, led to the latter's devaluing of the physical, material, and soul-ish, and the elevation of the intellectual, immaterial, and spirit-ual. The usual Western elevation of the mountaintop experience, of communing alone with one's deity, gets even more intense in Western Christianity, so that the "valley," the social realm of materiality (the body, relationships, sexuality, the arts), increasingly was treated negatively.

Other neo-Jungian historical revisionings are also appearing, such as Roger Woolger's (1978) exploration of the "dark" side of the lunar hero, and Howard Teich's recognition of the problem that "our patriarchal culture regularly identifies the sun-man as the establishment hero and relegates the moon-man to impotence and oblivion" (n.d.:2). Teich proposes that "the Solar Twin has become notoriously inflated in our society," since

> those qualities associated with "solar psychology" — clarity, willfulness, competitiveness, endurance, perfection, linear thinking, goal directed behavior — are labelled masculine, while the "lunar" qualities — tenderness, receptivity, intuitiveness, compassion, changeability, abandonment, frenzy, emotional availability for dance, song, and prayer — are said to be feminine and homosexual. Lunar masculine attributes, those spontaneously instinctual, reciprocal, and affectionate emotional behaviors, have long been perceived as a potential threat to a patriarchal order based on strict division of masculine and feminine behaviors. (3)

No wonder Teich is impressed with the Twin motif, which for him represents "a holistic model of male unity, transcendent of the disproportionate light/dark duality upon which so many male-male configurations are prefigured" (3).

Both Teich and Robert Hopcke (1990) agree that Twin imagery comes out at times when unconscious materials are arising anew. But what does that say about the masculine psyche of our own day? What sorts of unconscious but shared materials are coming into common consciousness? Why are so many men in the men's movement enamored of the drumming and Wildman chanting that mass media reporters treat so mockingly? What sorts of repressed or inflated materials have we locked away so that the three-piece grey suit won't look quite so dull and meaningless? Why do we need grey-flannel suits at all? Merely to suppress and reject models of communicative sharing that — if the mythic stories we have been studying have any validity — are loaded with false promises, after all?

Ours is not a time of clear answers to these or other questions, but in this chapter we have located a few chinks in our own suits of armor, and we have explored views of our hero-ing that indicate that it is time to develop more satisfactory models. Doubtless we are less closed than previous generations toward models of complementarity such as those represented by the Navajo Twins, so perhaps we are now ready to open ourselves to the discovery that other men need not be quite as threatening as they often seem to be. Neither Monster Slayer nor Child Born of Water could accomplish much when acting in total separation, but when the two of them *shared* their solar and lunar powers, the message is quite explicit: *Watch out Monsters!*

■ ■ ■ ■ ■

Sources of the Story

The Navajo myth was first published in 1943, along with commentary by mythologist Joseph Campbell (see the revised edition, King 1969); that boxed publication includes large silk-screened prints of the dry-paintings accompanying the myth and its prophylactic rituals, some of which are (poorly) printed in tiny reproductions in Campbell 1988, where Campbell radically abridges the myth (244–49). Campbell returns to the story in his videotaped *Transformations of Myth* lecture series, and a paperback reprint version of King 1969 is scheduled. Frank Waters (1950:213–22) gives an abridgment and an esoteric interpretation, as well as listing versions and Southwestern parallels. Many of the details of this chapter are derived also from Reichard 1950, Newcomb 1975, and Spencer 1957. Zolbrod 1984 represents state-of-the-art translation and annotation of the entire Emergence cycle.

Bibliography for Further Study

Kerényi 1959 has chapters on the Theban and the Spartan Dioskuroi, as well as references to many other Greek twin-pairs. Walker 1976 treats the same-sex double in an influential essay that includes discussion of Gilgamesh and Enkidu. McIntyre 1978 treats the dual figure in the American novel as a means of resolving dissatisfaction with the development of fictional male characters.

Chapter 10

Reintegrating Apollo and Dionysos

Background Information

While Hermes is paired with the goddess of the hearth, Hestia — hence the god of traveling contrasted to the goddess of the home — Apollo appears as her very antithesis since he is always the smooth-muscled young dude at the gym and is never connected with the everyday affairs of the household. Dionysos often plays the role of the absolute foreigner, the most different of the Olympians, who has no fixed Greek temple or city (his name, "the Zeus of Nysa," refers to a purely legendary mountain). Apollo and Dionysos are half-brothers, as one counts mythological relationships. Apollo's mother Leto was one of the earliest loves of Zeus; the daughter of Titans, she was pursued by jealous Hera and delivered Artemis on the island of Ortygia — the sister then helping her mother give birth to Apollo on Delos, after nine long days of labor. Still chased by Hera, she was attacked by a dragon, the python, at Delphi, but four-day-old Apollo killed it there where his famous temple was to be founded. The mother of Dionysos was the mortal Semele — or in variants, the goddess Persephone. Hera again responds jealously and causes Semele's death: Semele is persuaded by Hera (in the guise of a trusted neighbor woman) to demand that her lover Zeus appear before her not as just a handsome mortal, but as he would appear to Hera. Of course she is cremated by the flashing heat of his full divine majesty.

Summary

Twin to Artemis, a sun brother to the moon goddess whose powers he partly usurped, Apollo seems to have been originally a serpentine figure who gave oracles from the earth-womb (*delphys*; there is also a play in the name, Delphi, upon Apollo's theme animal, the dolphin, *delphis*). Exerting an extremely political form of masculine power, his priests formed a network of data-gathering across the nation, and hence provided well-informed prognostications when supplicants made pilgrimages to hear his oracles at Delphi.[1] A deity of youth and music like Hermes, Apollo fathers Asklepios, the divine physician, and hence is associated also with the medical arts. He accidentally kills his beloved Hyakinthos by a false throw of the discus, and his beloved Kyparissos grieves so over the death of a pet stag he has killed that Apollo turns him into the symbol of mourning, the cypress tree. Probably originally an Asiatic (Eastern, perhaps Hittite) deity, as were his mother, Leto, and his sister, Artemis, he is (again like Hermes) a deity both of flocks and of entrance ways. In Western thought he becomes an allegorical representative of speculative masculine rationality.

Dionysos (or Bakchos, Latin Bacchus) was a god of wine and vegetation generally, later associated with the Roman deity, Father Liber. Called "twice born" in the Greek materials, Dionysos (Zagreus) resulted from Zeus lying with Semele in the form of a snake. After his premature birth, Zeus's jealous wife Hera persuaded the Titans to tear the baby into bits and eat him, but Athena saved his heart and Hermes carried it to Zeus, sewing the six-month-old embryo into his thigh (euphemism for the genitals) for full-term gestation, hence a second birth.

Founder of an ecstatic religiosity that defied traditional Greek mores, Dionysos's followers included women — by no means the gender traditionally considered appropriate for public religious observances in Greek society — and represented a revisionist, enthusiastic type of religiosity. Over against the quite formal Greek state religion, the mysteries and the Dionysian cult stressed identifying with and actually experiencing the deity, so that Dionysiac religion, with its emphasis in his ceremonies upon the relaxing results of the wine imbibed and upon sexual liberation, came to be understood as the opposite of Apollonian restraint and rationality. Native to Thrace and Phrygia, the religion of Dionysos was "foreign" to masculinist ideas of the Greek ruling class; celebrating the earth's fertility and achieving oneness with the deity seemed "feminine" elements that could only be considered opposites to "normal" masculinity.

Homeric Hymn 7, "To Dionysos," relates the story of the pirates who sought to ransom the richly clad young Dionysos, but as punishment for failing to recognize his divinity found their ship immobilized by grapevines and the young lord turned into a fierce lion. Terrified, they jumped overboard and turned into Dionysos's animal totem, the dolphin. Euripides' *Bakchai* (newly translated by Evans 1988) relates how the normal masculine establishment figures also fail to recognize his power; the play remains one of the most powerful pieces of literature from antiquity, with a freshness not at all diminished as it relates to contemporary gendering issues.

Kynaithos's Homeric Hymn 3, "To Apollon,"[2] is one of the longest of these formal hymns from the line of the Homeric poets. It is an impressive catalogue of the many aspects of Apollo across ancient Greece, of the contradictory elements in this striking mythological figure: "both the pure and impure are at work in a god whose power is double, who is purifier and killer, a god who cures the plague and the sickness he himself brings to mortals" (Detienne 1986:51). The patron of homosexuals, he remains eternally the beautiful young adult just past the age appropriate to being a beloved (*eromenos*), and ready to take on the responsibilities of being a lover (*erastes*) — a mentor to adolescent males. But he also remains somewhat abstracted from the human condition, a god of prophecy who always speaks from afar or through someone else, and even the Olympian household share mortals' fear that Apollo's glance might not always be beneficent. He's called The Destroyer in the *Iliad*, and he is the god of the hated Trojans:

> I shall remember not to neglect Apollon who shoots afar.
> The gods of the house of Zeus tremble at his coming,
> and indeed all spring up from their seats
> as he approaches, stringing his splendid bow.
>   (Homeric Hymn 3:1–4, Athanassakis trans.;
>   see Clay 1989 on this hymn).

A solar god as contrasted with the dark Dionysos, Apollo sanctified divination from above for a culture that usually associates it with the underworld. A shepherd god, Apollo also officiates at the establishment of city foundations; as enthusiastic a scrapper as the young Greek male was supposed to be, he also portrays the characteristic tendency to go too far — Zeus had to intervene between Apollo and Herakles and between Apollo and Hermes when their competitive contests reached impasses. Yet the same deity was the most famous of the deities of music and is frequently represented as *Musagetēs*, the leader of his constant companions, the nine Muses. Companions of Dionysos were less delicate: the half-goat Satyrs, always sexually rampant and usually pursuing the Mainads, Dionysos's female devotees, and the older Seilenoi, figures of great oracular wisdom and musical skill, but often drunk on Dionysian wine or ecstasy.

Transmission of the Story

Thanks to some of the Romantic philosophers, copied by Friedrich Nietzsche and others, Apollo has come in modern times to represent the logical masculine, Dionysos the intuitive, even feminized masculine.[3] The distinction was encountered already in antiquity, when the

Dionysian cult represented a means for Greek women to participate in a sensual, experiential religiosity, whereas the name of Apollo came to stand increasingly for abstract rationality, non-religiosity, for the dry, rationalistic patriotism of official state religion. Ruth Benedict applied the Apollonian-Dionysian distinction to anthropology in 1934, and the dichotomy influenced ethnography strongly as it sought to understand cultures by means of looking at contrasting types of personality, a perspective soon discarded professionally, as in Margaret Mead's *Male and Female*, which is likewise a study from the discipline of anthropology, but which portrays a wide range of gendering representations and ideals and explicitly rejects simple gender dichotomies (1949:19).

C. P. Snow took the ancient distinction to new heights in his concept of the Two Cultures represented by the sciences and the humanities, a distinction that has little merit except to intimate that the two are methodologically separable and at war, rather than (in reality) sharing many crucial methodologies and intellectual history, but it provided the terms for a narrowing of debate about the nature and composition of intellectual endeavor that has contributed to the climate of competition between the sciences and the humanities that now threatens intellectual freedom in the university.[4] The dichotomy ignores the economic and political climate in which both the sciences and the humanities operate, and leaves both ignorant of the whole range of crucial information necessary to make reasoned moral judgments. In the immediate context that has meant a division between biological and psychological views of sexual orientation — the essentialist position that males are determined primarily by their physiological hormones and by early conditioning — and the long-range perspectives of the humanities that stress variations across periods in the ongoing history of the social construction of masculinity and the role of mythico-religious materials in establishing and amplifying such constructions, as well as the role of the media in conveying them.

The dualism between the experiential Dionysian and the intellectual Apollonian came to its high point in Greco-Roman Hellenism, at the end of the period when Greek mythological consciousness was most alive. Repression of the Dionysiac impulse accompanied the rise of the androcentric (male-centered) Western consciousness with its idealism of interiorized and self-reserved perfection, and its scapegoating of evil onto the repressed elements of society — women or those who do not make the economic grade, whether anciently in classical patriarchial society or recently in terms of Republican claims that the poor are impoverished because of their own inherent dispositions and lack of aggressive capitalist/masculinist orientations. The revision-ist Freudianism of Herbert Marcuse in the 1960s and Norman O. Brown in the 1970s proposed freeing the expressive-emotive elements of the personality that have been progressively repressed in the West-ern commercially oriented societies. Experiential therapy groups, and more recently the Recovery wing of the men's movement, stress the importance of emotional catharsis as a first step in overcoming the hypercontrolled abstract-arbitrary rationality that is often held up as the primary model of masculinity.

▪ ▪ ▪ ▪ ▪

In [the Archaic Age] of reorganization of the state and of the con-stitution of the individual, Apollo appealed to the few who sought stability through knowledge; Dionysus, to the many who needed release through action from the burden of their new selves — offer-ing a kind of athletic mental healing and preparing the participant for renewed efforts at living in an ever more lonely making world.
(Eisner 1989:117)

The Greeks, as long as we lack an answer to the question, "What is Dionysian?" remain as totally uncomprehended and unimag-inable as ever. (Preface to 1969 German edition of Kerényi's *Dionysos*, 1976: quoted from Roger J. Woolger's review, *Quadrant*, Summer 1978:76)

Adolescence is the time when all the gawkiness of the race comes to the fore: limbs akimbo, boys with a blush of cheek and genital hair stum-ble into just about any doorframe; girls giggle and flaunt their budding breasts and hips. Either gender is likely to burst out with tears or laugh-ter at what they feel are totally inappropriate times or to intuit that they are the only individuals ever to have had to undergo such trials as their human bodies impress upon them. The range from tough-guy to wimp seems inordinately short, and there's the constant fear that one may need to collapse at any moment into momma's lap because of shame caused by making the wrong move. This book is not about young girls or boys, but it does concern the manner in which adolescent choices and desires produce adult males, especially as today masculinity is both attacked and up for grabs, its very models now made questionable: Who plays out the archetypal masculine in our culture? John Wayne? Michael Jackson? Sports stars? Financiers such as Donald Trump? Presidents? Physicians? Actors?

The spectrum runs from a quiet "manly" heroism to a loud "girl-ish" extraversion, from models of keeping it cool to those of brutal slaughter of the enemy. In short, from the stereotypical "macho male" on the one hand to the "feminized sissy" on the other. Apollo and Dionysos represent that pairing, although in terms appropriate to the specific features of Greek culture; Apollo is never the rough-and-tumble muscular frontiersman that Herakles is, for instance. But Apollo does represent a strong contrast to Dionysos, who was described repeatedly as *arsenothēlys*, man-womanly or hermaphroditic, precisely because of the raft of feminine characteristics that came to be mapped onto his maleness.

The complex figures of Apollo and Dionysos have given rise to volumes of analyses, and there are so many competent accounts in studies of classical mythology that I will not discuss the legends of the two in any detail. Instead I focus upon two aspects: first, how it has been that the dualistic opposition of the features represented by the two deities has been so important in our society, what *functions* positing the opposition has had, and whether we might be ready to declare it bankrupt, in favor of a different interpretation that stresses complementarity rather than opposition.[5] And secondly I want to look at the ways in which masculinities are represented in the two figures, proposing along similar veins that their masculinities are likewise complementary, that indeed the sexuality represented by either seems almost dangerous in its mono-mania. The chapter also returns to themes addressed elsewhere in the book: the question of the gender boundaries that we live on and across, and the relation of crossing boundaries and human creativity.

To have become so familiar a dichotomy, the contrast of the Apol-lonian and the Dionysian had only a brief shelf-life in the writings of the antiquarian Friedrich Nietzsche: he developed it in his first book, translated as *The Birth of Tragedy* (1967 [1872]), and dropped it already by 1878 (in *Human, All Too Human*). The "Dionysiac" remains impor-tant for Nietzsche, but in meanings transfigured from the initial use in *The Birth of Tragedy*; his many reservations about *Birth* were ad-dressed in a self-critical preface to the 1886 edition. It becomes his own description of the worldview he developed, rather than merely signify-ing within the limited Apollonian-Dionysian dichotomy (see Mohr, in Gründer 1971:445).

Nietzsche was certainly not making up the dichotomy or the love of contrasting oppositions; indeed they were prominent within familiar Romantic schools of philosophy, especially in Schopenhauer's contrast between the Idea and the Will, which came to be represented in *The Birth of Tragedy* by Apollo and Dionysos respectively. Nor did Nietzsche denigrate the Apollonian nearly as much as subsequent Nietzscheans are inclined to argue. Walter Kaufmann, the contemporary expert translator and commentator on Nietzsche, suggests that he was in fact attempting to bring out its distinctive features by contrasting it with the Dionysian (Nietzsche 1967:9–10). Certainly a revisionist view in its attention to the "feminized" Dionysos of religious cultic practice, Nietzsche's contrast entered an important corrective to the position of early nineteenth-century classical scholarship that held Apollo to be the most Greek of the Greek gods. Modern scholarship recognizes that just such a Hellenic ideal is more the construction of later periods than of the earlier Hellenic period itself.

Nietzsche's Dionysian element emphasizes the group rather than the individual, promoting inspired frenzy rather than cool rationality. His Dionysian is no longer the stranger it was to earlier classical scholarship, since the aspects of ancient religions ignored by that scholarship have now been explored fully. Contemporary materials also see a "darker" side of Apollo than Nietzsche — radical for his day though he was — could recognize: "The bringer of plague, the striker from afar, the God of wolves, symbolized by serpents, and he who carries away mad prophetesses in maniacal, wind-driven frenzies — this is the darker Apollo about whom Kerényi chose to enlighten us" (Solomon, afterword to Kerényi 1983:63). Nor did Nietzsche recognize fully the correlation of the two figures:

> Nietzsche never honestly addressed Dionysos' residence at Delphi (Apollo's seat on Mt. Parnassus) during the four months each year while the god of the lyre was absent in the northern Hyperboreans. Dionysos, "god of disorder" was paradoxically the god who inspired the superbly ordered dithyramb. Apollo, "god of light and transcendence" could also shoot arrows of devastation. (Kimberley C. Patton, review of Kerényi 1983, *Journal of the American Academy of Religion* 54/3:590–92, at 591)

Nietzsche surely ignored the more feminine sides of Apollo, along with the excessive quality of the inspired artistic ecstasy and the death-dealing aspects. Perhaps Carl Jung was correct in suggesting that Nietzsche saw Dionysos more in the guise of the threatening Germanic Wotan than in terms of the Hellenic figure; certainly the author who described himself as "the last disciple and initiate of the god Dionysius" (quoted in Feder 1980:71) would have been appalled at the use of his concepts by the Nazis, the dark, destructive side of the Wotan of the North.

Writers such as Thomas Mann (in *Death in Venice* and *Dr. Faustus*), Norman O. Brown (in *Love's Body*), and contemporary apocalyptic novelists such as Thomas Pynchon and Carlos Fuentes have found in Dionysos a clarion call away from the isolation of normative Apollonian rationality toward collective concern for the social enjoyment of life — precisely the sort of ecstatic transcendence of the individual stressed in the plays *Dionysus in 69* (an adaptation of Euripides' *Bakchai*) and *Oh! Calcutta!*[6] The Dionysian almost always appears as the ideal of expressing creative emotions easily submerged beneath social veneers, but not in a merely idiosyncratic manner, since, as Lillian Feder notes, the motif of Dionysian frenzy not only "portrays the loss of individuation in ecstatic and destructive abandonment to primordial instinct, . . . it also conveys the self-knowledge and control that the release of instinctual aims can produce. Employed for either purpose, this myth depicts psychic incorporation and transformation of cultural, political, and social influences" (1980:68). Neither the overcoming of the restrictions imposed by individual self-consciousness nor the subsequent group ritualization ought to exist in isolation; Feder rightly stresses the contradictory nature of Nietzsche's combination of the two: "On the one hand, Apollo, the 'glorious divine image of the *principium individuationis*,' symbolizes the very principle which must 'collapse' if human beings are to reach a state of ecstatic harmony with the creative and destructive forces of nature. On the other hand, this undifferentiated state, without the intervention of the Apollonian, is a hazardous one, leading only to barbaric 'sensuality and cruelty' " (69).

The dichotomy between Apollo and Dionysos appears to be an allegory for that between the Freudian I or It (the ego or id) and the Transcendental I (the superego); or it maps the contrast between consciousness and instinct, rationality and emotionality, art and morality. Our recent history is the history of attempting to follow the liberal thought of the nineteenth and twentieth centuries in liberating the emotional, artistic, instinctual, while heeding the long-term importance of cultural traditions passed along through mythological and moral teachings. Bachofen's comment deserves reflection: "what is lacking in Dionysos will be found in Apollo" (quoted by Gründer 1971:443): how the best characteristics of each can be combined remains a pressing issue. Contemporary classicists today sniff condescendingly at Nietzsche's poor reconstruction of Greek thought and religious practice, although few would quarrel with Nietzsche's disparagement of what he called (not very accurately) the Socratic,[7] and perhaps with his allergies with respect to Christian admonitions to extirpate the passions and negate the importance of the present moment. I return to the issue of reintegration of the conflicting aspects at the end of this chapter, but first I turn to closer looks at Dionysos and Apollo, intending to re-examine those mythic heroes not just in terms of the Nietzschean dichotomy, but more broadly with respect to gender modeling.

Certainly we move immediately beyond the opposed terms of any dichotomy when we confront the essentially inclusive two-in-one sexuality of Dionysos, his double-sexed nature (I avoid the term "bisexual," because its use is primarily with respect to objects of erotic attachment, and I am working here with stories about the fundamental makeup of Dionysos, not those concerning his amours). Dionysos's sexuality, taken at its face value, in all its complexity and inclusiveness, ought to be reviewed just as carefully as was the case when Margaret Mead headed out to observe sexuality in seven Pacific island cultures; Mead found few biological givens, but many differences derived from local social differences (1949). Her example remains exemplary with respect to cultures that we can no longer visit; I often find methodological parallels between ethnography and mythography, although the disciplinary separatism of the contemporary university regulates against cooperative hermeneutics in the two disciplines.

Dionysos is dual-sexed from the beginning, perhaps as a result of his double-birth: he experiences gestation in a mortal woman, Semele, but she is consumed after six months by the flashing grandeur of Zeus, who snatches up the infant and sews it into his own thigh. Hence later Dionysos was born from this male womb as well.[8] This is an amusing parallel to the birth of Athena from the head of Zeus, although that goddess models the rational head-trip part of Zeus just as Dionysos apparently reflects his genitality.[9] There is something amusing about the womanly Dionysos having been born from a male, perhaps a mythological element that was felt to explain or compensate for his primary association with women in his cult; we are even told that his substitute mother, Ino, is required by Hermes to raise the child as a girl.

While Dionysos's womanly traits (the woman's full shawl or robe, *peplos*, is draped over his statues, on which he appears full-bearded) contrast him explicitly with the Apollo, whose oracular maxims include "Rule Over Women!" (Eisner 1989:142), these traits also provide continuity with Apollo, who never becomes a fully adult male either, since he remains associated with the (male) sexual titillations of the palaistra and gymnasion and never bonds lastingly with a woman. Apollo remains the paradigm of the lover, just as Ganymedes is the paradigm of the beloved, the love object (Downing 1993). Hence when Walter Otto contrasts the feminine world of Dionysos with the oh-so-masculine world of Apollo (1965:142), I think he is wide of the mark, since the masculine cult of boy love does not exhaust the extent of what the Greeks conceived as the masculine. Eisner strikes the right note:

> With few of his loves does Apollo succeed in procreating, in estab-
> lishing his line, in finding a productive expression for his eros. . . .
> Gods cannot die, but they may lead very lonely, isolated lives.
> Apollo embodies ageless male beauty; but mortal beauty does age,
> and where the years take a [mortal] boy Apollo cannot follow.
>
> (1989:143)

And Hillman likewise understands that the Apollonian model with respect to relationships was not a healthy one, since a low view of the Dionysian — and a corresponding high view of the Apollonian — seems tied to a low view of women, of the feminine as such (1972:270). Certainly a narcissist in the contemporary sense, Apollo represents not adult procreativity or long-lasting partnership but an ever-youthful sterility (Eisner 1989:141, 152–53). No wonder the severed head of Orpheus as it floated across the Aegean sang out a warning that Apollo's masculinity was not for mere mortals! (148). Perhaps we can discover other more healthy combinations, and perhaps the symbolism loaded in the dual-sex of Dionysos points toward a condition in which neither masculine nor feminine qualities will be disparaged or isolated.

I am struck by the fact that a number of authors stress independently of one another the contradictory characteristics of Apollo on the one hand, and Dionysos on the other.[10] Hardly a figure of singularity, the bearded male Dionysos wearing a woman's dress (*peplos*) is obviously multiplex, but Apollo's stories represent no less complexity and contradiction. Kerényi notes that Apollo represents simultaneously "the soul's darkness and the soul's clarity. His essence is such that he can be darkness and clarity at the same time"; and hence Kerényi is led to speak of "the two Apollos" (1983:58). While the white swan is his emblem in his lighter aspect, the raven, crow, and wolf are just as characteristic of his dark side. A god of healing, he also brings plagues and swift death (as does his sister Artemis). A cultured god of the noble art of music/poetry, he nonetheless punishes Marsyas, his challenger in a flute-playing contest, when the mortal is judged inferior, by having his skin flayed from his living body while roped to a tree.

Truly, Guthrie notices, "the more one looks at the ideas associated with the worship of Apollo, the stranger and more contradictory his character appears to be" (1949:183). Especially in light of his pre-Olympian status as the monster, or the killer of the monster at Delphi, Apollo is hardly "Apollonian" the way post-Nietzschean tradition has suggested. Nor does Apollonian ecstasy seem all that different from the Dionysian, except that it is individually experienced rather than being a group phenomenon. Later famous as the paradigm of Pindar and the philosophers, Apollo exhibits erratic qualities just as remarkably bizarre as those of his brother Dionysos. The violence of his sacrificial system certainly balances the rational ideal of Pythagoras and later Sokrates: "Apollo is without doubt the only divine power represented in vase-paintings with a butcher knife or a sacrificial knife raised above the head of one of his enemies"; Apollo is *lakeutes* and *mageiros*, a butcher-herald like Hermes (Detienne 1986:48, 46–47).

I am interested in how we lost sight of the dark side of Apollonian masculinity: how did the Greek philosophical tradition and then the Romans manage to repress so much complexity, so many dark sides? Is there something about the patriarchal view that suppresses the origins of sacrifice, that cannot abide the thought that obscurity and clarity can exist simultaneously? Certainly within the mythic tradition the god is already moving away from any sort of embodied darkness: his relationships with people are always at a distance, even when he was not greatly feared. He is "the god from afar" whose oracular pronouncements are heard from a distance, and even his famous death-bringing arrows kill from a distance, just like twentieth-century ballistics. His true mythical home is not at Delphi where he resides during the work year, but in the remote fantasy land of the Hyperboreans — to which he escapes during the intolerably hot Greek summer months. In contrast to the sunlit openness of Apollo's temple realm at Delphi, the sphere of Dionysos is that of nighttime rituals in the winter.

Such a contrast is related to the typification of Dionysos as in-every-way-strange, as the outsider; not like Hermes the god of boundaries or transitions, but the god of difference, of what comes to our experiences from elsewhere, the non-native. Such figures are said to break down walls, and since most Greek cities were surrounded by encompassing city walls, the wall-breaker is an anti-social character by definition. The boundary-breaker or the soul who goes beyond the boundaries can represent only the anti-norm; hence we begin to see just why Dionysos's sexuality was so threatening. "What this god means is the transgression of boundaries. Dionysos is the god not of the mean but of the extreme, the god of wine and ecstasy, madness and confusion. Among the many antitheses he confounds is that between masculine and feminine" (Downing 1993 cited from ms.).

But in addition to gender confusion there is also the human-divine confusion, because Dionysos is the type case of the *enthusiast,* a term indicating fusion between the object of worship and the worshiper. Such a condition was no less repugnant to the normal ancient Greek sensitivities concerning what was appropriately "religious" than it would be to the contemporary Protestant or Catholic: the appropriate limits of religious experience are clear in each case, and hence the merging of god and devotee represents a threat of some magnitude. "That the unsettling energy Dionysos embodies, the unrestrained instinctual passion, should be accepted as *divine* arouses violent opposition whenever he appears" (Downing 1993, cited from ms.)

And if we add the non-systematic schedule of this deity — he represents the unexpected appearings and disappearings of an energy incapable of being tamed who always comes from elsewhere — we begin to see why the Dionysian threatens so many people. If that energy is primarily a sexual energy emphasizing enjoyment rather than mere passing along of the seed, generation, as it is in the realm of Dionysos, then all the obvious social taboos will spring into action at any given moment (Evans 1988:37). And taboos relinquished become connectives: "in Dionysos, borders join that which we usually believe to be separated by borders"; Hillman's point catches the nub of the issue (1972:275). The borders are the confines of publicly acceptable behavior and symbolism, and the actualities of what is being symbolized: carrying erect phalli through the street in Dionysiac processions would today be less acceptable than in antiquity, perhaps, but the example gives a good parallel between what is unacceptable in our time and in antiquity. Imagine erecting a model of the male genitals in the lobby of a theater to celebrate victory by a male chorus! (Kerényi 1976:285). Or imagine that a phallic deity such as Dionysos was being represented as emasculated; again the record is clear (281). The very emblem of the cult, the thyrsos, a stalk topped with a pinecone, was "phallic" in our sense, and the intimate details of initiatory rites included the disclosure of emblematic phalli as well as models of the phallos later to be carried under one's arm as public parades honored Dionysos (illustrated in Dover 1978 and Keuls 1985).

Failure to worship Dionysos appropriately led — sweet vengeance! —

either to satyriasis or to eunuchism (Kerényi 1976:164, 277). Once again we have to ask what it means to worship an archetypal male figure, to worship a god of the phallos. Imagine an enormous penis the size of Picasso's iron figures in Chicago, or the soaring arc on the St. Louis skyline! Partly, of course, we recognize in such a situation the Christianized Western aversion to the body; but we are also dealing with an inability to comprehend masculinity in any other manifestation than the leather-swathed frontiersman, replete with scabbard knife and rifle (is there something "phallic" in either of those?).

The imagic, imaginal, aspects of phallic representations in antiquity (familiar not only in iconography of Dionysos, but also of Hermes) can remand us back to the element of artistic creativity that unites both Apollo and Dionysos. Apollo creates illusions that make it possible for us to go on living in the presence of ultimate nightmares such as the threat of nuclear annihilation; his realm is especially that of sculpture, "for it is the art of bringing form out of a raw conglomerate" (Eisner 1989:139). And at the same time Dionysos is the god of illusions as well, but in the sense of magical transformations — perhaps most visibly displayed when he is kidnapped by pirates whose boat he causes to be overgrown by grapevines.

The madness derived from the product of the fermented grape was no simple intoxication, nor is male intoxication with life or with sexuality the same as cheap alcoholic stupor, although there are always elements of society who desire a sort of psychedelic baby formula that will bring change and escape from the requirements of the present moment (Corneau 1991:87). The *suddenness* of the Dionysian enthusiasm (literally in Greek an en-godding) is still impressive: "The wonder of Dionysos is that he comes so suddenly [like Hermes — WGD], when all had seemed lost, dead, or at least boring" (Eisner 1989:118). Mass possession is nothing to be treated lightly, and we have already noted the tragedy of the appropriation of Nietzsche's *übermensch* concept by the Nazi regime, but Dionysian religiosity is a group religiosity that has largely been lost to us in the era of Protestant schismatic sects that stress their specific theological differences from other apparently similar sectarian groups. Just what Nietzsche was reacting to — the dangers of groupthink that George Orwell would pillory in *Animal Farm* — touch us today in a different manner. We are less worried about the Organization Men of the 1950s than about the fragmentation of the social communities in which our daily existences are situated. What sort of paradise (a term derived from the Persian term for a walled/boundaried city) awaits us when we are totally unable to enforce corporate commitments to minimal standards of environmental morality?[11]

And what sort of masculinities might be encompassed by Apollonian or Dionysian models today? Well, for one thing, we are not the ancient Greeks, and we are not immediately certain that the mainads (female followers of Dionysos) were wrong. The true madness may be buying into an androcentric world model, leaving the balanced Olympian world for the imbalances of the Soloflexed biceps and pectorals from the local Gold's Gym. It may be a sort of madness that is perfectly appropriate to a generation finally fed up with aggressor status in Vietnams and Iraqs, a generation receptive now to passivity as a normal blessing, not a curse; to death as the natural order of living things (constrasted starkly with the Apollonian mysteries of preservation of physical life at any emotional cost).

Narratives about both Dionysos and Apollo implicate the realms of death. For Dionysos that is a symbolic realm found for instance in the stories about Orpheus. The Orphic Dionysos was a fourth World Ruler (*Kosmokrator*), and Dionysos's realm is assimilated to the realm of death in some of his ritual festivals. Herakleitos proposed that "Hades and Dionysos . . . are one and the same." But how is the irrationality of the reign of Dionysos connected with death . . . and with creativity? Walter Otto's quirky study of Dionysos provides a clue:

> The creative phenomenon must be its own witness. And its testimony has only one meaning: that the human mind cannot become creative by itself, even under the most favorable circumstances, but that it needs to be touched and inspired by a wonderful Otherness; that the efficacy of this Otherness forms the most important part of the total creative process, no matter how gifted men are thought to be. This is what the creative ones have told us in all ages when they appealed to an inspiration which emanated from a higher being. (1965:25–26)

Robert Eisner provides yet another clue: Dionysos is the recovered shaman, the healed healer, in that having been wracked by Hera, and having recovered, he can provide aid to those who call upon him. After Hera drives him mad and he recovers, "Dionysus became the one who sends madness and panic on others; never again is he himself moved by irrational forces: that mania which was once outside him and inflicted upon him has become part of his essential nature" (Eisner 1989:109). Ultimately the Dionysian madness is not illness but health: "the madness which is called Dionysus is no sickness, no debility in life, but a companion of life at its healthiest" (Otto 1965:143). Euripides' *Bakchai* relates what happens when one resists the natural Dionysiac expressiveness of life, the extraversions that counter the introverted Apollonian. Dionysos as *Luaios*/Liberator counters the official Zeus cults that replicate only stereotypical masculinities (Evans 1988:68, 81, 106). Robert Woolger's question remains important: "Why, we may ask, does Dionysos so easily become the focus of projection for the hysterical and sensual shadow of our culture even among scholars and psychologists? Is it precisely because in our Apollonian culture we are *so* ungrounded in our instincts and the feeling function?" (review of Kerényi 1976, *Quadrant*, Summer 1976:97).

In the framework of the contemporary task of reimagining all that we have inherited as traditional, we may consider Guthrie's observation:

> The worship of Dionysos is something which can never be wholly explained. Historical research into his antecedents and the adduction of anthropological parallels have done much, but not all. It is useless to try to account for his nature by an origin in one single functional type, such as that of the vegetation-god. ... *Always there is something more.* (1949:145, my emphasis)

That "something more" is clearly comprised by the paradoxical features we have found characteristic of both Apollo and Dionysos. Paradox and otherness, and

> paradox belongs to the nature of everything that is creative. There is meaning here in the statement that man's most intimate activity is not his own, that an "otherness" allies itself with him in all creation, and that this "otherness" has far more significance than the sum total of everything he instinctively experiences as his own intentions and faculties. (Otto 1965:31)

Such self-awareness is opposed diametrically to narcissism, understood as a refusal to admit that a person's creativity comes from anywhere but one's own powers.

The Dionysian frenzy is prophylactic: it regulates and informs by means of the group what would otherwise be merely individual. It is a collective ecstasy not easily assimilated to the lone wolf Apollonian researcher, but it demands an erotic connection — not necessarily a genital/sexual connection — with the unconscious, with the long-term group, historical, mythological, and religious; in short, with the extended psyche that differentiates human from merely animal consciousness. Instead of the Nietzschean yearning for an eternal return to infantile omnipotence and omniscience in an orgy of (anti-Socratic, anti-institutional) Dionysian experiencing, we have tumbled onto a balancing of now-this, now-that that encompasses both the long range and the immediate; we have sighted a sexuality that does not boast of its single-genderedness but celebrates its duality. We have entered the presence of the raw creativity of the boundary-breaker and the community of followers necessary for long-range social survival ("Dionysian consciousness requires a *thiasos*, a community," Hillman 1972:296). And we have seen that the noble lord of reason, Apollo, is connected with suffering and sacrifice, with the infatuation of falling into loves one would as soon not engage.

René Girard notes that we ought not be misled by the Nietzschean and other traditions that idealized Apollonian restraint, but should remember the tremendous fear with which Apollo was regarded. He should not be regarded primarily as a "particularly benevolent, peaceful, or serene god," a point that Nietzsche overlooks (Girard 1986:46). Similarly Otto cautions against appropriations of Dionysos like Nietzsche's, which failed to recognize "the absolute terror of his reality" (1965:106): "no single Greek god even approaches Dionysos in the horror of his epithets, which bear witness to a savagery that is absolutely without mercy" (113). Such cautions are important to the extent that we live in a time dedicated to experiential immediacy, in a culture that has turned its back on saving for the future as opposed to having it now and faster. Our quest for change seems continuous and ongoing, and we turn to narcotics as to alcohol and nicotine and sugars for the sort of immediacy known earlier in Dionysiac religious experiences (Corneau 1991:87). The borderline experiences become the ordinary, and in light of this chapter we have to ask about the borderline experiences of gender also.

Are Apollonian males a possible model in a time that seeks to transcend earlier limitations on the transcendental and rational? Or can the Dionysian frenzies of the 1960s be recaptured in such ways as to develop now their ongoing psychological insights for contemporary modes of living? Somehow Eisner's comment that Dionysos "is the shadowside of Hades, and vice versa" (1989:119) haunts me. I wonder just how we will configure the Apollonian and Dionysian in 2100, a hundred years hence. Will we have attained any more satisfactory a resolution of what gender identifications mean? Will we have a richer, more satisfactory definition of masculinity and femininity? Or will we be stuck back with the early Nietzsche, seeing only the unbridgeable oppositions represented by the two Greek gods who were, even if only half-brothers, still united by a common family, by a brotherhood that might suggest to the alert observer that their similarities count for more than their differences. The dolphin that is the emblem of both gods flows with the tide, resists becoming only this or that symbol, yet remains an open-ended emblem of future transmogrifications, hence an open-ended sign in many fictions for the possibilities of gendering that are now only faintly imagined.

■ ■ ■ ■ ■

Sources of the Story

Evans 1988 is an engaging essay on Dionysos in the Indo-European and contemporary contexts along with a fresh translation of Euripides' *Bakchai*, one of the most important plays from Greek antiquity in terms of our ability to reconstruct classical religious sensitivities. Nonnos, in his *Dionysiaca* (1940), as late as the sixth century C.E., compiled all the Greek mythological stories about Dionysos he could find.

Bibliography for Further Study

Henrichs 1984 provides a sterling overview of the various attitudes taken in scholarship about Dionysos from the publication of Nietzsche's *Birth of Tragedy* in 1872 down to Girard's *Violence and the Sacred* of 1972. Feder 1980 is excellent as a summary of the Dionysian motif in modern literature. Dionysos was of particular interest to the later Greek tradition, and the account in Apollodoros's Hellenistic handbook, the *Library* (3:4.2–5.3) has the most extensive single account of his widely scattered adventures; I strongly recommend the Simpson 1976 version for this and other mythological summaries.

Chapter 11

Traditional Hero Myths
Confront the New Age

Never have we needed a Hero more than now: when our usual human greed and cowardice are so coupled with the possibility of fatal, final accidents. Never have we needed a miracle more — now that we know there are no miracles; now that we know that it is peace, not war, that "breaks out," and then only occasionally, in film, not in fact, and never Forever After.

A hero. A hero who is not put out to die at his Father's command. A hero who does not abandon his Mother. A hero who does not become his own Father, or an impersonal or dictatorial "Father" to other men. A hero who is not killed by his brothers and then worshiped afterward. A <u>hero such as we've never known: in whose name youth is not cannibalized and broken; a hero in whose name war is never declared, countries are never colonized, people are never enslaved, and women are never raped; a hero in whose time poverty, illiteracy, loneliness and conformity are unheard-of.</u> (Chesler 1978:251)

This penultimate chapter has a different shape because I work here with a representative or typical figure, rather than a specific mythic motif or individual. We might have looked at one hero figure — but which one? There are so many, and they appear in so many cultures, that I'd be hard pressed to say that this or that figure was the most representative hero. Nor can I begin the chapter with the same format I've used previously (Background, Summary), although Joseph Campbell's *The Hero with a Thousand Faces* provides an inclusive summary of elements of the Western heroic model (with characteristic themes or images in parentheses):

The mythological hero, setting forth from his commonday hut or castle, is lured, carried away, or else voluntarily proceeds, to the threshold of adventure. There he encounters a shadow presence that guards the passage. The hero may defeat or conciliate this power and go alive into the kingdom of the dark (brother-battle, dragon-battle; offering, charm) or be slain by the opponent and descend in death (dismemberment, crucifixion). Beyond the threshold, then, the hero journeys through a world of unfamiliar yet strangely intimate forces, some of which severely threaten him (tests), some of which give magical aid (helpers). When he arrives at the nadir of the mythological round, he undergoes a supreme ordeal and gains his reward. The triumph may be represented as the hero's sexual union with the goddess-mother of the world (sacred marriage), his recognition by his father-creator (father atonement), his own divinization (apotheosis), or again — if the powers have remained unfriendly to him — his theft of the boon he came to gain (bride-theft, fire-theft); intrinsically, it is an expansion of consciousness and therewith of being (illumination, transfiguration, freedom). The final work is that of the return. If the powers have blessed the hero, he now sets forth under their protection (emissary); if not, he flees and is pursued (transformation flight, obstacle flight). At the return threshold the transcendent powers must remain behind; the hero re-emerges from the kingdom of dread (return, resurrection). The boon that he brings restores the world (elixir). (245–46, there in italics)[1]

The Traditional Monomyth and Its Problems

According to Campbell's master-myth, Western male heroes break free of the constraints of society in order to prove themselves men through a series of trials. They are usually aided by various insignificant animals or women; they delve into otherwise forbidden territories, even into the underworld; and they bring back from their exploits some quality or material that becomes a boon to the society from which they've fled. In contrast, the contemporary Indiana Jones or the Rocky-type avenger hero familiar from recent American movies seems to operate in a manner antithetical to the achievements of the monomythic hero of tradition. These contemporary figures are not out to get a boon that restores or heals or completes the wounded or incomplete community, but are more likely to settle a personal or national score. Even if it is on behalf of his country, the hero now has to have some direct *emotional* connection; merely exhibiting the social or religious values obtained from education or political idealism no longer suffices. In contrast to the classical hero who restores the broken or threatened community, this recent sort of mass media hero generally operates in opposition to society rather than representing or healing it, and he is more likely to be celebrated for his individual gains rather than for how he helps others by defending an ideal. The emphasis upon the striking out from home or neighborhood and the developing of a strong individuality based upon proving oneself will be familiar to readers and viewers of Campbell's later writings and the several audio- and videotape series.

Campbell's monomyth works well as a pattern for analyzing much traditional literature, even for contemporary materials. It has been applied to the life of John F. Kennedy in some detail, and many advertisements repeat a similar pattern of a defeating problem, magical intervention by a hero, and resolution of the problem. In fact the hero monomyth seems to be an expansion of the fundamental threefold narrative pattern of our culture's literature: *problem, savior, resolution,* or of the phases of our most of our ritual sequences: *preliminal,* preparation and approach; *liminal,* trials and ecstasies; *postliminal,* reintegration of the community. Several years ago Alan Dundes (1990 [1976]) acerbically applied the pattern to the life of Jesus, taking the occasion to chide Christian scholars for not joining the ranks of literary and folklore comparativists generally.

It might be argued that the literary anti-hero figures from authors as diverse as Camus, Ionesco, Genet, Artaud, or even Hemingway already represent a *critique* of this Western monomythic pattern. Indeed Sean O'Faolain (1956) sees precursors in Scott's *Rob Roy* and Fielding's *Tom Jones,* and the picaresque or trickster figure extends back to *Don Quixote,* a figure echoed today in the characters of Thomas Pynchon, Carlos Fuentes, or J. G. Ballard. But a full-scale attack was mounted only in 1989 in the section of Robin Morgan's *The Demon Lover* dedicated to excoriating Campbell's views as representative of the masculine dominance responsible for most of what's wrong with Western culture. "The terrorist mystique is twin brother to the manhood mystique, and the mythic father of both is the hero. The terrorist has charisma *because* he is the technological-age manifestation of the hero." The hero myth makes any act of violence "not only possible but inevitable: the rapist is transformed into the seducer, the tyrant rules by divine right, the terrorist reconstitutes the hero" (56).

According to Morgan, Campbell's own work on the hero is ruled by three central misperceptions: first, he ignores the fact that every culture is ethnocentric, its heroes unable to move people beyond that condition; second, he argues wrongly that a universalized hero will be able, as merely local figures are not, to bring world peace; and third, the androcentricism revealed in his language and in his choice of males for 90 percent of his examples erases the experience of over half of the human race. Arguing the feminist point that material, embodied differences ought never be displaced by spiritualistic abstractions, Morgan finds that the thousand-faced hero ultimately wears only the single artificial face of the monomythic male and ignores the embodied differences of actual historical-material experience. Such a figure promises only inappropriate psychic inflation to your average Joe, who ignores the suffering in the streets as he clicks through the TV channels.

Another profile has been documented, that of the international terrorists themselves: they are overwhelmingly single males, about twenty-two to twenty-five years of age, the children of middle-class professionals, about two-thirds of them educated at the university level. Many are extremely ideological or religious, many place great weight on the achievements of the sciences, and many survived early-childhood traumas by developing a Manichean vision of the universe in which issues are simplistically either wholly good or wholly bad. Morgan's implication is that the developing-adolescent hero pattern of the monomyth mirrors the normal profiles of terrorists.

We can be grateful to Morgan and others for exposing *the shadowy side* of the hero, the dark dualistic patriarchial side that seeks domination of every living thing and stresses only "prowess, competition, and strength exercised for the exclusion of others for political, social, and economic control"; I am quoting Gregory Vogt, whose *Return to Father* (1991) attempts to recover a Positive Patriarch beyond the dualistic figures that have held sway for so long. As malfunctional a picture of the traditional hero model as Morgan's is presented in another book, Mark Gerzon's *A Choice of Heroes* (1982), which is a solid, important study of American models of masculinity. Until now every American generation has faced war, and since participation in warfare confirmed one's status as a man, men for generations have had imprinted upon them the equation of warrior-hood and man-hood. Gerzon notes that that equation has skewed masculinity toward aggressiveness, since soldiers must learn to repress fear and concern for others, who are generalized into "the enemy." Treated as the most dispensable commodity in warfare, the male soldier develops an armoring shell against vulnerability, sensitivity, and compassion. The soldier quickly learns that emotions should be restricted to patriotism and anger — the berserker qualities that were certainly functional when protohistoricals clobbered one another, but are now merely liabilities as an increasingly internationalized world calls for cooperation and mutual understanding.

Amur-i-kun Heroes

No wonder, Gerzon observes, that the very character traits that both women's and men's liberation movements have urged us to abandon as no longer healthy — toughness, aggressiveness, insensitivity — seem "naturally" what our culture expects males/warriors to exhibit (35) and that "we have sacrificed other traits — gentleness, openness, softness — because they were liabilities, not assets, in war. We have left them to women" (34). Just such oppositions between women's and men's "appropriate" behaviors underlie the roots of the American psyche's identification of true masculinity as what is exemplified by *the conquering hero* rather than, say, *the competent politician*.

Indeed Ronald Reagan, who stated that he was "a sucker for hero worship" (*Tuscaloosa News*, 8 May 1985), focused his 1981 inaugural address on the heroism of Martin Treptow, a World War I soldier killed in action. Repeatedly in his speeches Reagan recounted emotional stories about American heroes instead of formulating substantive steps toward changes in the runaway society that he and other conservatives seem to regard as hopeless. His successor George Bush felt that as Presidential Hero he hardly needed to confer with the elected Congress before killing over three hundred thousand people in the Persian Gulf. Political commentators have suggested that his astonishing public militarism was fabricated by his political advisors to overcome an impression that he had appeared too (womanishly) sensitive for an American president.

The most thoroughgoing treatment of American heroic mythology (and American ways of treating myth generally) remains Jewett and Lawrence's *The American Monomyth* (1989), referred to in Chapter 9. These authors suggest that the American version of the traditional monomyth represents a shift from emphasis on the maturation of the traditional people's-hero in initiation rites to religious tales of redemption by an extraordinary savior. Hence the American monomyth represents a secularizing of Judeo-Christian redemption dramas, the new hero figure becoming a replacement for the Christ figure of traditional Christianity.[2] Such a figure is motivated not by the *quest for self* of the classical monomyth, but a sort of *selflessness:* he operates outside the traditional context of the established social community. And he is typically a frontiersman-defender of that idealized Garden of Eden thought to lie behind the Main Street of every Midwestern town — although the Noble Frontier imagery was essentially a post-1940s myth designed to justify America's increasing socio-political interventions abroad.

An outsider, the American monomythic hero seldom achieves sexual satisfaction, or at any rate he doesn't achieve the *hieros gamos* (the sacred marriage of ritual) or produce offspring, but rides off grandly into the stunning Western sunset. He's an outsider who intervenes to help the community repel other outside agitators; more recently he's been an apocalyptic champion of the local community against the monster state or national government, or in Rambo-form, manages to get even for slights to his government in unwinnable battles, or conquers his loss of self-esteem at returning from Southeast Asia and finding that he's considered no hero-warrior at all, but a miserable warmonger despised by a liberalized, now anti-war society. Susan Jeffords documents (1989) how films in the post–Vietnam War period sought desperately to re-masculinize American society, reflecting or causing the outbreak of militarism that directly supported the enormous defense budgets of Reagan and the early years of the Bush administration.

Jewett and Lawrence worry about American monomythicism because they see it typifying the ethical dualism by which evil is denied in oneself and projected outward onto shadow figures. The enemy is considered so powerful that only a strong savior-leader or a posse of lawbreaking vigilantes can counter it: nearly any Western movie will provide examples, and there are many manifestations of this sort of myth-making as it is expressed repeatedly in historical novels and popular legend. But I want to reaffirm the importance of such mass-mediations of our underlying heroic ideals and models: the symbolic language of folk tales, legends, and myths is always significant far beyond any rational or historical argument — try convincing children that their peers' hero/ine models might be maladaptive in the long run, or persuading an American police worker to relinquish the almighty firearm, monomythically sanctified in countless Western movies. Precisely because we live in a society where we are conscious of the many manipulations of semiotic values for purely commercial and nationalist ends, we need to remain alert to the human ethical values conveyed by *Star Wars* or *Death Wish* or *The Exterminator*, and they are hardly those of peaceful dialogue or sensitive attention to the positions of the other side.

Postmodern Polymythic Heroes

From looking at dimensions of the heroic *mono* myth, the shift here is to the heroic *poly* myths that increasingly characterize our own day, from the singular heroic standard to the multiple diversities that confront anyone trying to describe "the" hero today. To be sure there are still elements of the traditional monomyth that are highly influential in our society, as one might document by means of rhetorical analyses of political campaigns in which each candidate tries to outdo the others in masculinity. But I have found it increasingly difficult to comprehend all the shadings of literary and filmic heroes under the restrictive categories of the monomyth. I suggest that we turn instead to the postmodern experience of multiplicity and plurality that frequently leaves us puzzling just what sort of hero/ines we have just read about or seen on the screen: Is the main character of *My Private Idaho*, with his epileptic seizures, part-friendships, and apparent defeat at the end of the movie, *a hero?* In what sense?

Or the protagonist of *Blue Velvet*, whose voyeurism almost does him in? Its "heroine," who sometimes saves the "hero," yet is the subjugated moll of the evil doper? Or T., the multi-named hero of Ballard's *The Atrocity Exhibition*, whose very name changes (always beginning with the letter *T:* Travis, Trabert, Talbot . . .) from chapter to chapter, in a novel focused upon his psychotic breakdown? And what about the figure of David Wojnarowicz, autobiographically remaking himself vis-à-vis street life, drugs, AIDS, homosexuality, and politics in *Close to the Knives: A Memoir of Disintegration?* Or Roger, in Paul Monette's remarkable bestseller reflecting on the death of his lover, *Borrowed Time: An AIDS Memoir* (1988)?

But instead of pursuing the unique qualities of postmodern hero figures, I want here to suggest that we reflect upon some of the ways the heroic figure can be recognized today. When teaching hero/ine workshops I use a typology that contains over thirty items or types, but even that typology will doubtless become more complex as our fictions/lives shape and are shaped by the culture of the twenty-first century. Obviously there are the frontier/cowboy hero, the professional athlete or bodybuilder; but also today the avenger hero who gets even for injustice, the sensitive hero (as in *Dances with Wolves*), the martyr-hero (such as Oliver North, regarded from the hawkish perspective, or Ralph Nader or Morris Dees, regarded from a leftist orientation). And what we might term the postmodern anti-hero, the figure who finds within himself the energy to regulate his life in a way that goes against the grain of the society — Richard Ford's *Sportswriter* provides an excellent example.

The celebrity hero is prominent, a hero manufactured by the entertainment industry and mass communications media, and abandoned by them just as quickly; and there are financial whizzes such as Donald Trump. Politicians and religious leaders (where does Martin Luther King, Jr., fit?); even intellectual and professional heroes such as Robert Coles, Linus Pauling, Marshall MacLuhan; physicians, scientists, technological heroes such as the astronauts. Entertainers and musicians, even soap-opera starlets and hunks. The list goes on and on, but it is a list even richer in variety of appearance than the many faces of the hero in Campbell's influential book.

My initial typology grows from year to year as the hero/ines multiply in accord with our increasingly fragmented and multiply-oriented existences: all we learned about the rigid progression toward "normal maturation" through adolescence to young adulthood now shatters upon the panopticon of multi-channel cable TV where one can see portrayals of any conceivable level of immaturity or type of behavior. Taught to take charge of our own destinies, we escape monomythic sameness by switching to another channel, cancel one subscription for another, leave one career for its opposite (not always voluntarily), relinquish moral commitment by moving to a different suburb, reprogram the psyche by joining a different affinity group, drop one charity for one whose hit-people call less frequently.

Such a list merely articulates the polyphasic/polymythic nature of contemporary culture; it seems less and less likely that any traditional monomyth can begin to encompass the recent transformations of the hero/ine pattern. In fact the plural contexts of many contemporary lives are so distant from any earlier sense of shared social experience that we ought now, finally, to recognize why so many young minds are bored by the monomythic sameness, having been trained by television's constantly changing commercial breaks to consume anything *but* sameness or tradition. How could our psyche-models remain Tom-Sawyerishly the same after *Twin Peaks* or the Persian Gulf or Nixon's resignation?

Furthermore we need to challenge the dependence of our culture upon what are almost overwhelmingly *adolescent* hero materials. Campbell notes that the traditional hero path he charts with such verve and insight is a model *for the adolescent.* One wonders then if the traditional hero model so widely celebrated in America isn't something that is no longer appropriate for adults. How can it be that so much of our mass entertainment (with its Cowboy or Vice Squad or Ninja Assassin) apparently is fixated at a *teenage* level of development? Campbell proposed that the hero "evolves as the culture evolves" (1988:135), but unfortunately he did not show us what he meant by that remark, nor did he develop adequately the corresponding monomyth of the evolved *heroine.*

One sort of evolution would be a re-visioning of the hero toward more psychological and mystical directions. Perhaps attention to something like the various metaphysical levels (*padmas* or *chakras*) articulated in Kundalini Yoga might help us to rise beyond the needs and concerns of the adolescent-hero: Campbell observes that only the first three of the seven chakras have to do with the development of hero strengths, but in order to reach more adult stages of development, the higher chakras require the sacrifice of the hero-form itself (1974:490). The goal of every yoga/religion is to go into the ultimate zones of what Buddhists term the Mother Light, the mystical experience, not merely as part of the bliss of the individual, but as participation in the ultimate society. A new heroicism on this model would strengthen the planetary, not the individual ego; it would involve not merely fighting the demons of constricting institutionalism but those of the egoic denial of others that often characterizes the pop-psychology or pop-spirituality leaders who blithely tout the universalism of Joseph Campbell. Homophobic phantoms still mitigate against comfort with same-sex relationships, and even the well-intentioned male has to work very hard to learn the feminist mode of governing by consensus.

Where we need most help today is in finding hero/ines whose selves consciously unfold *from* the supportive community, not solar heroes who strike out *against* the community (now seen as "the Other"), as their first proof of manhood. And we need help in defining the very postmodern community itself: Is it any longer possible to conceive of an ongoing community in any traditional sense? A community in which one is born, lives, dies, in continuity with the historical traditions of the past and their anticipations of the future? Which future? Oriented toward which heroic longings? If, as I suggested earlier, the postmodern *means change,* it means harkening to changes so fundamental as to make traditional forms of "community" meaningless — as in the postmodern economic concept of *teletopical* statehood, a condition in which reality is based upon international electronic circulation of funds: "It's not simply a locality in the old sense of what would constitute a state" (Ronell 1991:145); one must let go of the concept that "the state is the site or locus for realizing or fulfilling the need for community," and hence we have to face comprehensively the issue of *where* the community or state exists today, where the "polis" of the political lies, and how hero/oines appropriate to the new forms of community may be modeled.

New Hero/ine Modeling

In the light of the problems raised by media manipulation of ideological models and by apparently dysfunctional aspects of the traditional Western hero model, and gathering all the categories represented today as heroic ideals, we might develop an inclusive typology and then set about to critique each type. But what seems most useful here is to look first at new models of the heroine, at what may be called *women's new-quest models.* Carol Christ's 1980 work on spiritual quests developed in fiction and poetry by five women writers (Kate Chopin, Margaret Atwood, Doris Lessing, Adrienne Rich, and Ntozake Shange) broke new ground in suggesting that an orientation characteristic of women's experience was grounded in an experience of nothingness, and moved on through mystical experience and identification, to a new naming of self and reality: "women's quest is for a wholeness in which the oppositions between body and soul, nature and spirit or freedom, rationality and emotion are overcome" (26).

And in her survey of fiction written by British and American women, Annis Pratt (1991) has distinguished several stages in the "social quest" aspect of the female hero, comprised of the Experience of the Green World (a longing for nature), leaving the parental household, finding a non-patriarchal fantasy lover, the Rape Trauma, Enclosure in Patriarchy (the threat of conformity to marital and other gender norms), and Completion of the Quest, with its Achievement of Erotic and Vocational Wholeness. The second half of the heroine's journey likewise has several stages: Persona Rejection (growing dissatisfaction with the social roles forced upon her), Encountering the Shadow (a socially conformist figure, even a horrific male partner, such as the gynophobic "horrible husband"), coming to terms with and transcending family ties, reconnection with nature, the Green World Lover who serves as an initiatory guide, acceptance of the Maternal Archetype, and finally the Return to Society. Attaining the social quest, and "filled with sexual pleasure, competence, self-love, and courage, the female hero is now a Crone, or Wise Woman" (217).

Others have developed additional aspects of the newly identified heroine-quest. A key essay by Mara Donaldson (1987) focuses upon the difference between Campbell's monomythic pattern for male heroes and the heroines of both Margaret Atwood and Maxine Hong Kingston. Instead of the arrogant young journeyman who returns humbled of his pride, the sort of heroine Donaldson points to likewise experiences separation, initiation, and return, "but her personal transformation is from self-negation to self-affirmation, from lack of pride to self-pride," that is, from playing a supportive ego-negating role "to an ego-self which is separate and independent from the expectations of others" (106). Since so much of the male pattern was determined by Augustinian teachings about sin as pridefulness, women may have double difficulty following a heroine path that promotes full self-assertion.

But then another comment on the work of Atwood, one of the novelist-poets whom Christ treats, by Estella Lauter (1984), suggests that "what is finally mythologized in Atwood's poems is the possibility of *altering* myths that are so basic that we can scarcely dream of existence without them." In fact, according to Lauter the cycle of Atwood's Circe/Mud Poems "is part of a long process of rearranging the elements of the quest myth into a shape which may finally negate the idea of questing, as we now understand it, in order to embrace an idea of self-acceptance and relationship quite different from the traditional ideal of self-transcendence and attainment perpetuated by the [male] quest" (77).

Later in her book Lauter highlights a number of "trouble spots" for women in Western mythology that particularly challenge traditionally conceived visions of (masculine) heroics:

> the emphasis on the masculine in our images of God; the confinement of the mother to the realm of intimate relationships; the emphasis on the seductress in every woman; the definition of creativity in terms of a heroic (masculine) quest; the identification of woman with nature to the detriment of both; the assumption that woman is the guardian of love; the hierarchical arrangement of the species, as if the ladder were the most "natural" principle of relationship; and the dichotomizing tendencies of our language and thought, as if it were really true that "without contraries there is no progression," or as if "progression" were the only viable option. (1980:204)

And finally we may mention Maureen Murdock's attempt (1990) to work out a monomyth of the heroine's journey in which ten stages move (clockwise, not counterclockwise, as Campbell's do) from Separation from the Feminine, through Identification with the Masculine, Finding the Boon of Success, Initiation and Descent to the Goddess, Healing the Mother/Daughter Split, and others, leading finally to Integration of Masculine and Feminine. Quite in contrast to the emphasis upon *linear* progression identified by Lauter in the previous quotation, Murdock emphasizes the *circularity* of typical women's imagery, particularly as the shape of her monomythic pattern itself is circular or non-dualistic; the emphasis is not upon this/the other world, up/down, as in the classical monomyth, but upon the inclusion of the natural order, or the secular *and* the sacred, upon linking and collaborating rather than dominating, and in general transcendence of the gender dualism that has marked Western thought.

Reclaiming the Lunar Hero

Long-term cultural models are now exhausted, and hence, in Murdock's words, "the old story is over," implying that a new story has begun, or is about to begin, as demonstrated by these examples of remythologizing *heroine* mythologies. And perhaps there are changes possible for the *hero* mythologies as well: one of the first indications of the change deals with reaching beyond the masculinist/macho hero, specifically beyond the *solar* to the *lunar* hero archetype, as we saw toward the conclusion of Chapter 9. Roger Woolger's article "Death and the Hero" suggests that the traditional hero's major task "is no less than the total transformation of the old order of things, which has become degenerate and is in need of renewal" (1978:37); he must first of all overcome the deadly power of the maternal through his striving, effort, fighting, overcoming — all the elements belonging to competitive Western individualism.

In our forward-looking culture, turning from the upward path of brightness means to "fall" into the darkness of failure and depression — into the valley of the feminine soul (anima), which is resolutely embodied and *social*. Jung rather than Freud helped the West recognize the importance of the Dark Night of the Soul, the Night Sea Journey, as it is frequently represented in religious mythology, although Jung like Freud stressed the development of heroic feats of the individual ego who could overcome it.

Rationality or domination, spiritual enlightenment — the "solar" — characterizes this sort of strong egoic hero, but Woolger argues for reclaiming the importance of the "lunar," stressing the importance of the themes of "suffering, passion, and willing union with death" (47). Passivity, then, is not necessarily only a feminine trait, but a "heroic" valence as well, and at this point in our culture it might balance the overweening aggressivity and dominance of the traditional solar hero: "Lunar heroic figures like Ishtar/Inanna and Persephone, in their entirely passive and unassertive descents into the underworld, are ... the cultural compensations for the overly hybristic drive of the solar, conquering heroes" (46).

And the same author hints suggestively that "the whole range of 'dying gods' (Tammuz, Attis, Adonis, Osiris, Dionysus, Christ)," figures treated by classical psychology as being insufficiently differentiated from the Mothers, might more properly "be seen as a *superior* stage of psycho-spiritual development, since in their androgynous and sacrificial nature they incorporate both the solar and lunar modes and transcend them in death" (47, 48). They disclose not the necessity of overcoming the feminine or one's natural instincts generally, but the importance of "*the sacrifice of the ego itself* to a higher spiritual principle," that is, to the principle known in Jungian psychology as the archetype of the Self — a complex figure containing all opposites and represented by only a few historical figures such as Jesus. Thus we are reminded of the importance of passivity and allowing things to happen, as Woolger articulates all too briefly something of the heroism of not-doing that is already familiar in much of Eastern psychological, religious, and philosophical thought.

This is a highly symbolic use of language, but important in its re-visioning of some of the gender associations to which we've become unconscious. The lunar and solar polarity has been discussed also by Howard Teich, who notes how *solar* has usually been represented as masculine in the West, *lunar* as feminine, and the qualities associated with each likewise gendered: "Those qualities associated with 'solar psychology' — clarity, willfulness, competitiveness, endurance — have been labeled 'masculine.' The 'lunar' qualities — tenderness, recep-tivity, intuitiveness, compassion, emotional availability — conversely have been designated 'feminine'" (1991:124; see also Teich 1993) across Western thought, although prior to the ascendency of patriarchal traditions, the majority of mythologies considered the overarching *so-lar* principle to be feminine, and vice versa (a typical representation is of the blue, female Nut arching her body over that of the green, recumbent, masculine Geb, in Egyptian iconography).

In many mythological *twin heroes* the solar and lunar form a com-posite whole. However, "the sacrifice or suppression of the Lunar Twin runs so deep in our culture that most of us are unaware that nearly every central male hero was originally a Twin" (128). For many of us today, as individuals, the lunar twin has been submerged into the dark, inferior "shadow" of the personality and can be recognized only when it is pro-jected onto others; hence "men tend to project their Lunar Twin onto other men, seeing it as 'effeminate' and 'homosexual'" (129). Only when the lunar side of the heroic personality can affect the solar is the combined twinship able "to experience the mysterious, numinous qualities of his being" (129); and the connection to the spiritual is very clear in images such as the Egyptian Hawk/Horus, who when powerfully transformed, sees with purified vision out of both his moon eye and his sun eye. The Navajo Hero Twins, as we saw in Chapter 9, likewise combine these traits.

If indeed the Western masculine God/Hero concept is breaking down, we may well need to rediscover images of more holistic personality in the lunar-solar Twins. Reconnection with the masculine lunar hero may help us correct the over-identification with the solar hero- ics that have led (arguably) to the brutal nightmares of our century. Our situation invokes careful naming of the same-sex double who appears not as a foreign, extraneous heroic image, but as a companion, a complement to our ordinary sense of self.

Mitchell Walker's creative essay of 1976, cited earlier, deals with the "double," the powerful helper of one's dreams and fantasies, the figure who appears "with an aura of beauty, youth, and perfection or near-perfection," and facilitates a sense of rapport with the world, as well as a sense of self-love and self-confidence. It is not necessarily a homosexual archetype, although in a homophobic culture such as our own, it will receive negative projections if not recognized appropriately. Then even male friendships will be treated with a suspicion they hardly deserve, the supportive embrace suspected, and the attempt to connect honestly with another male treated guardedly. But then we lack the sorts of etiquettes of friendships that guided men in previous eras, and it would be useful to redevelop them for our own time, and I argue elsewhere the importance of organizing guidelines for male-male friendships into a discipline or athletics of friendship (Doty 1993c). We need an aesthetics of male bonding that is not necessarily erotic-sexual but compassion- ate and mentoring and creatively and enjoyably egalitarian. Such an aesthetics will include attention to the connecting and reconnecting of fathers and sons, to mentoring and friendships at work; it will recount and learn from literary accounts and artistic representations, as well as from the human sciences of sociology and psychology.

The Gentle Warriors of the New Age

Writers from New Age orientations quickly reinforce the ideal of the "gentle warrior," and several of the journals appealing to "the new spirituality" today have had features on reconceiving ways of being a masculine hero in our time. The model is generally a "softer" hero who is likely to be involved with shared parenting, who has learned to nurture expression of his own emotional side and to support the full maturation and independence of his mate. Repeatedly such personality development is named by the apparent oxymoron "gentle warrior," or sometimes just "the new warrior," who has undergone "mind-body" training. Such a figure will have faced his own weaknesses and in particular those negative aspects usually projected outward onto others. He will have learned to deal responsibly with anger and physical or emotional violence, especially that passed along in his own family; and he will have learned that being vulnerable results in being receptive to more aspects of the human experience than it is possible to experience when defensively guarded or heavily armored.

Generally the term "warrior" is being reclaimed by a number of voices from its customary association with crass brutality and mayhem. Richard Heckler, akido master, psychologist, and author of *In Search of the Warrior Spirit* (1990), claims that "a true warrior is oriented toward life and creativity, not death and destruction" (Miller 1990:12). Features of the martial arts wisdom Heckler preaches include discipline, orderliness, integrity, service, selflessness, and moral courage. And the Tibetan Buddhist teacher Chögyam Trungpa, Rinpoche, in his *Shambhala: The Sacred Path of the Warrior* (1984), specifically works against traditional definitions: "Warriorship here does not refer to making war on others. Aggression is the source of our problems, not the solution. Here the word 'warrior' is taken from the Tibetan *pawo*, which literally means 'one who is brave' "; "the point of warriorship is to become a gentle and tamed human being who can make a genuine contribution to this world" (8, 98). The warrior is "sensitive to every aspect of phenomena — sight, smell, sound, feelings. He appreciates everything that goes on in his world as an artist does"; he is meek, perky, outrageous, and inscrutable, a family person who avoids ambition and frivolity, a person who learns "to rest in a complete state of simplicity . . . egolessness," and one who understands that it is not the extraordinary hero tale but the ordinary daily reality that usually offers training for the "continual journey" of warriorship, which is "to learn to be genuine in every moment" (42, 47, 48).

Neither a Buddhist practitioner nor a devotee of the Naropa Institute (which the Rinpoche founded), I am often impatient with the quietism if not ethical naiveté of Trungpa's teachings, but the characteristics of the new warrior he advocates do typify many of the New Age teachings about the hero-warrior, and their simplifications. I find just such simplification in Robert Moore and Douglas Gillette's *King, Warrior, Magician,*

Lover (1990). A more satisfactory set of models is found in Carol Pearson's *The Hero Within* (1989) in an emphasis that the various stages
of the hero pathways charted can be approached as a three-dimensional
spiral across which an individual may progress on now this, now that
level — a model more appropriate than Campbell's monomyth with its
apparent lockstep progression. But then Pearson's flexibility seems natural insofar as "what we imagine immediately when we think of the
hero really is only one heroic archetype: the Warrior," and "in our culture, the heroic ideal of the Warrior has been reserved for men — usually
only white men at that" (1989:1–2). So Pearson sets out explicitly to
counter the Campbell-ian model, the elitist myth from which women,
working-class men, and minority men easily feel excluded.

Six primary archetypal manifestations of the hero are sketched in
the *The Hero Within*: "The Innocent lives in the prefallen state of grace;
the Orphan confronts the reality of the Fall.... The Wanderer begins
the task of finding oneself apart from others," and so forth. In Pearson's
later *Awakening the Heroes Within* (1991), the six hero figures are expanded to twelve (Caregiver, Seeker, Destroyer, Lover, Creator, Ruler,
Sage, and Fool, are added, with Wanderer and Martyr disappearing),
now accompanied by such trivializing suggestions as "You can literally
ask the archetype to come into your life" and elaborate charts and scor-
ing devices that make the whole enterprise look like pop-psychology's
self-help blather, but I appreciate the fact that Pearson recognizes the
complexity of including both the positive and negative sides and does
not allow the types to rigidify, as Campbell's monomyth did in many
secondary studies.

It seems a long way from the elevated figures of Campbell's heroes
to the flow charts and numerical scores of Pearson's handbooks, but I
cannot complain too much if such works (and those of Bolen) ultimately
draw attention to the major thematics of our civilization by asking that
we heed more carefully the hero/ine modeling that too often remains
implicit, trivialized, or ignored. For my own part, I would add as well
outrageous science fiction and fantasy such as C. J. Cherryh's *The Kiff
Strike Back*, which casts women in the important interstellar leadership positions because males are so prone to go berserk under pressure,
demonstrating the obvious, that men are indeed the weaker gender!

From Yesterday's to Today's Hero/ines

One other exploration of hero modeling remains to be mentioned, that
by Mark Gerzon, whose probing denunciation (in *A Choice of Heroes*,

205 of our culture's militarism expressed in traditional warrior imagery

1982) of our culture's militarism expressed in traditional warrior imagery was cited earlier. Gerzon is clear that *the nuclear age we live in*, willy-nilly, *"has shifted the meaning of heroism.* If we annihilate ourselves, it will not be because we were cowards. It will be because we were still trying to be *yesterday's heroes"*; "we should not be worried if masculinity is changing. We should be worried if it were not" (1982:43, 7, my emphasis). True heroism involves "the courage to explore oneself deeply and to act with self-awareness"; and to do that adequately, new models of heroism will be constantly evolving as the culture changes. Given our cultural framework, such models will probably continue to be models of masculine heroism, but not just what Gerzon calls "yesterday's heroes."

Figures such as those Gerzon chronicles from the past — the Frontiersman, Soldier, and Lord — give way to emerging models, but "unlike the old archetypes, which were for men only, the emerging masculinities are not. They are, in fact emerging humanities" (262; "humanities" meaning, of course, non-gendered ways of being human). Already there are models that "transcend sexual identity," namely those of the Healer, Companion, Mediator, Colleague, and Nurturer, and they are based less on traditional models than on contemporary reflection and experience (237). The Healer is particularly relevant with respect to the ecological nightmare we seem so easily to ignore; the Companion is situated in the post-feminist shared-Breadwinner household; the Mediator has to do with the avoidance of violence instead of the enthrallment of the Soldier; the Colleague with mentoring and sharing instead of competition between Experts; and the Nurturer with Erik Erikson's concept of generativity — aiding the creativity of others — rather than with the self-aggrandizement of the traditional capitalist.

Models of tomorrow's hero/ine figures developing today reflect the complexities of our contemporary experience. No single hero/ine model can do justice to all the historical experiences, or personality types, or even the abilities now mapped by learning theorists.[3] Nor can any single developmental model encompass all the ways of knitting together our experiences and our abilities into unique individual holisms. Perhaps Jean Clift and Wallace Clift are on the right track, in their book about hero figures in dreams (1988), in suggesting that instead of following a single hero journey, each of us goes on many hero/ine journeys during a lifetime (or maybe "during each year").

The various new figures need elaboration, and the hero journey of today is not supplied with trail markers since the new trails are still being cleared. Holographically seen, the trails overlap and cross one another endlessly; holistically regarded, the trails to be defined are but part of the overall moral dilemma interfacing the contemporary world. That dilemma does not consist of gender enactment alone, or of any simple manner of charting self-improvement. It is the dilemma of survival, moral survival, in a world for which we are responsible. The hero/ines of tomorrow will take responsibility for the needs of justice and equality among citizens of an interconnected global society, the likes of which we are only beginning to imagine.

Our need is not for a hero monomyth, but for models of spiraling paths undertaken as part of the training for the politics and nurturing of the commonweal, and on which each of our many intelligences enables us to nurture now this, now that dimension of the common life. Perhaps "hero/ine" can become the adult model once again, a model not of self-aggrandizement but of community-enhancement, a model in which the maleness or the femaleness of the heroic figure no longer matters very much, a model realized not in exclusion but in inclusion, not domination but cooperation, growing together rather than towering over. The Proto-Indo-European root of hero is *ser-, to protect, cognate with *servant:* maybe we need to go all the way back to this linguistic beginning in order to recognize that *hero* need not mean merely one who struggles heroically for one's own desires.

Chapter 12

Where Do We Go from Here?

I suggest to the new men to form antirape squads (as women did back in 1972), interfere when you hear a cry for help, male or female. Don't be just a "consumer" of yet another fashionable living room topic, "the men's movement." Make it a real movement; don't let it be just a workshop cult for the few. Reach out to your poorer men's groups. Formulate ideas that can attract the black and yellow and brown and red men as well. Manifest men's centers, where courses are free. Manifest marches against violence, battle the "Shadow Man" openly and tame/absorb him. This is truly your challenge. Your sisters and mothers and lovers depend on your full awakening. We have waited for you so long! (Budapest 1992:90)

At no point have I thought to speak for all men or to presume any normative definition of masculinity. That would go against the entire tenor of the book; several chapters include open-ended questions that are not merely rhetorical devices, but honest seekings (question is from the Latin *quaestus*, to seek or ask) that evoke readers' experiences and knowledge alongside my own. Remembering the significance to my own life work of encountering feminist thought, and aware of how I have learned to consider whatever I produce through feminist perspectives, I wonder if twenty years from now a corresponding "new masculine" perspective will be identifiable, and if it will have produced such a fundamental social and intellectual reconceiving of our past and ourselves as feminism did, somewhat along the lines of what I sketched in Chapter 2. (Twenty years is not so long a period: a faculty member at Colgate tells me that twenty years after the university went co-educational, older male faculty still talk about how different it is to have women on the campus!)

As I finished the manuscript, a long conversation with a journal editor who keeps track of what is transpiring across the many branches of the men's movements reminded me of the extraordinary fervor with which an anti-feminist animus is being expressed within parts of that

207

movement. I find it tragic and ironic that feminism generally would be cast into a male-hating position. To be sure, simplistic equation of feminism with an anti-male perspective is represented at the fringes of the women's movements, and I have experienced it myself more than once, but it is never an equation made by the most important voices. Sometimes I wonder if people equating women as a whole with male-baiting have any experience whatsoever with the various voices of feminism or associated critiques — Emmanuel Reynaud, for instance, who reminds us of the significance of what has been learned over the last twenty-some years. In particular we ought to remember that the setting up of the two genders in strict opposition is very problematic:

> one of the achievements of the feminist movement is to have shown that the antagonism between the sexes, far from being limited to conflicts between isolated individuals, is part of a well-defined social structure — patriarchy. Thus the categories "man" and "woman" are not simply entities which could be tinkered with in order to solve the problem of oppression; they are the product and the instrument of patriarchal power. (1983:7)

What seems most discouraging is that males and females still might distrust each other today so much that such false, know-nothing misconceptions could arise.

My pro-feminist, gay-affirmative posture is in no manner anti-male, nor do I find other serious, mainstream writers trashing men today, even when the common enemy is indeed a patriarchal despotism that ought not remain viable in a world that has changed so much since it began to be the dominant cultural value (the "hegemonic," to use a postmodernist term I appreciate, but have tried to avoid in this book). It saddens me that within the men's movements there are currents that bend any particular contribution into corners identified as anti- or pro-this-or-that instead of hearing fully and fairly what such contributions have to offer to us all. On the other hand, I am clear about where I am coming from, namely, a long-term appreciation of feminist thought in which I have learned when to shut up and when to acknowledge what massive achievements feminist advocates have brought to the self-consciousness of the human enterprise. My primary docket is where we go from here, not possible sidetracks that lead to nowhere, and the positions I've taken here remain those I'd defend against those whose lack of historical and political perspective leaves them supposing that "pro-male" advocates have suddenly discovered positions never before conceived.

■■■

A comment in a friend's essay on contemporary American poetry has accompanied the revisions of this book: Hank Lazer writes about the danger of the poet remaining in the realm of what an audience might be expecting; he suggests that the standard claim that the good poet is the one who can speak to everyone is now dead in the water (1990:521). Instead of looking as readers for materials that speak to us *as we are*, Lazer suggests, when faced with a particular work that strikes us as strange, we ought to try to become those to whom the work is not strange. Such an imaginative exercise is important alongside the mythic revisionings in this book, because it has to do with learning to appreciate difference, with retraining our receptors — whether for contemporary poetry or for figures of mythical antiquity.

Where we have come from is tied to where we are headed: the two directions are inescapably linked in language, metaphor, image, narrative, and experience. We need to train our capacity to become receptors with broadened imaginations, and with a desire for another, different, poem or book next time. "Education by difference," Lazer's term, will have us scouting out not the works cheaply reprinted and widely available because their authors sell well, but the chap books and small-press publications that are often going against the mainstream. We will be reading the tradition anew and aslant, exploring not the familiar engendered cultural productions but those that open up and challenge gender specifications and restrictions, and such contemporary works will often be by gay and lesbian poets, minority voices, African American or Native American writers. An obvious next step here would be to examine contemporary representations of masculinity in fiction, poetry, and the arts, a project that will need many hands; a volume of essays edited by Steve Craig (*Men, Masculinity, and the Media*, 1992) demonstrates how few analytical tools have been developed sufficiently, but its contributors also point out important directions for future research.

Customary shapes of masculinity no longer seem "naturally" self-evident when one has viewed them from a wide range of competing definitions of masculinity. Myths no longer seem so cut and dried when explored from the perspectives of contemporary issues and different cultures. And heroes become nothing but celebrities when they turn into merely repetitive examples of media hype. The revisioning called for by this book sends one out the door with rich resources already present across the cultural traditions represented in myths and traditional images. Such images are not exhausted and ready for the

210 · Toward New Heroes and Heroines

junk heap, as a society focused only on the most recent might suppose, but readily available for reinterpretation and utilization in newly appropriate fashions. But we have to re-member them carefully, and avoid the problematic ways in which they have been used earlier to sustain a hierarchy of privilege based on an assumption of masculine superiority.

The destination of such cultural revisionings is less clear today than it has been for centuries in the West; we only know that social and technological change has accelerated to the point where we can no longer plan adequately for a single future. But it is also clear that the destination is not the stage we have already attained, but something yet to be fashioned. Already in the first decade of the century, Franz Kafka, in the parable entitled "My Destination" ("Das Ziel"), recognized that all our provisioning fails us as we set out toward the destination that can be named only as Away-From-Here (weg-von-hier).[1] Leaving home with no apparent supplies, the master is questioned about this unnamed destination by the stable attendant who brings him his horse. But he recognizes that sometimes one can discover the destination only by undertaking the journey, and that no provisions would ever be sufficient. It is a process rather than an achievement, a quality of the journeying whose discipline one learns only en route, but whose entry point is the one clear direction, weg-von-hier. Instead of hoary assurances that the culture's achievements are sufficient, projections of future needs remain half-attained and partial, and hence somewhat threatening, as most of our journeying through this century has seemed. Yet Kafka's traveler combines his realistic sense of the extent of the journey ahead with the irony that its difficulty is just what makes it a blessing: "Kein Eßvorrat kann mich retten. Es ist ja zum Glück eine ungeheurere Reise. / No provisions can save me. For it is, fortunately, a truly immense journey."

■ ■ ■

The excitement of working on a movement involving wide-reaching social and intellectual change is balanced by the frustration of one's desire to treat every possible angle. Before I adjusted fully to the reality of producing this book, I had planned another chapter that would have treated a miscellany of other topics, some of them intimately tied to mythological stories or heroic images, and others to experiences and conditions shared every day. Some of the topics that I hope to engage elsewhere, or that others will be stimulated to engage, can be listed here as a means of indicating some of the many issues remaining to be addressed as the men's movements develop.

These are some initiating gestures toward another book that readers can help me to write in the course of our immense journey:

- The Pantheon, the Golf Course, the Sweat Lodge. Men passing spirit/soul to one another. How to evolve a discipline within the male group so that outside stereotypes do not inhibit what can happen among the brothers. The roles of sharing, intimacy, timing, and leadership.

- *Homo fabricans:* Prometheus and Hephaistos and Daidalos. Learning passively to accept gifts may be the deceit that wrecks technology — imagine recycling holiday gifts instead of consuming something new! Why do we presuppose that we have to *produce* endlessly? Overconstruction/overproduction is an important male defense against castration anxieties, but *no one* needs to be as driven to produce, always to have more, as so many men seem to be today.

- Eros/Amor/the Cupids: Freud and Valentine's Day. Cute cherubs, "oversexed" adolescent boys, and the absolute terror of falling in love. Differences between love and sexuality; exploring what the erotic means today as so many of the traditional restrictions upon relationships and sexuality are ignored.

- Osiris and Seth. Male competition and fraternal aggression within the close family scene. Exploring the disciplines of rhetoric, the rules of debate and argument, and brotherly politics.

- Nadleh the Hermaphrodite: the Berdache in Native North America. The male house person, the ambiguity of religious sexuality, and the ambisexual nature of the androgyne. How does the figure on the borderline clarify those in the middle? What do they have to contribute to those at the center? Where/what is the center?

- Those Nasty Statues in the Garden. Pan, Faunus, Priapos, and earlier Dionysos and Hermes. What goes beyond the limits of acceptable gender display? The Mapplethorpe controversy: to what extent is the phallos to be displayed? Phallic iconography and masculine imagery generally. Has the phallic signifier become nothing but another empty signifier in a critical discourse that speaks freely of vaginal politics and invaginated writing?

- Folk/Fairy/Wondertales. Why are the boys always so stupid or nasty? What sexist positions are determinative of folk tale collections, study, and interpretations?

- Fathering and Sonning. Including second-marriage and split-household fathering. Getting beyond the son's natural anger against the father's regime.

- Mentors Mentoring. From Homer to the academic counselor. Men's roles in working with younger men individually and in groups.

- Initiation. What contemporary shapings are not stupid, but appropriate? Who leads? Gender issues in schools and athletics.

- The Many Amours of Zeus: How does one explain the countless love affairs of the Greek goddesses and gods? What does one learn about coupling, relating, from all these stories?

- Socially Constructed Males. What are our ideals and whence are they derived? Learning from the ways masculinities have been constructed variously at different times in different social strata and economies, the ways gender behaviors and expectations vary according to economic status, age, and ethnicity.

- Friendships at Work, at Play. The role of cooperation as contrasted with competition. What a truly integrated or interdisciplinary methodology might entail with respect to getting the credit a man needs. Balancing various levels of intensity in friendships with other males and females.

- Spirituality and Ritual. Historical review of specifically masculine religious elements. Ritualizing attempts today. Given the widespread "return to the Goddesses," ought/will there be a return to the Father Gods? Why is that a counter-intuitive question?

▪ ▪ ▪

Many other issues could be named, and for many of them extensive bibliography is available already. The following recommendations for an initiation into the topic are from my working bibliography of several hundred titles; full bibliographic information will be found in the References, immediately following the Notes. The most extensive published bibliography, primarily keyed to counseling and psychotherapy, and not annotated, is reprinted in Moore 1990:313–56; a second edition of a widely used bibliography on Men's Studies, August 1985, is in preparation.

- *Iron John: A Book about Men* (Bly 1990): A bestseller that the author simmered long enough for it to have real substance; example of approaching a folk tale from a new masculinity perspective.

- *Gods in Everyman* (Bolen 1989): I am not fond of the way Bolen plasters elements of myths so freely onto contemporary types of people, but her introductory remarks on connecting with mythological materials is very helpful.

- "Hard and Heavy: Toward a New Sociology of Masculinity" (Carrigan 1987): An extremely inclusive and acute review of social science approaches to masculinity, in a bibliographic critique.

- *About Men* (Chesler 1978): Not sure why this feminist work has not had more influence; it deserves to have an impact. Freudian perspective with analysis of images, interviews, and — a rarity — a well-annotated bibliography.

- *Contemporary Perspectives on Masculinity* (Clatterbaugh 1990): The most inclusive overview of the many branches of the men's movements.

- *Absent Fathers, Lost Sons: The Search for Masculine Identity* (Corneau 1991): Jungian without being inaccessible; excellent insights on problematic issues such as alcoholism and relationship to fathers.

- *A Man's Place: Masculinity in Transition* (Dubbert 1979): One of the best historical accounts of the feeling-tone of masculinity in various periods from the nineteenth century to the 1970s.

- *The Man in Me* (Firestone 1992 [1978]) and *The Myth of American Manhood* (Kriegel 1978): Collections of fictions directly relevant to male experience.

- *A Choice of Heroes: The Changing Face of American Manhood* (Gerzon 1982): Crucial study of the dysfunctional hero models we've been living with; looks toward new models.

- *Manhood in the Making: Cultural Concepts of Masculinity* (Gilmore 1990): I would like much better theoretical reflection, but it is useful as an account of manhood as an achieved social status in a number of countries and cultures.

- *Wingspan: Inside the Men's Movement* (Harding 1992): A wide-ranging, well-illustrated reader introducing several aspects of the men's movement, from the pages of the journal *Wingspan*, which Harding edits, other movement periodicals, and materials written specifically for the reader.

- *Men's Dreams, Men's Healing* (Hopcke 1990) and *He: Understanding Masculine Psychology* (Johnson 1974): Both Jungian in orientation, but both are helpful, the latter for exemplifying the Jungian approach to folk materials (the legend of Parsifal and the Grail), and the former for its effort to reclaim a positive regard for the masculine.

- *Beyond Patriarchy* (Kaufman 1987): Out of a number of anthologies, this is one of the best, with several outstanding contributions (Carrigan 1987 among them).

- *Knights without Armor* (Kipnis 1991): Strongly pro-male perspective, beginning with evidence of male-bashing and moving on to twelve agendas for recovering a positive masculinity.

- *The Sexuality of Men* (Metcalf 1985): As good a collection on sexuality as I've seen. Chapters on pornography, infancy-conditioning toward machismo, gay relationships, etc. from a British context, but transferable observations and suggestions.

- *Phallos: Sacred Image of the Masculine* (Monick 1987): In a series in Jungian psychology by Jungian analysts, so one may not expect elementary reading, but it is well worth wrestling with the technical terminology in this fine book.

- *The Intimate Connection* (Nelson 1988): The best book to come out from professional religious contexts. As healthy a perspective on sexuality as one might wish.

- *Finding Our Fathers: The Unfinished Business of Manhood* (Osherson 1986): A very moving book about the male need to hold and be held, to honor the father's values yet move on to being a sensitive, caring father and friend on one's own.

- *Holy Virility: The Social Construction of Masculinity* (Reynaud 1983): A stunning account of the images and factors of masculinity involved in patriarchy that recognizes that how power is exerted is always the key element. Sample suggestions: Today male sexuality needs to be released to spread throughout the body; fear of homosexuality is fear of sexuality as such. A book that ought to be reissued and widely read.

- *American Manhood: Transformations in Masculinity from the Revolution to the Modern Era* (Rotundo 1993): The "social-construction-of-gender" folks sometimes omit the solid socio-historical reconstructions that document just *how* gendering has been shaped. Rotundo never does, and these accounts are "must" reading (see the earlier Rotundo 1983, 1987).

- *Slow Motion: Changing Masculinities, Changing Men* (Segal 1990): One of those "if you can read just one, read this" books. Extraordinarily up to date and powerful on the socio-historical-economic situation of masculinity. Social constructionist and leftist in orientation.

- *Rediscovering Masculinity: Reason, Language, and Sexuality* (Seidler 1989): And this is another of those "just one" books, but more philosophical in tone than Segal. Best in terms of comprehending the gender politics of the period from the late 1950s to the mid-1980s.

- *Sexuality* (Weeks 1986): Not necessarily the best of his several benchmark studies of sexuality in the modern West, but a brief account that summarizes others of his very important works.

■ ■ ■

The last words in this account of the underlying mythic patterns of masculinities are ultimately utopian; they come from the final pages of Emmanuel Reynaud's remarkable *Holy Virility* (1983:110, 113–115):

> Up till now, men have always guarded power well, either as they benefited by submitting to it, or as they have reproduced it by fighting it. . . . Today patriarchy is at the end of its history; in its most developed form, it has created many ways of freeing people from natural alienation, whilst at the same time reproducing, to a degree of extreme sophistication, the most inhuman law of nature: that of the survival of the fittest. The struggle for power between men has made the world unfit to live in; where people do not die of hunger, life is reduced to waiting for death, day by day, amidst an accumulation of commodities and pollution. . . . The death warrant of patriarchy will come about either in nuclear self-destruction (will it then be able to rise from its ashes?) or in the actions of free and autonomous individuals, united in their common desire to live without power. . . . The pleasure of living without power may give the push that will finally tip the scales of history.

Idealistic visions of the world aside, determining where the power is remains crucial as we make our way from day to day. This book has been looking indirectly at a shift in power represented in modern gendering, and it has shared Reynaud's utopian hopes that the positive benefits for all of our culture to be gained from revisioning our gender proscriptions will be shared soon, before it becomes too late to tip the scales of history.

Notes

Preface

1. Adrienne Rich, "When We Dead Awaken: Writing as Re-Vision," *College English* 34/1 (October 1972): 18–19; now revised in Rich 1979:35. Hillman 1975 (*Re-Visioning Psychology*) is such a powerful reconstructive work that its very title has worked its way into many aspects of work in the humanities and social sciences. Hillman 1989 provides an excellent cross-section of the themes in Hillman's many writings. The term "re-visioning" is used in the masculinity context as a subtitle to Matthews 1991, *Choirs of the God: Revisioning Masculinity.*

Chapter 1:
Introducing Heroic Masculinity in Myths and Contemporary Culture

1. For materials related to Robert Bly's approach, contact Ally Press Center, 524 Orleans Street, St. Paul, MN 55107. Academic titles in Men's Studies are especially well represented in the Gender and Women Studies publications of Routledge, Chapman and Hall, Inc.

2. In a conference on world peace, David Miller notes that both stereotype and archetype "describe pattern. A stereotype is common knowledge, usually oversimplified, often tired and worn. An archetype is an original model, an ideal form, to which similar things or actions are compared. Stereotypes may or may not be accurate reflections of the archetypal original; often they carry the implication of inferiority. Stereotypic conditioning is so pervasive that one cannot help but fall into it in one's thinking and writing, even when one intends the opposite." Miller's remarks are cited by Monick 1991:23.

3. The most creative approach to the technical terminology is Remy 1990, with its attempted distinctions between patriarchy, androcracy, or fratriarchy on the one hand, and gynocracy, matriarchy, or sororiarchy on the other. Hearn 1987: Chapter 3 treats patriarchy from Marxian perspectives.

4. Segal argues that " 'masculinity' . . . is best understood as transcending the personal, as a heterogeneous set of ideas, constructed around assumptions of social *power*, which are lived out and reinforced, or perhaps denied and challenged, in multiple and diverse ways within a whole social system in which relations of authority, work, and domestic life are organized, in the main, along hierarchical gender lines" (288). Likewise British socialist and feminist philosopher Victor Seidler argues "for the reclamation of masculinity as a social and

217

historical experience" as he recognizes "the existence of different masculinities" (1989:12); and the British socialist sociologist Arthur Brittan agrees: "we
cannot talk of masculinity, only masculinities" (1989:1).

5. Kann 1991 argues that "individualism is more problem than promise
in America. The problem is that males are usually considered too passionate and selfish to be trusted with individual rights. The liberal solution is to
condition men's individualism with civic virtue. Historically, Americans look
to fatherhood to prompt male sobriety, consent, and patriotism. They rely on
constructions of womanhood to urge lovers, wives, and mothers to sacrifice
their own individuality to tame men's appetites and ensure that men heed the
nation's call to arms." Obviously Kann's book fits right in the line of my calls to
action with respect to what seems to me to be a disease of individualism; but I
found his work fairly impenetrable except to the experienced political scientist.

6. Shewey 1992, originally appearing in *The Village Voice*, and Dowden
1992, represent well-grounded positive alternatives to the coverage in most of
the mass media; cf. Johnson 1992 (she is a regular columnist for the same
periodical), a vituperative, ad hominem trashing of Bly.

7. A comprehensive on-line academic bibliographic service will be invaluable to keep up with the large number of new works in the field. A search for
the keyword "masculinity" at the research library of the University of Michigan
at Ann Arbor brought up 121 "hits" or titles; my local resource, NOTIS, at the
University of Alabama, brought up 93 — and note that 26 of them were published within 1990–91. Clearly we are just experiencing the initial interest in
a form of cultural change in our experience of gendering that will engage many
competing voices in this decade.

Chapter 2:
The Myth . . . and the Myths . . . of Masculinities

1. See for instance Rotundo 1983, 1987, 1993; Carnes 1989; Dubbert 1979;
Jeffords 1989; Kimmel 1987; Mangan 1987; Pleck 1980.

2. To my amazement, I heard a conference lecturer use "inversion" as if it
had never been a crucial term to the early twentieth-century sexologists, as if it
had not accrued a totally negative signification in gay scholarship. A good dose
of the historical revisionist scholarship of Jeffrey Weeks is imperative.

3. See Monick 1987 for a sensitive Jungian treatment of the religiosity of the
phallos as existentially experienced; Nelson 1988, for a useful treatment of sexuality within contemporary Protestantism; Carmody n.d., for a bold wrestling
with the Roman Catholic position on gender; Scroggs 1983 for a liberal Christian position on the New Testament and homosexuality; and Brod 1988 for a
miscellany from Jewish perspectives.

Chapter 3:
Masculinity in Media Images, Gender,
and the Men's Movements

1. Malone 1979 is insightful concerning the public stereotype of masculinity down to about 1976, and Garfinkel is unsurpassed for the period down to

the present. His résumé of the male stereotype provides an inclusive outline for analysis of films as well as other cultural productions, 1985:110:

The message of the media man can be summed up in six points:

- Winning — whether it is a gun duel or a top corporate position — is everything. Accomplishment is all.

- In order to win, a man must be ready to resort to violent or otherwise aggressive behavior.

- Because the rise to the top can be so brutal emotionally a man must hide his pain behind a wall of silence and inexpressiveness.

- Maintaining that wall of silence requires an independent stance.

- Living up to the model of the Media Man, like living up to expectations of fathers, mentors, and older brothers, is practically impossible — which only reinforces a man's inferiority in the shadow of other men.

- The image of masculinity is ambiguous, out-of-focus, elusive, and evasive. The outer form is emphasized over the inner.

2. Hamill 1978 usefully tracks American frontier machismo as one such script. Stengel 1992:72 notes how the roles have changed as men's bodies are now emphasized the way women's were formerly: "traditionally, men have traded power for women. But as the balance of power between the sexes begins to shift, men are having to rely on their looks."

3. Answering some of these questions will require a long period of theoretical reflection, comparable, no doubt, to the extended period in which "desire" has been a major topic within feminist theory. Some steps toward what he called "a sociology of desire" were developed by Karatheodoris (1992). Preliminary steps toward the necessary theorizing include recognition that desire is socially produced at the point where sexual difference is institutionalized in a binary system of gender stratification. Freud's theory of the masculinity of the libido, the social enforcing of desire as a social construct, recent articulation of the directed male "gaze," and linguistic intersections between sexual difference and gender stratification are all of concern as Karatheodoris crafts an initial explanation about how men are interpolated into the social-gender machinery.

4. See Strathern 1988:45 and n. 1; for the widest perspective, see Illich 1982, a work of bibliographic largesse such as is seldom seen in American publications.

5. For a brief historical sketch, see Astrachan 1984. Hearn 1987 and Seidler 1991 survey the British men's movements, and Faludi 1991 documents how few of the feminist demands have been satisfied today.

6. "Essentialism" is defined variously today, but I think the definitional statement in Hall 1991:2 is useful: The essentialist argument sees sex as a natural urge or instinct, and sees masculinity and femininity as "essentially different and unchanging throughout history and in all different societies. Under this schema (to be simplistic) males are forceful, aggressive, promiscuous, 'instrumental,' while females are nurturing, maternal, monogamous, 'expressive.'

At its most reductive, men have innate sexual desires and women have the innate capacity to arouse them. Any attempt to change this order of things given by either God or Nature is doomed to failure."

7. A reader edited by Victor Seidler (1991) from the socialist collective that produced the journal *Achilles' Heel* includes materials published from 1978 to 1984, with contemporary revisions and additions. See also Chapman 1988 on contemporary Marxist approaches to masculinity.

Chapter 4:
Friendship at the Beginning: Gilgamesh and Enkidu

1. In a professional survey (±4% margin of error), 90 percent of men answered "Who is a man's best friend?" with: *my wife* (*Men's Life* [Fall 1990]: 65).

2. Lewis Hyde's distinction between *erōs* as the connective principle opposed to the separating, differentiating *logos* is useful (1983:xiv). Eros is synthetic (60), and fights the distancing aspects of the boundaries: "logos-trade draws the boundary, eros-trade erases it" (61). Hyde turns immediately to the *moral* consequences of such distinctions, as demonstrated in the Ford Motor Company's decision not to add safety features to the Pinto models that killed so many persons (62–65), or in the instance of the logos-dominated couple who tried to exchange their baby for a used Corvette valued in 1980 at $8,800 (96n).

Chapter 5:
Herakles the Heroic Trickster

1. Seltzer 1990 clarifies ways attitudes toward the human body were reshaped by the growth of machine technologies in the late nineteenth century, and how simultaneously "nature" was reconceived. Turn-of-the-century youth movements combined both, the muscle-building regimen for machining the body, and the "return to nature" in camping and outdoors activities.

2. Slater's perspective on Herakles is rather negative, although he sees evolution in the character, paralleling the development of Greek culture, just as Brown 1947 finds it in the figure of Hermes: "One can perhaps best summarize the myth's evolution by saying that Herakles changes (although not altogether) from a bumptious, impulsive, gross, immoderate, and quarrelsome hero, appropriate to a coarse and uncivilized era, to a hag-ridden sufferer — persecuted, unstable, and self-defeating. Narcissism and sex antagonism are present throughout, but are increasingly elaborated; while other themes, such as sibling rivalry, tend to diminish in importance or are suppressed. . . . Heracles, more than any other figure, was a symbol of Greece itself. His progress from Gargantuan bully to suffering culture-hero, and from hero to deity, reflects the development of Greek civilization out of [pre-Achaian] Dorian vulgarity" (Slater 1968:387).

Chapter 6:
Narcissus and the Narcotic of the Self/Body Image

1. The single ill-fated issue of *Men's Life* (Fall 1990: 135) included exercises for the pubococcygeus muscle in the male groin, promising to help overcome

incontinence and reduce urinary tract infections, but especially to increase sexual endurance by as much as 50 percent, in order to produce more frequent erections and to increase orgasms for women (partners, one presumes).

2. In Greek society, the appearance of hair on the face and backside marked the transition between being available as the sexual object of older men, and turning sexually to men younger than oneself.

3. Brenkman 1976 deconstructs Ovid's narrative treatment of Narcissus in order to explicate its consummate dialogic structures.

4. In Latin an echo is *imago vocis*, the mere "image of a voice," similar to the Hebrew *bat qol*, "the daughter of the voice."

5. In another variant, Pan was in love with Echo, and unable either to persuade her or to overtake her, he sent madness upon the shepherds with whom he associated, and they tore her into pieces, only her voice surviving: see Rose 1959:169.

6. The terms "extravert" (now "extrovert") and "introvert" stem from Jung's psychology, but one need not be a Jungian to see the need for balancing both vectors, as well as recognizing the element of personal change over time.

7. Lesley Hall 1991 corroborates Weeks's point in a very useful analysis of the ways male sexuality was approached between about 1900 and 1950. She notes: "There is an assumption that male sexuality is not subject to the problems and complications which are understood to be an intrinsic part of female sexual functioning. . . . The very male organs are regarded as less complex and less liable to malfunction than those of the female," and hence they were represented in terms of healthy functioning while those of the female were approached in terms of pathology (114). This was in the face of estimates that as many as 50 percent of males faced problems of sexual dysfunction, but the same situation applies with respect to the birth of modern psychology, which focused upon the hysteria of *women* until the World Wars created masses of shell-shocked male troops who had to be healed.

Chapter 7:
Phallic Hermes between the Realms

1. As I mention in Doty 1978, there are many parallels to the Hermes figure across the world's mythologies, certainly more than I can discuss here. One about an Aztec deity is so striking in this immediate context that I cannot refrain from citing it (Hultkrantz 1979:271): "The merchants had their Mercury, the pathfinder Yacatecuhtli, presumably the same god as the one who, under a different name, guided the journeys of Mayan tradesmen."

2. The German term *Gymnasium* still has this wider sense: it refers to a college preparatory secondary school, to which physical athletics may be entirely ancillary.

3. Walker 1983:395 compares Hermes to Ardhanarisvara, the union of Kali and Shiva in one body, and hence the original hermaphrodite. She reports that priests of Hermes wore artificial breasts and female garments to preside over Aphrodite's temple in the guise of the god Hermaphroditos. In what follows I continue to be instructed by the "Peaks and Vales" article of James Hillman 1979; although there have been many explorations of the ways our society

has constructed the essential differences between masculinity and femininity, I still find this essay the most important in demonstrations of the ties between worldview and ethics and gendering.

4. Christians learned from the Angel of Death, Michael, when Michael replaced Hermes with similar functions: a hill originally sacred to Hermes/ Mercury now bears the name Saint Michael-Mont-Mercure in France; its counterpart across the Channel is Michael's Mount in England. Walker 1983:398.

Chapter 8:
Ares the Aggressive Militarist

1. Accepting *Areios pagos* as the source, rather than as Graves would have it from " 'the hill of the propitiating Goddess,' *areia* being one of Athene's titles" (1955:§19.b.2).

2. The threat of another forced national draft because of that military theater was treated casually in my daily paper as one answer to Alabama's persistent need for new prisons (Doris Flora, "Draft Could Ease Prison Population," *Tuscaloosa News,* 7 Dec. 1990: 1B, 3B). "Desert Storm" was a triumph of one technological machine over another, with the smallest amount of face-to-face combat in history. Media coverage of the actual carnage and destruction faced by the losers in the war and its aftermath was insignificant by comparison with the extent of coverage of the war-making machinery and engineering involved. As the first Independence Day subsequent to the operation approached, a Vermont hobby shop ad for flags, rockets, and other ways to "Celebrate!" included videotapes that could be purchased, on "Stealth Fighter, Battle Tanks, etc." First it was "Star Wars," now it's "Desert Storm." A review of the available videocassette versions of the conflict criticizes them very strongly because of their damping of the brutality of the war by introducing musical scorings and by almost totally ignoring what happened to the thousands of Iraqis killed (James Gorman, "Miss the War? Here's How to Catch Up," *New York Times,* 30 June 1991; Arts and Leisure section: 19).

3. Just as in Latin "virtue" is the quality of the *vir,* male. The Greek hero's story or *aristeia* is stereotypical: ideally he fights single-handedly, distinguishing himself thanks to divine inspiration, and becomes a "hero" when he wins his duel with another champion; see Schnappe-Gourbeillon 1991:416. I won't develop etymological arguments further, although it is amusing to note that as usual Plato also got on board: in the *Kratylos* (407.d), where he is giving etymologies of the names of the deities (from the standpoint of contemporary etymological knowledge, they are often hilariously derived), he suggests "Ares may be called [i.e., derived], if you will, from his manhood (*arrēn*) and manliness, or if you please, from his hard and unchangeable nature, which is the meaning of [a homonym] *arratos;* the latter is a derivation in every way appropriate to the god of war" (Plato 1961:444, my additions in brackets).

4. The following essay in the same encyclopedia, Schnappe-Gourbeillon 1991, is also very useful in understanding the ideological regulating of warfare. Paris 1986:39 and Graves 1955:§18, show similar aspects of Ares' relationship to Aphrodite, and Hillman 1991:11–13 describes the voluptuous side of Ares.

5. Fontenrose 1959:329, who suggests that Ares may have been "a death god before he became primarily associated with war."

Chapter 9:
Connecting the Active and the Passive: Monster Slayer and Child Born of Water

1. Myths of interaction between two different siblings apparently date back to the literary *débat* genre that originated about 3000 B.C.E. in Sumer, and I suggest that they come forward into issues of contemporary masculinity as a whole.

2. One part of the social background should be mentioned: the Navajo "have for the stage of babyhood but one name which is neither masculine nor feminine: the 'just born,' the 'newly arrived,'" but with the onset of puberty gender discriminations are established (Moon 1970:115–16).

Of course I am not using "macho" or "machismo" here or elsewhere in this book in the original sense, meaning, neutrally, "robust, masculine" in contrast to *manso*, "meek, soft," but rather with the acquired and negative connotations it has assumed in the English-speaking world. See Hamill 1978, and Goldwert 1983, who attributes the American beginnings of the concept of machismo to the repressive Spanish Conquistadores.

3. The Seneca story, "Brother Red and Brother Black," in Bierhorst 1976:91–94, portrays sibling death as the result of one sib's inability to accept the evil in the other.

4. Perfect reduplication is found in the number twelve, and one of the ritual paintings for this myth — I think the most beautiful — has twelve panels that go with a twelve-word song. What I am calling "ritual paintings" are drypaintings, in this instance dried crushed pigments laid out on specially prepared buckskin. The usual Navajo ritual painting is made by dribbling crushed elements between the fingers onto a smooth bed of fine sand, hence a "sandpainting."

5. They dominate the Navajo Curriculum Center presentation of Navajo history, for instance; see Yazzie 1971.

6. Some of the literary works he studies include: O'Neill, Jamie and Edmund in *Long Day's Journey into Night*; Miller, Biff and Happy in *Death of a Salesman*; Wolfe, Luke and Eugene Gant in *Look Homeward, Angel*; Faulkner, in both *The Sound and the Fury* and *Absalom, Absalom!*; Steinbeck, three generations of brothers in *East of Eden*; Guest, *Ordinary People*; and Cheever, *Falconer*. And some films: *Butch Cassidy and the Sundance Kid* and *The Sting*; *Dog Day Afternoon* (79–80); I'd add *Midnight Cowboy*.

Chapter 10:
Reintegrating Apollo and Dionysos

1. The oracular system was quite an impressive means of coordinating planting with likely harvest needs, identifying the real holders of power in various towns, and keeping materials in circulation. The maxims inscribed within his temple represent the more abstract moralistic teachings that came to be associated with Apollonian rationality; Guthrie's list cited by Eisner 1987:

142 includes: Abstain from inauspicious words; Fear authority; Do not glory in strength; Make obeisance to the divine; Hate hybris; Govern your spirit; Observe the limit; and Nothing in excess.

2. The proper transliteration of the Greek would include the final *nu*, but likewise the "long-o," *omega*, hence Apollōn; but the usual spelling is so entrenched, I have given up my preference for the Greek, rather than the Latinized names. For both Hymns, I recommend the translation and annotations of Athanassakis 1976.

3. See the terse but inclusive account of the views of Schlegel, Cruezer, Baur, Schelling, Bachofen, and Ritschl by Gründer 1971:441–45. Typical of many contemporary treatments, Holton 1974 makes a passing reference to the Greek materials and immediately skips to the situation of the 1970s, ignoring the philosophical tradition. The dichotomy influenced earlier ethnography strongly as it sought to understand cultures by means of looking at personality types, a perspective soon discarded professionally. Although the classical philologist Nietzsche used *Apollinisch*, "Apollonian" has become customary, and is the usage I follow; the normative discussion is Nietzsche's *The Birth of Tragedy from the Spirit of Music* (1967), first published in 1872.

4. No single voice or shared universe of discourse any longer, the contemporary university is more an academic corral of intellectually competing stallions, each of which struggles mightily to capture the dwindling capital now expended by a society that increasingly turns away from social welfare to accumulation of individual wealth. Connecting such an attitude with the patriarchal set of values, we see that gender models have a direct impact upon society.

5. An indirect resource here has been the section of *Re-visioning Psychology* (1975) where James Hillman notes how the dualistic male-female opposition, with its consequent stronger-weaker characterizations, has led to the repeated emphasis in medicine and psychology upon women's pathology (see also Hall 1991). Hillman seeks to revision psychology from the Dionysian rather than the Apollonian perspective in such a way as to emphasize the innate conjunction of both passive-aggressive and masculine-feminine within the psyche. Elsewhere Hillman also notes the importance of the Apollo-Dionysos contrast for the work of the imagination: "If 'Apollo' *versus* 'Dionysus' is merely a Romantic fantasy in the eyes of academic scholarship, the validity for psychology of these terms lies just in the fantasy" (1972:267).

6. Centuries are compressed: as I wrote this chapter, I read in *Civil Liberties: The National Newsletter of the ACLU* (no. 376, 1992:4) of attempts by the city of Chattanooga to ban performances of *Oh! Calcutta!*, first presented in 1969, and still almost fifteen years later evidently too Dionysian for some audiences. At my own university the musical *Hair*, famous for on-stage nudity, was revived in 1993 with no bare bottoms whatsoever.

7. It is actually the "Socratic" that Nietzsche despises, not the Apollonian: "The spirit of Socrates, the 'archetype and progenitor' of scientific rationalism, dominated Western life and art until Nietzsche's own time. It is in opposition to what he names 'Socratic' or 'Alexandrian' culture that he calls upon his own age to restore 'Dionysian magic' " (Feder 1980:70).

8. Alternative versions abound: for example, after he has been born as Za-

greus, from Persephone, Hera has the Titans tear him to bits; but his heart is saved and fed by Zeus to Semele, who provides the second birth.

9. Downing 1993 notes, however, that Dionysos does not represent unbridled sexuality but is in fact devoted to women: alone among the Greek gods Dionysos is never accused of seduction or rape or infidelity, and remains the constant spouse of Ariadne. Otto proposes that "the one thing which sets him off from all of the truly masculine gods, whose passions are cooled by transient moments of possession, is the fact that his love is ecstatic and binds him to the loved one forever" (1965:177).

10. Compare Guirand 1968:113, "the legend of Apollo and his functions reveal divergences which are sometimes even contradictory"; his functions "are so multiple and complex that it is often hard to connect one with another"; 116, "So many varying functions lead one to suspect that in Apollo there were many personalities." And with respect to Dionysos, Henrichs 1984:236 stresses the dualities and oppositions encompassed; the composite nature of this figure, 205; so many traits that the figure defies definition, 209; and its complexity, 212.

11. A child of the Second World War period, but then also of the 1960s and later decades, I can hardly believe the retreat from responsibility for the global environment represented by the Reagan and Bush administrations. Are we so unable to learn from the past that we elevate immediate profit over long-term ecological responsibility for Planet Earth? Apparently so, although the success of such a patriarchal perspective that can understand Nature only as waiting to be subjugated and destroyed ought to be untenable at this point.

Chapter 11:
Traditional Hero Myths Confront the New Age

1. The sketch of the monomyth can be supplemented by Leeming 1973, which gathers an additional assortment of myths arranged according to Campbell's categories, and by Leeming 1990: Part III, Hero Myths. A much longer and more formal academic version of this chapter appears as Doty 1993b.

2. I repeat here some of my earlier summary, Doty 1986:176–78. Jewett and Lawrence's book is an invaluable guide to the ways myths operate within societies, as well as to American popular religious mythologies. Some of my own work on the analysis and uses of myths as an aspect of social production will appear in an essay entitled "Silent Myths Singing in the Blood: The Sites of Production and Consumption of Myths in a 'Mythless' Society."

3. Howard Gardner's theory that has challenged the standard I.Q. prognostications provides for some *seven* types of intelligence: linguistic, logical-mathematical, musical, bodily-kinesthetic, spatial, inter-, and intrapersonal (Winn 1990:28). Perhaps there ought to be a congeries of hero/ine models, one for each of the seven types.

Chapter 12:
Where Do We Go from Here?

1. The text is cited from Kafka 1958:188–89.

References

Anderson, William. 1990. *Green Man: The Archetype of Our Oneness with the Earth.* San Francisco: HarperCollins.

Apollodoros. 1976. *Gods and Heroes of the Greeks. The Library of Apollodorus.* Trans. with notes, Michael Simpson. Amherst: University of Massachusetts Press.

Apollonios of Rhodes. 1959. *The Voyage of Argo.* Trans. E. V. Rieu. Baltimore: Penguin.

Artemidoros. 1975. *The Interpretation of Dreams. Oneirocritica by Artemidorus [Daldianus].* Trans. Robert J. White. Park Ridge, N.J.: Noyes Press.

Astrachan, Anthony. 1984. "Men: A Movement of Their Own." *Ms.* August:91–94.

————. 1986. *How Men Feel: Their Response to Women's Demands for Equality and Power.* Garden City, N.Y.: Doubleday.

Athanassakis, Apostolos N. 1976. *The Homeric Hymns: Text, Translation, and Notes.* Baltimore: Johns Hopkins University Press.

August, Eugene. 1985. *Men's Studies: A Selected and Annotated Interdisciplinary Bibliography.* Littleton, Colo.: Libraries Unlimited.

Babcock, Barbara A. 1980. "Reflexivity: Definitions and Discriminations." *Semiotica* 30/1–2:1–14.

Bellah, Robert N., Richard Madsen, William H. Sullivan, Ann Swidler, and Steven M. Tipton. 1985. *Habits of the Heart: Individualism and Commitment in American Life.* New York: HarperCollins.

Bierhorst, John, ed. 1976. *The Red Swan: Myths and Tales of the American Indians.* New York: Noonday.

Bly, Robert. 1987. "The Erosion of Male Confidence." In Louise Carus Mahdi, Steven Foster, and Meredith Little, eds. *Betwixt and Between: Patterns of Masculine and Feminine Initiation.* Chicago: Open Court; 189–96.

————. 1990. *Iron John: A Book about Men.* Reading, Mass.: Addison Wesley.

————, and Keith Thompson. 1985 [1982]. "What Men Really Want." In John Welwood, ed. *Challenge of the Heart: Love, Sex, and Intimacy in Changing Times.* Boston: Shambhala; 100–116.

Bolen, Jean Shinoda. 1984. *Goddesses in Everywoman: A New Psychology of Women.* San Francisco: HarperCollins.

————. 1989. *Gods in Everyman: A New Psychology of Men's Lives and Loves.* San Francisco: HarperCollins.

Bonnefoy, Ives, ed. 1991. *Mythologies.* English trans. ed. by Wendy Doniger. Chicago: University of Chicago Press.

228 • *References*

Boone, Joseph A., and Michael Cadden, eds. 1990. *Engendering Men: The Question of Male Feminist Criticism*. New York: Routledge.
Boswell, Fred, and Jeanetta Boswell. 1980. *What Men or Gods Are These? A Genealogical Approach to Classical Mythology*. Metuchen, N.J.: Scarecrow.
Boyd, Kelly. 1991. "Knowing Your Place: The Tensions of Manliness in Boys' Story Papers, 1818–39." In Roper 145–67.
Brain, Robert. 1976. *Friends and Lovers*. London: Hart-Davis, MacGibbon.
Brenkman, John. 1976. "Narcissus in the Text." *The Georgia Review* 30/2:293–327.
Brenton, Myron. 1966. *The American Male*. New York: Coward-McCann.
Brittan, Arthur. 1989. *Masculinity and Power*. New York: Blackwell.
Brod, Harry, ed. 1987. *The Making of Masculinities: The New Men's Studies*. Boston: Allen and Unwin.
———, ed. 1988. *A Mensch among Men: Explorations in Jewish Masculinity*. Freedom, Calif.: Crossing Press.
Brown, Norman O. 1947. *Hermes the Thief: The Evolution of a Myth*. New York: Vintage.
Brown, Richard Harvey. 1989. *Social Science as Civic Discourse: Essays on the Invention, Legitimation, and Uses of Social Theory*. Chicago: University of Chicago Press.
Budapest, Zsuzsanna Emese. 1992. "In Search of the Lunar Male: Contemporary Rituals of Men's Mysteries." In Kay Leigh Hagan, ed. *Women Respond to the Men's Movement: A Feminist Collection*. New York: HarperCollins; 83–91.
Butters, Ronald R., John M. Clum, and Michael Moon, eds. 1989. *Displacing Homophobia: Gay Male Perspectives in Literature and Culture*. Durham: Duke University Press.
Cafferata, John, comp. 1975. *Rites*. New York: McGraw-Hill.
Campbell, Joseph. 1968 [1949]. *The Hero with a Thousand Faces*. 2nd ed. Bollingen series, 17. Princeton: Princeton University Press.
———. 1974. *The Mythic Image*. Princeton: Princeton University Press.
———. 1988. *Mythologies of the Great Hunt*. Historical Atlas of World Mythology 1/2. New York: HarperCollins.
———, and Bill Moyers. 1988. *The Power of Myth*. Ed. Betty Sue Flowers. New York: Doubleday.
Carmody, John. N.d. [based on 1987 lectures]. *Toward a Male Spirituality*. Mystic, Conn.: Twenty-Third Publications.
Carnes, Mark C. 1989. *Secret Ritual and Manhood in Victorian America*. New Haven: Yale University Press.
Carrigan, Tim, Bob Connell, and John Lee. 1987. "Hard and Heavy: Toward a New Sociology of Masculinity." In Kaufman 139–63 [orig. publ. in *Theory and Society* 1985; also repr. in Brod 1987:63–100].
Castiglia, Christopher. 1990. "Rebel without a Closet." In Boone 207–21.
Chapman, Rowena, and John Rutherford, eds. 1988. *Male Order: Unwrapping Masculinity*. London: Lawrence & Wishart.
Chesler, Phyllis. 1978. *About Men*. New York: Simon and Schuster.
Christ, Carol. 1980. *Diving Deep and Surfacing: Women Writers on Spiritual Quest*. Boston: Beacon.

Clarke, Norma. 1991. "Strenuous Idleness: Thomas Carlyle and the Man of Letters as Hero." In Roper 25–43.

Clatterbaugh, Kenneth. 1989. "Masculinist Perspectives." *Changing Man* 20:4–6.

———. 1990. *Contemporary Perspectives on Masculinity: Men, Women, and Politics in Modern Society.* Boulder, Colo.: Westview Press.

Clay, Jenny Strauss. 1989. *The Politics of Olympus: Form and Meaning in the Major Homeric Hymns.* Princeton: Princeton University Press.

Clift, Jean Dalby, and Wallace B. Clift. 1988. *The Hero Journey in Dreams.* New York: Crossroad.

Cohen, David. 1991. *Law, Sexuality, and Society: The Enforcement of Morals in Classical Athens.* New York: Cambridge University Press.

Corneau, Guy. 1991. *Absent Fathers, Lost Sons: The Search for Masculine Identity.* Boston: Shambhala.

Cosby, Bill. 1986. *Fatherhood.* Garden City, N.Y.: Doubleday.

Craig, Steve, ed. 1992. *Men, Masculinity, and the Media.* Research on Men and Masculinities, 2. Newbury Park, Calif.: Sage.

Dalley, Stephanie. 1989. *Myths from Mesopotamia: Creation, The Flood, Gilgamesh, and Others.* New York: Oxford University Press.

Darmon, Jean-Pierre. 1991. "The Powers of War: Ares and Athena in Greek Mythology." In Bonnefoy 414–15.

Dawson, Graham. 1991. "The Blond Bedouin: Lawrence of Arabia, Imperial Adventure, and the Imagining of English-British Masculinity." In Roper 113–44.

Dellamora, Richard. 1990. *Masculine Desire: The Sexual Politics of Victorian Aestheticism.* Chapel Hill: University of North Carolina Press.

Detienne, Marcel. 1986. "Apollo's Slaughterhouse." Trans. Anne Doueihi. *Diacritics: A Review of Contemporary Criticism* 16/2:46–53.

Dittes, James. 1991. "A Men's Movement for the Church?" *Christian Century* 29 May–5 June; 588–90.

Donaldson, Mara E. 1987. "Woman as Hero in Margaret Atwood's *Surfacing* and Maxine Hong Kingston's *The Woman Warrior.*" In Pat Browne, ed. *Heroines of Popular Culture.* Bowling Green: Bowling Green Popular Press; 101–13.

Doty, William G. 1978. "Hermes Guide of Souls." *The Journal of Analytical Psychology* 23/4:358–64.

———. 1986. *Mythography: The Study of Myths and Rituals.* Tuscaloosa: University of Alabama Press.

———. 1980. "Hermes' Heteronymous Appellations." In James Hillman, ed., *Facing the Gods.* Irving, Tex.: Spring Publications; 115–33.

———. 1987. "Revising Our Myths of Masculinity." *The University of Dayton Review* 18/2:67–82.

———. 1993a. "A Lifetime of Trouble-Making: Hermes as Trickster." In Hynes 46–65.

———. 1993b. "From the Traditional Monomythic Hero to the Contemporary Polymythic Hero/ine." In Bernard Scott and John L. White, eds. *"Through the Looking Glass": Essays in Honor of a Precursor.* Festschrift for Robert W. Funk. *Foundations and Facets Forum.*

————. 1993c. "'Companionship Thick as Trees': Our Myths of Friendship." *The Journal of Men's Studies* 1/4:359–82.

Dover, K. J. 1978. *Greek Homosexuality.* Cambridge: Harvard University Press.

Dowden, Graham. 1992. "Into the Black with Meade and Bly." *Thunder Stick* 2/1:3–5, 18–19.

Downing, Christine. 1981. *The Goddess: Mythological Images of the Feminine.* New York: Crossroad.

————, ed. 1991. *Mirrors of the Self: Archetypal Images that Shape Your Life.* A New Consciousness Reader. Los Angeles: Tarcher.

————. 1993. *Gods in Our Midst: Mythological Images of the Masculine: A Woman's View.* New York: Crossroad.

Drummond, Hugh. 1987. "The Ultimate Erector Set." *Mother Jones* 12/11:8–9.

Dubbert, Joe L. 1979. *A Man's Place: Masculinity in Transition.* Englewood Cliffs, N.J.: Prentice-Hall.

Dürrenmatt, Friedrich. 1985. *Herkules und der Stall des Augias: Eine Komödie.* Zurich: Die Arche.

Dundes, Alan. 1990 [1976]. "The Hero Pattern and the Life of Jesus." In Rank 177–223.

Dyer, Richard. 1985. "Male Sexuality in the Media." In Metcalf 28–43, 183–84.

————. 1990. *Now You See It: Studies on Lesbian and Gay Film.* New York: Routledge.

Eagleton, Terry. 1991. *Ideology: An Introduction.* New York: Verso.

Easlea, Brian. 1983. *Fathering the Unthinkable: Masculinity, Scientists, and the Nuclear Arms Race.* London: Pluto.

Easthope, Anthony. 1990. *What a Man's Gotta Do: The Masculine Myth in Popular Culture.* Boston: Unwin Hyman; rev. ed.

Eisner, Robert. 1987. *The Road to Daulis: Psychoanalysis, Psychology, and Classical Mythology.* Syracuse: Syracuse University Press.

Elder, George R. 1987. "Phallus." In *The Encyclopedia of Religion.* Ed. Mircea Eliade. New York: Macmillan; vol. 1:263–69.

Evans, Arthur. 1988. *The God of Ecstasy: Sex-Roles and the Madness of Dionysos.* New York: St. Martin's.

Everitt, David, and Harold Schechter. 1982. *The Manly Handbook.* New York: Berkley.

Faludi, Susan. 1991. *Backlash: The Undeclared War against American Women.* New York: Crown.

Farnell, Lewis Richard. 1921. *Greek Hero Cults and Ideas of Immortality.* The Gifford Lectures. Oxford: Clarendon Press.

Feder, Lillian. 1980. "Mythical Symbols of the Dissolution and Reconstitution of the Self in Twentieth-Century Literature." In Wendell M. Aycock and Theodore M. Klein, eds. *Classical Mythology in Twentieth-Century Thought and Literature.* Proceedings, Comparative Literature Symposium, Texas Tech University, XI. Lubbock: Texas Tech Press; 67–87.

Ferry, David. 1993. *Gilgamesh: A New Rendering in English Verse.* New York: Farrar, Straus & Giroux.

Fiedler, Leslie A. 1962. *Love and Death in the American Novel.* Cleveland: World.

Firestone, Ross, ed. 1992 [1978]. *The Man in Me: Versions of the Male Experience.* Orig. title *A Book of Men.* San Francisco: HarperCollins.

Fontenrose, Joseph. 1959. *Python: A Study of Delphic Myth and its Origins.* Berkeley: University of California Press.

Ford, Richard. 1976. *A Piece of My Heart.* Vintage Contemporaries. New York: Random House.

Foucault, Michel. 1985. *The Use of Pleasure.* Trans. Robert Hurley. The History of Sexuality, vol. 2. New York: Pantheon.

Friday, Nancy. 1980. *Men in Love. Men's Sexual Fantasies: The Triumph of Love over Rage.* New York: Delacorte.

Galinsky, G. Karl. 1972. *The Herakles Theme: The Adaptations of the Hero in Literature from Homer to the Twentieth Century.* Totowa, N.J.: Rowman and Littlefield.

Gardner, John, and John Maier. 1984. *Gilgamesh: The Sîn-Leqi-Unninnî Version.* New York: Random House.

Garfinkel, Perry. 1985. *In a Man's World: Father, Son, Brother, Friend, and Other Roles Men Play.* New York: New American Library.

Gerzon, Mark. 1982. *A Choice of Heroes: The Changing Face of American Manhood.* Boston: Houghton Mifflin.

Gilmore, David D. 1990. *Manhood in the Making: Cultural Concepts of Masculinity.* New Haven: Yale University Press.

Gingold, Alfred. 1991. *Fire in the John: The Manly Man in the Age of Sissification.* New York: St. Martin's.

Girard, René. 1986. *The Scapegoat.* Trans. Yvonne Freccero. Baltimore: Johns Hopkins University Press.

Goffman, Irving. 1979. *Gender Advertisements.* New York: Harper.

Goldberg, Jonathan. 1992. "Recalling Totalities: The Mirrored Stages of Arnold Schwarzenegger." *Differences: A Journal of Feminist Cultural Studies* 4/1:172–204.

Goldwert, Marvin. 1983. *Machismo and Conquest: The Case of Mexico.* Lanham, Md.: University Press of America.

Graves, Robert. 1955. *The Greek Myths.* Baltimore: Penguin; 2 vols. [References are to sections, not pages.]

Green, Peter. 1986. "Hellenistic Technology: Eye, Hand, and Animated Tool." *Southern Humanities Review* 20/2:101–13.

Gründer, Karlfried, and J. Mohr. 1971. "Apollinisch/dionysisch." In Joachim Ritter, ed. *Historisches Wörterbuch der Philosophie.* Basel/Stuttgart: Schwabe and Co., vol. 1:442–45.

Guirand, Felix. 1968. "Apollo." In Guirand, ed. *New Larousse Encyclopedia of Mythology.* Trans. Richard Aldington and Delano Ames. New York: Prometheus Press; 109–13.

Guthrie, W. C. K. 1949. *The Greeks and Their Gods.* Boston: Beacon.

Hall, Lesley A. 1991. *Hidden Anxieties: Male Sexuality, 1900–1950.* Family Life Series. Cambridge, U.K.: Polity Press.

Halperin, David M. 1990. *One Hundred Years of Homosexuality and Other Essays on Greek Love.* The New Ancient World. New York: Routledge.

————, John J. Winkler, and Froma I. Zeitlin, eds. 1990. *Before Sexuality: The Construction of Erotic Experience in the Ancient Greek World*. Princeton: Princeton University Press.

Hamill, Pete. 1978. "A Farewell to Machismo." In Kriegel 392–407.

Hammond, Dorothy, and Alta Jablow. 1987. "Gilgamesh and the Sundance Kid: The Myth of Male Friendship." In Brod 241–58.

Harding, Chris, ed. 1992. *Wingspan: Inside the Men's Movement*. New York: St. Martin's Press.

Hearn, Jeff. 1987. *The Gender of Oppression: Men, Masculinity, and the Critique of Marxism*. London: Wheatsheaf.

————, and David Morgan, eds. 1990. *Men, Masculinities, and Social Theory*. London: Unwin Hyman.

Heath, Stephen. 1987. "Male Feminism." In Alice Jardine and Paul Smith, eds. *Men in Feminism*. New York: Methuen; 1–32.

Heckler, Richard Strozzi. 1990. *In Search of the Warrior Spirit*. Berkeley, Calif.: North Atlantic.

Henrichs, Albert. 1984. "Loss of Self, Suffering, Violence: The Modern View of Dionysus from Nietzsche to Girard." *Harvard Studies in Classical Philology* 88:205–40.

Herdt, Gilbert. 1981. *Guardians of the Flutes: Idioms of Masculinity. A Study of Ritualized Homosexual Behavior*. New York: McGraw-Hill.

————, ed. 1982. *Rituals of Manhood: Male Initiation in Papua New Guinea*. Berkeley: University of California Press.

Herek, Gregory M. 1987. "On Heterosexual Masculinity: Some Psychical Consequences of the Social Construction of Gender and Sexuality." In Michael S. Kimmel, ed. *Changing Men: New Directions in Research on Men and Masculinity*. Newbury Park, Calif.: Sage; 68–82.

Hill, Geoffrey. 1992. *Illuminating Shadows: The Mythic Power of Film*. Boston: Shambhala.

Hillman, James. 1972. *The Myth of Analysis: Three Essays in Archetypal Psychology*. Studies in Jungian Thought. Evanston: Northwestern University Press.

————. 1975. *Re-Visioning Psychology*. New York: HarperCollins.

————. 1979 [1976]. "Peaks and Vales: The Soul/Spirit Distinction as Basis for the Differences between Psychotherapy and Spiritual Discipline." In Hillman and others. *Puer Papers*. Dallas: Spring Publications; 54–74.

————. 1979 [1972]. "Notes on Opportunism." In Hillman and others. *Puer Papers*. Dallas: Spring Publications; 152–65.

————. 1985. *Anima: An Anatomy of a Personified Notion*. Dallas: Spring Publications.

————. 1987. "Wars, Arms, Rams, Mars: On the Love of War." In Valerie Andres, Robert Bosnak, and Karen Walter Goodwin, eds. *Facing Apocalypse*. Dallas: Spring Publications; 118–36.

————. 1989. *A Blue Fire: Selected Writings*. Intro. and ed. Thomas Moore. New York: HarperCollins.

————. 1991. "City, Sport, and Violence." *Inroads* 7:10–18.

Hite, Shere. 1981. *The Hite Report on Male Sexuality*. New York: Knopf.

Holton, Gerald. 1974. "On Being Caught between Dionysians and Apolloni-ans." *Daedalus* 103/3:65–81.

Hopcke, Robert H. 1989. *Jung, Jungians, and Homosexuality.* Boston: Shambhala.

———. 1990. *Men's Dreams, Men's Healing.* Boston: Shambhala.

Hultkrantz, Åke. 1979. *The Religions of the American Indians.* Trans. Monica Setterwall. Hermeneutics: Studies in the History of Religions, 7. Berkeley: University of California Press.

Hyde, Lewis. 1983. *The Gift: Imagination and the Erotic Life of Property.* New York: Vintage.

Hynes, William J., and William G. Doty, eds. 1993. *Mythical Trickster Figures: Contours, Contents, and Criticisms.* Tuscaloosa: University of Alabama Press.

Illich, Ivan. 1982. *Gender.* New York: Random House.

Jeffords, Susan. 1989. *The Remasculinization of America: Gender and the Vietnam War.* Bloomington: Indiana University Press.

Jewett, Robert, and John Shelton Lawrence. 1989. *The American Monomyth.* 2nd ed. Lanham, Md.: University Press of America.

Johns, Catherine. 1982. *Sex or Symbol: Erotic Images of Greece and Rome.* A Colonnade Book. London: British Museum Publications.

Johnson, Jill. 1992. "Why Iron John Is No Gift to Women." *New York Times Book Review,* 23 February:1, 28–29, 31–33.

Johnson, Robert A. 1974. *He: Understanding Masculine Psychology. Based on the Legend of Parsifal and His Search for the Grail, Using Jungian Psychological Concepts.* New York: HarperCollins.

Kafka, Franz. 1958. *Parables and Paradoxes.* Ed. Nahum Glatzer. New York: Schocken.

Kann, Mark E. 1991. *On the Man Question: Gender and Civic Virtue in America.* Philadelphia: Temple University Press.

Karatheodoris, Stephen. 1992. "Male Desire in the Political Economy of Sexual Difference." Ed. William G. Doty. *Gender, Race, and Identity: Proceedings of the 1991 Southern Humanities Conference.* Chattanooga: Southern Humanities Press.

Kaufman, Michael, ed. 1987. *Beyond Patriarchy: Essays by Men on Pleasure, Power, and Change.* New York: Oxford University Press.

Kerényi, Karl. 1959. *The Heroes of the Greeks.* Trans. H. J. Rose. London: Thames and Hudson.

———. 1976. *Dionysos: Archetypal Image of Indestructible Life.* Trans. Ralph Mannheim. Bollingen series, 65/2. Princeton: Princeton University Press.

———. 1976. *Hermes Guide of Souls: The Mythologem of the Masculine Source of Life.* Trans. Murray Stein. Zurich: Spring Publications.

———. 1983. *Apollo: The Wind, the Spirit, and the God. Four Studies.* Trans. Jon Solomon. Dunquin Series, 16. Dallas: Spring Publications.

Keuls, Era C. 1985. *The Reign of the Phallus: Sexual Politics in Ancient Athens.* New York: HarperCollins.

Keyes, Roger. 1989. *The Male Journey in Japanese Prints.* Berkeley: University of California Press, in assoc. with the Fine Arts Museums of San Francisco.

Kimmel, Michael S. 1987. "The Cult of Masculinity: American Social Character and the Legacy of the Cowboy." In Kaufman 235–49.

King, Jeff, Maude Oakes, and Joseph Campbell. 1969 [1943]. *Where the Two Came to Their Father: A Navaho War Ceremonial.* Bollingen series, 1. 2nd ed. Princeton: Princeton University Press.

Kipnis, Aaron R. 1991. *Knights without Armor: A Practical Guide for Men in Quest of Masculine Soul.* Los Angeles: Tarcher.

Kirk, Geoffrey S. N.d. [from Urbino conference, 1973]. "Methodological Reflexions on the Myths of Heracles." In Bruno Gentili and Giuseppe Paioni, eds. *Il Mito Greco: Atti del Convegno Internazionale.* Rome: Edizioni dell'Ateneo and Bizzarri.

Kovacs, Maureen Gallery. 1989. *The Epic of Gilgamesh.* Stanford, Calif.: Stanford University Press.

Kriegel, Leonard, ed. 1978. *The Myth of American Manhood.* New York: Dell.

Lasch, Christopher. 1979. *The Culture of Narcissism.* New York: Norton.

Lattimore, Richmond, trans. 1960. *Greek Lyrics.* 2nd ed. Chicago: University of Chicago Press.

Lauter, Estella. 1984. *Women as Mythmakers: Poetry and Visual Art by Twentieth-Century Women.* Bloomington: Indiana University Press.

Lawlor, Robert. 1991. *Earth Honoring: The New Male Sexuality.* Rochester, Vt.: Park Street Press.

Lazer, Hank. 1990. "The Politics of Form and Poetry's Other Subjects: Reading Contemporary American Poetry." *American Literary History* 2/3:503–27.

Le Guin, Ursula K. 1969. *The Left Hand of Darkness.* New York: HarperCollins.

Leeming, David A. 1973. *Mythology: The Voyage of the Hero.* Philadelphia: Lippincott.

———. 1990. *The World of Myth: An Anthology.* New York: Oxford University Press.

Leo, John R. 1989. "The Familialism of 'Man' in American Television Melodrama." In Butters 31–51.

Loraux, Nicole. 1990. "Herakles: The Super-Male and the Feminine." In Halperin 21–52.

Malone, Michael. 1979. *Heroes of Eros: Male Sexuality in the Movies.* New York: E. P. Dutton.

McIntyre, John P., S.J. 1978. "The Brothers." *Semeia: An Experimental Journal for Biblical Criticism* 13:75–90.

Mangan, J. A., and James Walvin, eds. 1987. *Manliness and Morality: Middle-Class Masculinity in Britain and America.* Manchester: Manchester University Press.

Mason, Herbert, trans. 1970. *Gilgamesh: A Verse Narrative.* New York: New American Library.

Matthews, John, ed. 1991. *Choirs of the God: Revisioning Masculinity.* London: HarperCollins.

Mead, Margaret. 1949. *Male and Female: A Study of the Sexes in a Changing World.* New York: Viking.

Mellen, Joan. 1977. *Big Bad Wolves: Masculinity in the American Film.* New York: Pantheon.

Metcalf, Andy, and Martin Humphries, eds. 1985. *The Sexuality of Men*. London: Pluto.

Meyer, Richard. 1991. "Rock Hudson's Body." In Diana Fuss, ed. *Inside/Out: Lesbian Theories, Gay Theories*. New York: Routledge; 258–88.

Miller, D. Patrick. 1990. "Mastering the Enemy Within: An Interview with Richard Strozzi Heckler." *The Sun*, no. 180 (November): 6–13.

Miller, Jason. 1972. *That Championship Season*. New York: Dramatists Play Service Inc.

Miller, Stuart. 1983. *Men and Friendship*. Los Angeles: Tarcher.

Minnich, Elizabeth Karmarck. 1990. *Transforming Knowledge*. Philadelphia: Temple University Press.

Mishkind, Marc E., Judith Rodin, Lisa R. Silberstein, and Ruth H. Striegel-Moore. 1987. "The Embodiment of Masculinity: Cultural, Psychological, and Behavioral Dimensions." In Michael S. Kimmel, ed. *Changing Men: New Directions in Research on Men and Masculinity*. Newbury Park, Calif.: Sage; 37–52.

Monette, Paul. 1988a. *Borrowed Time: An AIDS Memoir*. San Diego: Harcourt Brace Jovanovich.

———. 1988b. *Love Alone: 18 Elegies for Rog*. New York: St. Martin's Press.

Monick, Eugene. 1987. *Phallos: Sacred Image of the Masculine*. Studies in Jungian Psychology by Jungian Analysts, 27. Toronto: Inner City Books.

———. 1991. *Castration and Male Rage: The Phallic Wound*. Studies in Jungian Psychology by Jungian Analysts, 50. Toronto: Inner City Books.

Moon, Sheila. 1970. *A Magic Dwells: A Poetic and Psychological Study of the Navaho Emergence Myth*. Middletown, Conn.: Wesleyan University Press.

Moore, Dwight, and Fred Leafgren, eds. 1990. *Problem Solving Strategies and Interventions for Men in Conflict*. Alexandria, Va.: American Association for Counseling and Development.

Moore, John H. 1989. *But What about Men? After Women's Lib*. Bath: Ashgrove.

Moore, Robert, and Douglas Gillette. 1990. *King, Warrior, Magician, Lover: Rediscovering the Archetypes of the Mature Masculine*. San Francisco: HarperCollins.

Moore, Thomas W. 1976. "Narcissus." *Parabola: Myth and the Quest for Meaning* 1/2:50–55.

———. 1990. "Eros and the Male Spirit." In Franklin Abbott, ed. *Men and Intimacy: Personal Accounts Exploring the Dilemmas of Modern Male Sexuality*. Freedom, Calif.: Crossing Press; 125–33.

———. 1992. *Care of the Soul: A Guide for Cultivating Depth and Sacredness in Everyday Life*. New York: HarperCollins.

Morgan, Robin. 1989. *The Demon Lover: On the Sexuality of Terrorism*. New York: Norton.

Murdock, Maureen. 1990. *The Heroine's Journey*. Boston: Shambhala.

Nagy, Gregory. 1979. *The Best of the Achaeans: Concepts of the Hero in Archaic Greek Poetry*. Baltimore: Johns Hopkins University Press.

Nelson, James. 1988. *The Intimate Connection: Male Sexuality, Masculine Spirituality*. Philadelphia: Westminster.

Neumann, Erich. 1962 [1954]. *The Origin and History of Consciousness.* New York: HarperCollins.

Newcomb, Franc J., and Gladys A. Reichard. 1975. *Sandpaintings of the Navajo Shooting Chant.* New York: Dover.

Nietzsche, Friedrich. 1967 [1872, 1888]. *The Birth of Tragedy and the Case of Wagner.* Trans. with commentary, Walter Kaufmann. New York: Vintage.

Nilsson, Martin P. 1972 [1932]. "Heracles." *The Mycenaean Origin of Greek Mythology.* Berkeley: University of California Press; chapter 3.

Nonnos. 1940. *Dionysiaca.* Trans. W. H. D. Rouse; mythological intro. and notes, H. J. Rose; notes on textual crit., L. R. Lind. Cambridge: Harvard University Press, 3 vols.

O'Faolain, Sean. 1956. *The Vanishing Hero: Studies of the Hero in the Modern Novel.* New York: Grosset and Dunlap.

Osherson, Samuel. 1986. *Finding Our Fathers: The Unfinished Business of Manhood.* New York: Macmillan.

Otto, Walter. 1954. *The Homeric Gods: The Spiritual Significance of Greek Religion.* Trans. Moses Hadas. New York: Pantheon.

———. 1965. *Dionysus: Myth and Cult.* Trans. Robert B. Palmer. Bloomington: Indiana University Press.

Pareles, Jon. 1991. "As MTV Turns 10, Pop Goes the World." *New York Times,* 7 July; Arts and Leisure section: 1, 19.

Paris, Ginette. 1986. *Pagan Meditations: The Worlds of Aphrodite, Artemis, and Hestia.* Trans. Gwendolyn Moore. Dallas: Spring Publications.

———. 1990. *Pagan Grace: Dionysos, Hermes, and Goddess Memory in Daily Life.* Trans. Joanna Mott. Dallas: Spring Publications.

Pearson, Carol. 1989 [1986]. *The Hero Within: Six Archetypes We Live By.* San Francisco: HarperCollins; expanded ed.

———. 1991. *Awakening the Heroes Within: Twelve Archetypes to Help Us Find Ourselves and Transform Our World.* San Francisco: HarperCollins.

Plato. 1961. *The Collected Dialogues of Plato Including the Letters.* Ed. Edith Hamilton and Huntington Cairns; trans. various. Bollingen series, 71. Princeton: Princeton University Press.

Pleck, Elizabeth H., and Joseph H. Pleck, eds. 1980. *The American Man.* Englewood Cliffs, N.J.: Prentice-Hall.

Postman, Neil. 1985. *Amusing Ourselves to Death: Public Discourse in the Age of Show Business.* New York: Viking.

Pratt, Annis. 1991. "The Female Hero." In Downing 1991:213–18.

Prinz, Friedrich. 1974. "Herakles." Pauly-Wissowa-Krell, *Real-Encyclopädie,* Suppl. 14.136–96.

Radin, Paul. 1950. "The Basic Myth of the North American Indians." *Eranos-Jahrbuch* 17:359–419.

———. 1955. *The Trickster: A Study in American Indian Mythology.* New York: Schocken.

Rank, Otto, F. R. R. S. Raglan, Alan Dundes, and Robert A. Segal. 1990. *In Quest of the Hero.* Princeton: Princeton University Press.

Reichard, Gladys A. 1950. *Navaho Religion: A Study of Symbolism.* Bollingen series, 18. Princeton: Princeton University Press.

Remy, John. 1990. "Patriarchy and Fratriarchy as Forms of Androcracy." In Hearn and Morgan 43–54.

Reynaud, Emmanuel. 1983 [1981]. *Holy Virility: The Social Construction of Masculinity*. Trans. Ros Schwartz. London: Pluto Press.

Rich, Adrienne. 1979. *On Lies, Secrets, and Silence*. New York: Norton.

Rochlin, Gregory. 1980. *The Masculine Dilemma: A Psychology of Masculinity*. Boston: Little, Brown and Company.

Ronell, Avital. 1991. Interview, in Andrea Juno and V. Vale, eds. *Angry Women. Re/Search* no. 13:127–53. San Francisco: Re/Search Publications.

Roper, Michael, and John Tosh, eds. 1991. *Manful Assertions: Masculinities in Britain since 1800*. New York: Routledge.

Rose, H. J. 1959. *A Handbook of Greek Mythology Including Its Extension to Rome*. New York: E. P. Dutton.

Ross, Andrew. 1986. "Masculinity and *Miami Vice*." *Oxford Literary Review* 8:143–54.

———. 1990. "Cowboys, Cadillacs, and Cosmonauts: Families, Film Genres, and Technocultures." In Boone 87–101.

Rotundo, E. Anthony. 1983. "Body and Soul: Changing Ideals of American Middle-Class Manhood, 1770–1920." *Journal of Social History* (Summer): 23–38.

———. 1987. "Patriarchs and Participants: A Historical Perspective on Fatherhood in the United States." In Kaufman 64–80.

———. 1993. *American Manhood: Transformations in Masculinity from the Revolution to the Modern Era*. New York: HarperCollins.

Rowan, John. 1987. *The Horned God: Feminism and Men as Wounding and Healing*. London: Routledge & Kegan Paul.

Saikaku, Ihara. 1990 [1687]. *The Great Mirror of Male Love*. Trans. with intro. Paul Gordon Schalow. Stanford: Stanford University Press.

Samuels, Andrew, ed. 1985. *The Father: Contemporary Jungian Perspectives*. New York: New York University Press.

Sandars, N. K. 1972. *The Epic of Gilgamesh: An English Version with an Introduction*. New York: Penguin Books.

Sappho. 1958. *Sappho: A New Translation*. Trans. Mary Barnard. Berkeley: University of California Press.

Schnappe-Gourbeillon, Annie. 1991. "Heroes and Gods of War in the Greek Epic." In Bonnefoy 415–18.

Scroggs, Robin. 1983. *The New Testament and Homosexuality*. Philadelphia: Fortress.

Sedgwick, Eve Kosofsky. 1985. *Between Men: English Literature and Male Homosocial Desire*. New York: Columbia University Press.

———. 1990. *Epistemology of the Closet*. Berkeley: University of California Press.

Segal, Lynne. 1990. *Slow Motion: Changing Masculinities, Changing Men*. New Brunswick, N.J.: Rutgers University Press.

Seidler, Victor J. 1987. "Reason, Desire, and Male Sexuality." In Pat Caplan, ed. *The Cultural Construction of Sexuality*. New York: Tavistock; 82–112.

———. 1989. *Rediscovering Masculinity: Reason, Language, and Sexuality*. New York: Routledge.

————, ed. 1991. *The Achilles Heel Reader: Men, Sexual Politics, and Socialism*. Male Orders. New York: Routledge.

Seltzer, Mark. "The Love-Master." In Boone 140–58.

Sergent, Bernard. 1986. *Homosexuality in Greek Myth*. Trans. Arthur Gold-hammer. Boston: Beacon.

Shewey, Don, 1992. *In Defense of the Men's Movements*. Minneapolis: Ally Press; Dragonsmoke Pamphlet 1.

Showalter, Elaine. 1985. "Shooting the Rapids: Feminist Criticism in the Mainstream." *The Oxford Literary Review* 8/1–2:218–24.

Silko, Leslie Marmon. 1977. *Ceremony*. New York: Signet.

Silverberg, Robert. 1984. *Gilgamesh the King*. New York: Bantam.

————. 1990. *To the Land of the Living*. New York: Warner.

Simpson, Michael, trans. and annotator. 1976. *Gods and Heroes of the Greeks: The Library of Apollodorus*. Amherst: University of Massachusetts Press.

Slater, Philip E. 1968. *The Glory of Hera: Greek Mythology and the Greek Family*. Boston: Beacon.

Slochower, Harry. 1970. *Mythopoesis: Mythic Forms in the Literary Classics*. Detroit: Wayne State University Press.

Snodgrass, Jon, ed. 1977. *For Men against Sexism: A Book of Readings*. Albion, Calif.: Times Change Press.

Spencer, Katherine. 1957. *Reflection of Social Life in the Navaho Origin Myth*. UNM Publications in Anthropology, 3. Albuquerque: University of New Mexico Press.

Spivak, Gayatri Chakravorty. 1989. *In Other Worlds: Essays in Cultural Politics*. New York: Routledge.

Spotnitz, Hyman, and Philip Resnikoff. 1954. "The Myths of Narcissus." *Psychoanalytic Review* 41/2:173–81.

Stanford, W. B. 1963. *The Ulysses Theme: A Study in the Adaptability of a Traditional Hero*. 2nd ed. Ann Arbor: University of Michigan Press.

Stein, Murray. 1976. "Narcissus." *Spring: An Annual of Archetypal Psychology and Jungian Thought*; 32–53.

Stengel, Richard. 1992. "Men as Sex Objects." *M* 9/10:72–79.

Strathern, Marilyn. 1988. *The Gender of the Gift: Problems with Women and Problems with Society in Melanesia*. Studies in Melanesian Anthropology, 6. Berkeley: University of California Press.

Strage, Mark. 1980. *The Durable Fig Leaf: A Historical, Cultural, Medical, Social, Literary, and Iconographic Account of Man's Relations with His Penis*. New York: Morrow.

Stuart, Grace. 1956. *Narcissus: A Psychological Study of Self-Love*. London: Allen and Unwin.

Tacey, David J. 1991. "Attacking Patriarchy, Redeeming Masculinity." *San Francisco Jung Institute Library Journal* 10/1:25–41.

Tedlock, Dennis. 1983. *The Spoken Word and the Work of Interpretation*. University of Pennsylvania Publications in Conduct and Communication. Philadelphia: University of Pennsylvania Press.

Teich, Howard. 1991. "The Twins: An Archetypal Perspective." In Downing 1991: 124–32.

————. N.d. "Homovision: The Solar/Lunar Twin-Ego." Unpublished paper, 1991. [See Teich, 1993: same title, in Robert H. Hopcke, Karin Loftus Carrington, and Scott Wirth, eds. *Same-Sex Love and the Path to Wholeness.* Boston: Shambhala; 136–50.]

Trungpa, Chögyam. 1984. *Shambhala: The Sacred Path of the Warrior.* New York: Bantam; Bantam New Age Books.

Thompson, William Irwin. 1981. *The Time Falling Bodies Take to Light: Mythology, Sexuality, and the Origins of Culture.* Lindisfarne series. New York: St. Martin's.

Tiger, Lionel. 1969. *Men in Groups.* New York: Random House.

Vidal-Naquet, Pierre. 1986. *The Black Hunter: Forms of Thought and Forms of Society in the Greek World.* Trans. Andrew Szegedy-Maszak. Baltimore: Johns Hopkins University Press.

Vinge, Louise. 1967. *The Narcissus Theme in Western European Literature up to the Early 19th Century.* Trans. Robert Dewsnap. Lund: Gleerups.

Vogt, Gregory Max. 1991. *Return to Father: Archetypal Dimensions of the Patriarch.* Dallas: Spring Publications.

————, and Stephen T. Sirridge. 1991. *Like Son, Like Father: Healing the Father-Son Wound in Men's Lives.* New York: Plenum.

Walker, Barbara G. 1983. *The Woman's Encyclopedia of Myths and Secrets.* San Francisco: HarperCollins.

Walker, Mitchell. 1976. "The Double: An Archetypal Configuration." *Spring: An Annual of Archetypal Psychology and Jungian Thought;* 165–75.

————. 1991. "Jung and Homophobia." *Spring: A Journal of Archetype and Culture* 51:55–70.

Waters, Frank. 1950. *Masked Gods: Navaho and Pueblo Ceremonialism.* New York: Ballantine.

Watrous, Peter. 1991. "Pop Turns the Tables — With Beefcake." *New York Times,* 10 February, Arts and Leisure section; 1, 27.

Weeks, Jeffrey. 1986. *Sexuality.* New York: Routledge.

Wernick, Andrew. 1987. "From Voyeur to Narcissist: Imaging Men in Contemporary Advertising." In Kaufman 277–97.

Whitmont, Edward C. 1982. *Return of the Goddess.* New York: Crossroad.

Williams, Walter L. 1986. *The Spirit and the Flesh: Sexual Diversity in American Indian Culture.* Boston: Beacon.

Winkler, John J. 1990. *The Constraints of Desire: The Anthropology of Sex and Gender in Ancient Greece.* The New Ancient World. New York: Routledge.

Winn, Marie. 1990. "New Views of Human Intelligence." *New York Times Magazine,* 29 April; Part 2:16–17, 28, 30.

Woolger, Roger. 1978. "Death and the Hero." *Archē: Notes and Papers on Archaic Studies* 2:36–50.

Yazzie, Ethelou, ed. 1971. *Navajo History.* Many Farms, Ariz: Navajo Community College Press, vol. 1.

Zolbrod, Paul G. 1984. *Diné bahane': The Navajo Creation Story.* Albuquerque: University of New Mexico Press.

Index